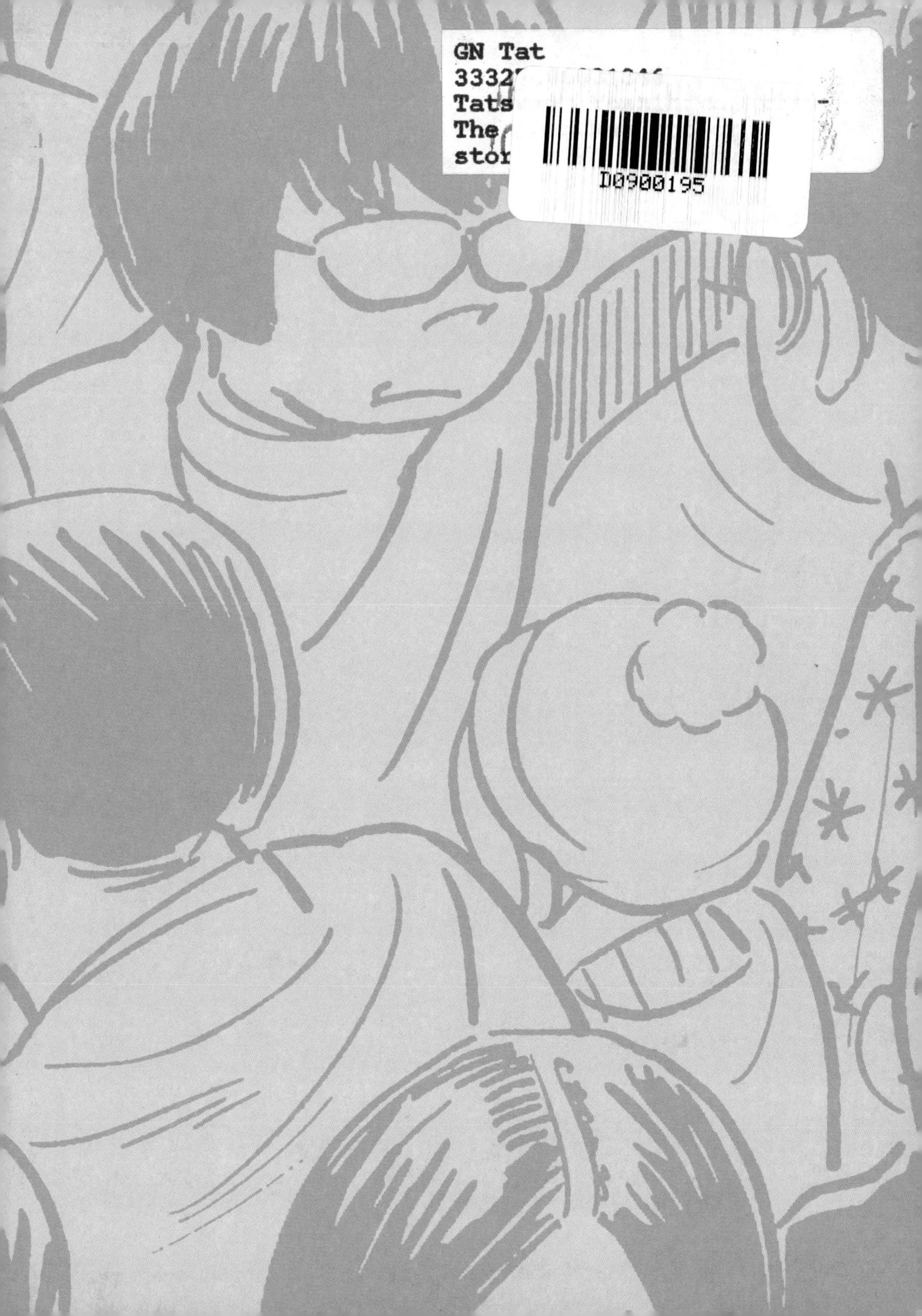

辰巳ヨシヒロ

Edited, designed, and lettered by Adrian Tomine.
Translated by Yuji Oniki.
Production by Melissa Meyer, Bernie Mireault, Chris Oliveros and Yoshihiro Tatsumi.

Drawn & Quarterly
Post Office Box 48056
Montreal, Quebec
Canada H2V 4S8
www.drawnandquarterly.com

Publisher: Chris Oliveros.
Publicity: Peggy Burns.

First hardcover edition: September 2005.
Printed in Singapore.
10 9 8 7 6 5 4 3 2 1

This edition supported in part by The Japan Foundation.

Library and Archives Canada Cataloguing in Publication
Tatsumi, Yoshihiro, 1935-
    The Push Man and other stories / Yoshihiro Tatsumi.
ISBN 1-896597-85-8
    1. City and town life--Japan--Comic books, strips, etc. I. Title.
PN6790.J33T38 2005   741.5'952   C2005-900136-4

Distributed in the USA and abroad by:
Farrar, Straus and Giroux
19 Union Square West
New York, NY 10003
Orders: 888.330.8477

Distributed in Canada by:
Raincoast Books
9050 Shaughnessy Street
Vancouver, BC V6P 6E5
Orders: 800.663.5714

THE PUSH MAN

and other stories

INTRODUCTION

In 1988, at the age of 14, I experienced a crisis of faith. Except, instead of doubting long–held religious beliefs, I was suddenly questioning my life–long love of comic books. I found myself ritualistically purchasing the latest issue of, say, *Web of Spider–Man*, filing it away in protective mylar and acid–free cardboard, but increasingly skipping the step of actually reading the thing. I became depressed by the possibility that comics were yet another childhood hobby, like skateboards or action figures, that I'd suddenly outgrown. In a last–ditch effort to resuscitate my interest and justify my weekly trips to the comic store, I began a process of wild experimentation, giving almost anything that seemed unusual or "alternative" a try. For every five (or ten) disappointments, there was usually one gem, and one such find was *Good–Bye and Other Stories*[1] by Yoshihiro Tatsumi. This book (along with others such as *Love and Rockets*, *Weirdo*, and *RAW*) not only re–ignited my passion for comics, but made very clear to me the now–commonplace fact that comics were simply a medium, just as capable of expressing personal, artistic stories for adults as they were of indulging childhood fantasy.

At the time, Tatsumi's work seemed to me like a refreshing, eye–opening rebellion against

everything I'd come to expect from comics. Unlike the garish, full–color, action–packed comic art I'd grown up with, Tatsumi's visuals were restrained, minimal, and stylized in a manner that seemed appealingly foreign. The potentially discordant placement of slightly cartoon–y characters within realistic backgrounds worked beautifully, communicating a sense of place and emotion that more photo–realistic comics couldn't approach. Instead of epic, ever–continuing storylines, Tatsumi's work was comprised of compact, elliptical short stories which, like the best modern prose fiction, were simultaneously satisfying and open–ended. The stories' focus alternated between stretches of mundane daily life and moments of surprising violence and sexuality, and both extremes were equally refreshing and unsettling to me. In place of one–dimensional heroes and villains, there were real people: faces in a crowd, seemingly plucked at random and then examined down to their darkest, most private moments. Characters didn't recur from story to story, but the depiction of an overwhelming, alienating modern world remained constant. I had seen some Japanese comics, or *manga*, before, but none of it had appealed to me in the way that Tatsumi's did.

In the fifteen years since that discovery, I've

---

[1] Published in 1987 by Catalan Communications, this was, until now, the only English–language edition of Tatsumi's work. Much of the art was poorly reproduced, and the writing was twice translated: first from Japanese into Spanish, and then from Spanish into English. Shockingly, this edition was published with neither Tatsumi's permission nor knowledge: he learned of its existence only when a friend discovered it while traveling in America.

managed to become a cartoonist myself, and examining Tatsumi's work now, I'm pleased to find that it holds up just as well as it did upon my first exposure to it. But instead of viewing it in relation to the sub–par comics I was attempting to replace at the time, I see it simply as a significant work of modern cartooning. Like all my favorite comics, from *Peanuts* to *Yummy Fur* to *Eightball*, it reads like the direct expression of a personality that is keenly observant, deeply self–critical, and constantly torn between sympathy and misanthropy. The durability of Tatsumi's work is impressive: today's reader, if not previously informed, would surely be surprised to learn that these stories were created thirty–six years ago. In terms of tone and style, this work shares an obvious kinship with the "alternative" or "literary" comics that began proliferating in North America in the mid–1980s (and continue to thrive today), yet it predates much of that work by as much as three decades. (I should also point out that the stories in this book predate my very birth by five years!) Critics have always been eager to identify the various influences that are so apparent in my comics, and I've never denied my great debt to American artists such as the Hernandez brothers and Daniel Clowes. In revisiting the work of Tatsumi, it's now apparent to me how much his comics also impacted me, and I'm sure that elements of his style continue to influence my work to this day.

I traveled to Tokyo in the Summer of 2003 to promote a Japanese translation of some of my comics, and while there, my gracious hosts arranged for me to meet with Mr. Tatsumi. My adult life has been punctuated by the kind of experiences that make me think, "If the teenage me could see me now...", and this was one of the more potent examples. I had been forewarned that Mr. Tatsumi was a bit of a recluse, and that

he might be impersonal or reticent. But, on the contrary, I found him to be much like all the other great cartoonists I've had the pleasure to meet: friendly, polite, generous, and perhaps a bit shy. We met for tea in a cavernous, underground cafe in the *Jimbocho* district, and with the help of an interpreter, Mr. Tatsumi and I soon found ourselves chatting amiably about the kinds of things that could only be of interest to other cartoonists.[2] For several years prior I had been attempting to get more of Tatsumi's stories translated into English. It proved to be a surprisingly complicated and troubled process, but this informal meeting seemed to finalize the arrangement through which the book you presently hold could see print. I left the cafe feeling honored both to have met Mr. Tatsumi and to have been given the opportunity to help bring his work to a wider audience.

In spite of having met him face–to–face and having studied his work at length, I still don't know that much about Yoshihiro Tatsumi. I know that he was born in 1935 in Osaka. I know that he is considered the "grandfather of Japanese alternative comics," and that in 1957, he coined the term *gekiga* to differentiate the gritty, naturalistic style of cartooning he helped pioneer from that of the more commercial, youth–oriented *manga*. Other tid–bits I've learned about him arrived through the haze of translation, but my understanding is that he runs a small book shop and that he continues to write and draw comics. Someone told me they believed he was working on a long–form autobiography. More as a curious fan than an editor, I recently sent Mr. Tatsumi a handful of questions, and received a prompt, insightful reply. This brief but illuminating interview is reprinted in full following the stories in this volume.

As plans for this translation project began to

---

2 Other cartoonists and the more curious reader are invited to read a transcript of this conversation on the Drawn & Quarterly website: www.drawnandquarterly.com/tatsumi.

get off the ground, it soon became apparent that a comprehensive reprinting of Tatsumi's work would be literally impossible. With a career spanning from the 1950s to the present day, and with a work ethic that yielded up to twelve pages in a week (and, with the help of assistants, fifty pages in one night!), Mr. Tatsumi has produced a mind–bogglingly immense body of work. So this will be a selective survey of his best work, beginning, at Mr. Tatsumi's request, with the year 1969. Our hope is to release one volume per year, each focusing on a single year in Mr. Tatsumi's career.

A brief note about the translation: As you may or may not know, Japanese comics are designed to be read in a manner that Western readers would consider reversed (this pertains to both the binding of pages as well as the arrangement of the panels). It was initially suggested that we maintain the original, Japanese–style layout for this edition, and perhaps include instructions on how to read it. But unfortunately, there is still somewhat of a cultural prejudice against comics in North America, and if a comic book (or "graphic novel") is to reach as wide an audience as possible, the last thing it needs is another obstacle for new readers to surmount. So with the consultation of various cartoonists, publishers, and Mr. Tatsumi himself, it was agreed that the best solution was to re–format the book to the Western style. To achieve this, Japanese comics have, in the past, been "flopped." That is, each page is printed as a mirror image of the original. This is clearly the simplest, most efficient method, but as a cartoonist who has seen his own artwork "flopped," I know that this can often cause a perfectly good drawing to suddenly look bad. Mr. Tatsumi apparently concurred, and he painstakingly re–arranged the panels on each page so that they would be read in the proper order, without being "flopped." In certain isolated cases in which it was necessary (such as panels in which more than one character speaks, thus making the order of their lines of dialogue paramount), some "flopping" was committed. Yes, this is a compromise, and indeed, this art is no longer exactly the same as when it was created, but such is the nature of translation. Those who cannot read the work in its original language must make do with the best possible approximation, and I believe that's what we've arrived at.

This project has been assisted, guided, and encouraged by the following people, to whom I am deeply grateful: Mitsuhiro Asakawa, Sarah Brennan, Peggy Burns, Tom Devlin, Paul Gravett, Maki Hakui, Tim Hensley, Beatrice Marechal, Melissa Meyer, Yasutaka Minegishi, Bernie Mireault, Chris Oliveros, Yuji Oniki, Yuji Yamada, and most of all, Yoshihiro Tatsumi.

Coincidental to the onset of this project (and unbeknownst to me), there was a sudden surge of interest in Tatsumi's work around the world. Thick collections of his stories were being reissued in Japan, translation rights were being procured in a number of European countries, and at least one other North American publisher attempted to compete with us at the last minute for the English–language rights. I'm not sure how to account for this synchronicity, but I couldn't be happier about it. I'm glad that more people will now be exposed to this timelessly fascinating work, and that Mr. Tatsumi will receive the wider respect and acclaim he deserves. But mostly I'm excited for selfish reasons: as someone who unfortunately cannot read Japanese, this will be my chance to finally have more stories by one of my favorite cartoonists. I hope you enjoy them as much as I do.

ADRIAN TOMINE
Brooklyn, New York
January 2005

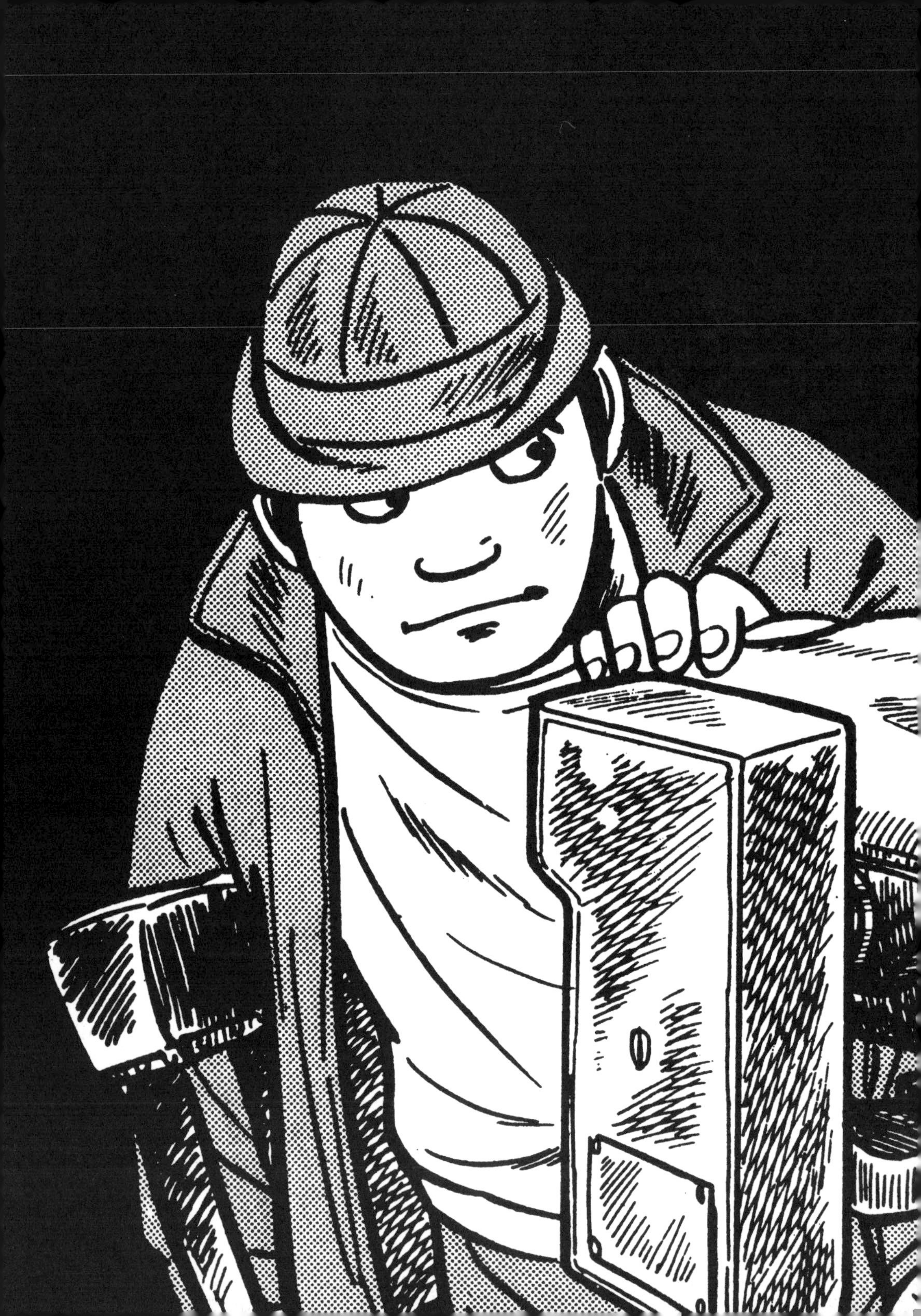

YOSHIHIRO TATSUMI

THE PUSH MAN and other stories

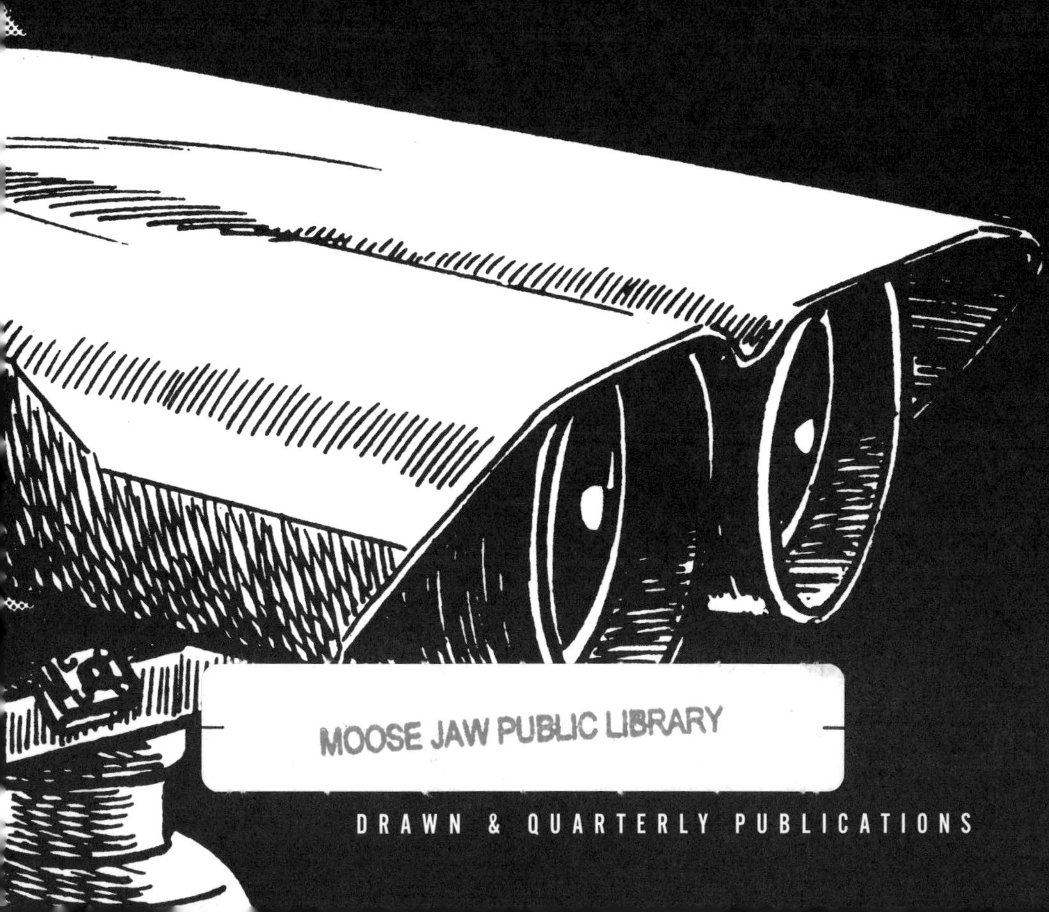

DRAWN & QUARTERLY PUBLICATIONS

CONTENTS

PIRANHA

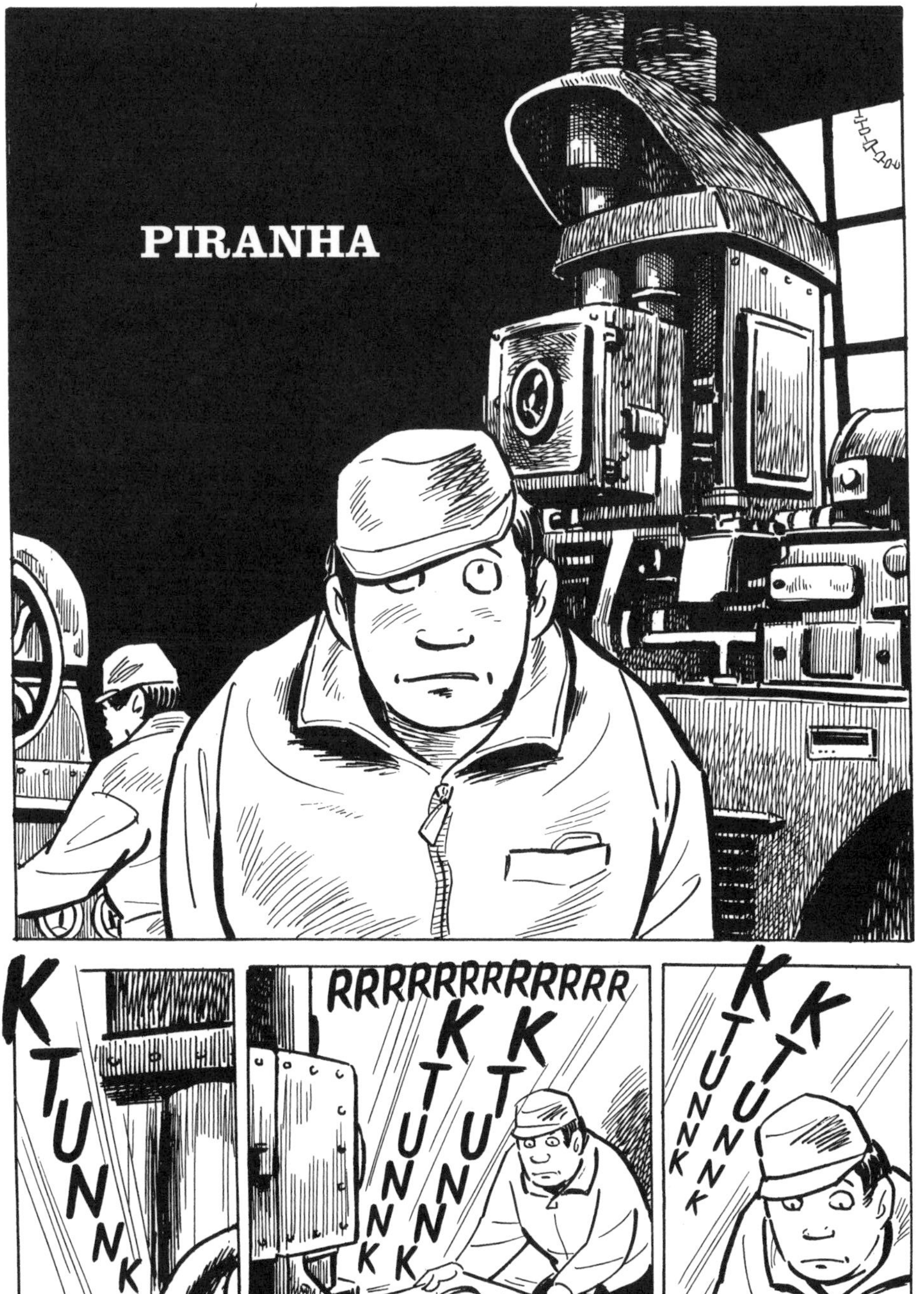
KTUNNNK
RRRRRRRRRRRRR
KTUNNNK
KTUNNNK
KTUNNNK
KTUNNNK

OH, HI.

I MADE DINNER. YOU'RE ON YOUR OWN TONIGHT.

SIGN: FACTORY/ OX INDUSTRIES CORP.

SORRY... IT'S NOT MUCH.

BUT IT'LL HAVE TO DO.

I HAVE TO HURRY. DON'T WANT TO UPSET THE BOSS.

...

HEY...ANY CHANCE YOU COULD SCRAPE UP A MILLION YEN?

I WANT TO RUN MY OWN BUSINESS.

OF COURSE YOU CAN'T. I DON'T KNOW WHY I EVEN BOTHER ASKING.

AFTER ALL, YOU JUST WORK AT A PLANT.

14

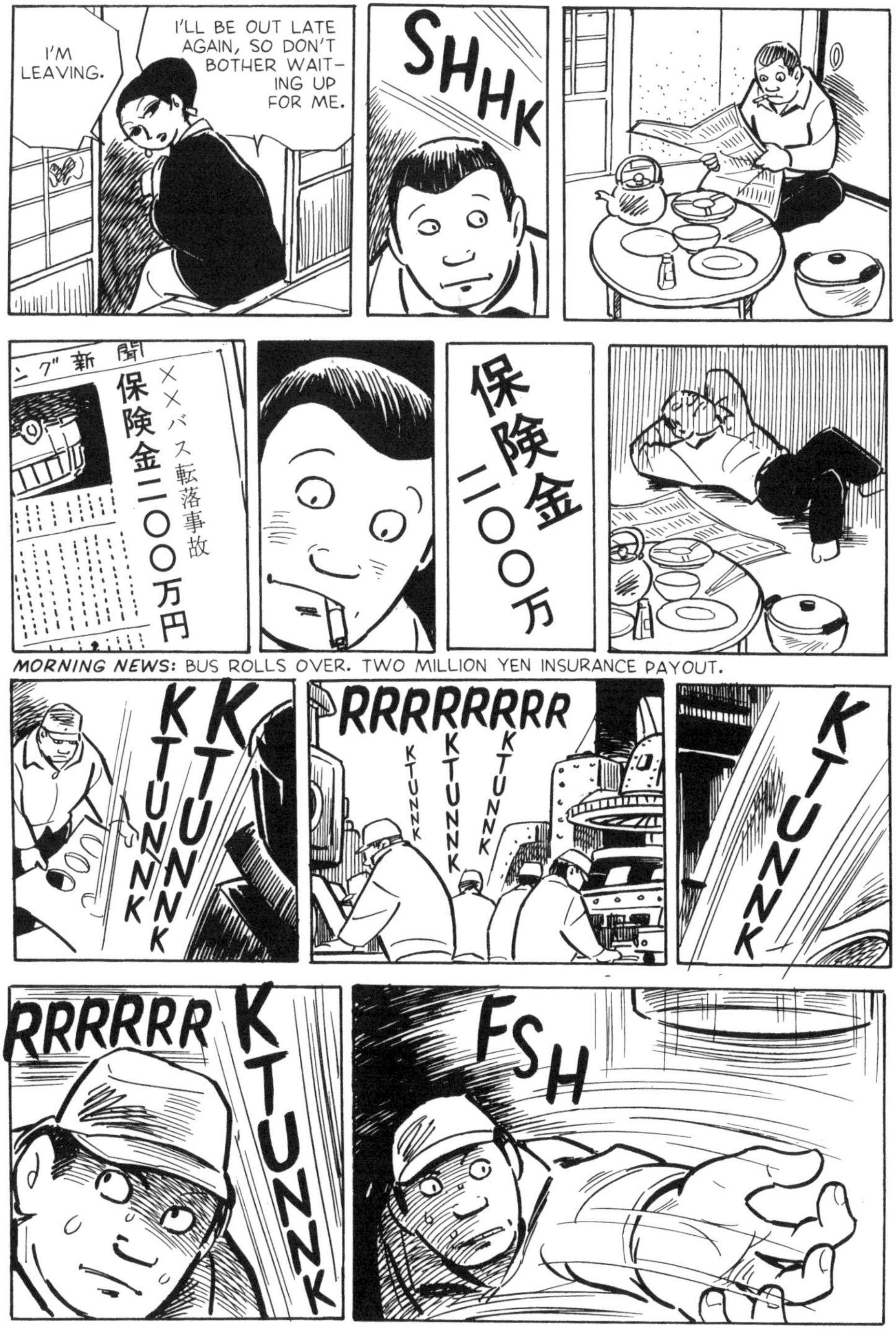
I'M LEAVING.
I'LL BE OUT LATE AGAIN, SO DON'T BOTHER WAITING UP FOR ME.
SHHK
ング新聞
××バス転落事故
保険金二〇〇万円
保険金二〇〇万
MORNING NEWS: BUS ROLLS OVER. TWO MILLION YEN INSURANCE PAYOUT.
KTUNNK
KTUNNNK
RRRRRRRR
KTUNNK
KTUNNK
KTUNNK
KTUNNK
RRRRRR
KTUNNK
FSH

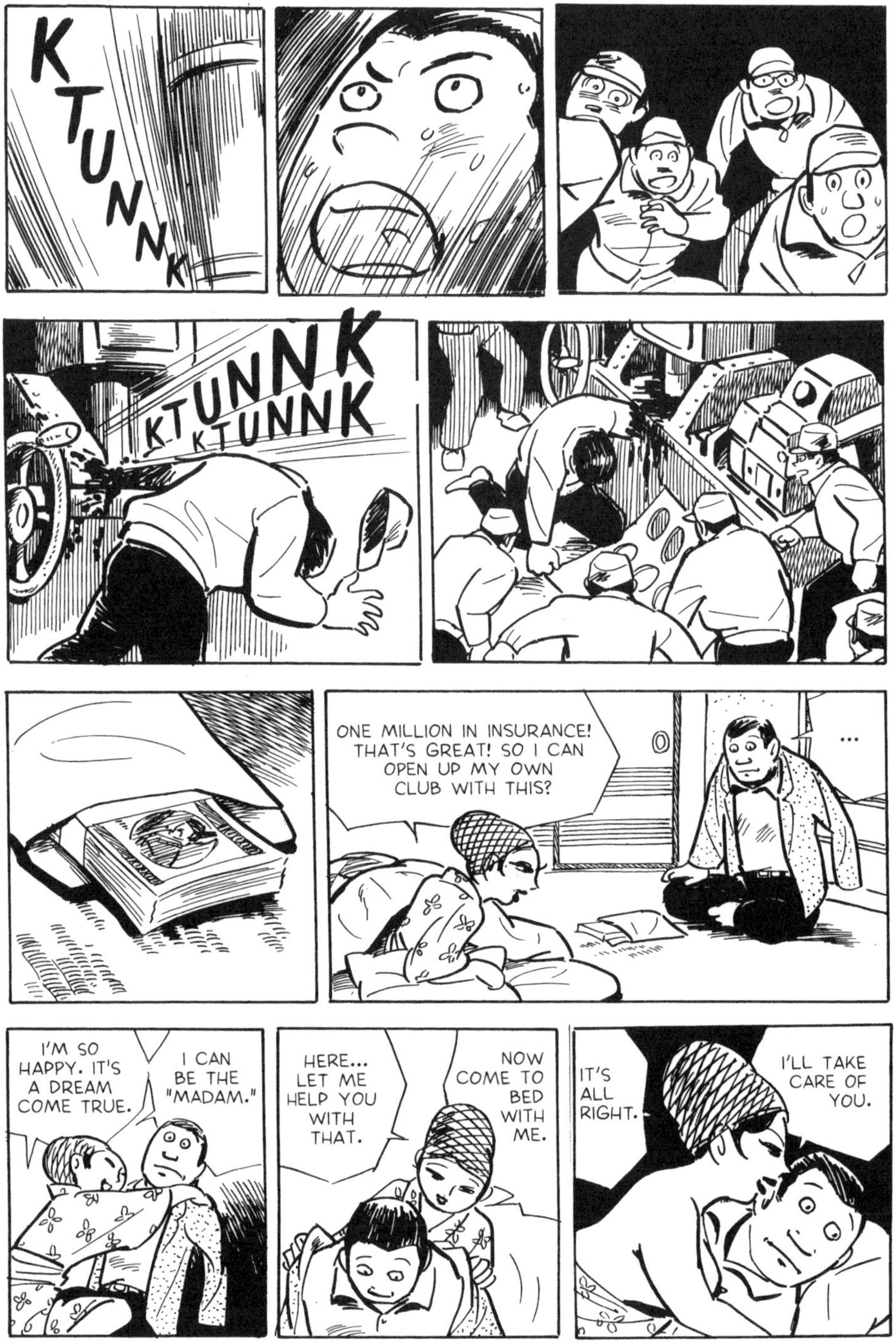
KTUNNNK
KTUNNK
KTUNNK
KTUNNK
ONE MILLION IN INSURANCE! THAT'S GREAT! SO I CAN OPEN UP MY OWN CLUB WITH THIS?
...
I'M SO HAPPY. IT'S A DREAM COME TRUE.
I CAN BE THE "MADAM."
HERE... LET ME HELP YOU WITH THAT.
NOW COME TO BED WITH ME.
IT'S ALL RIGHT.
I'LL TAKE CARE OF YOU.

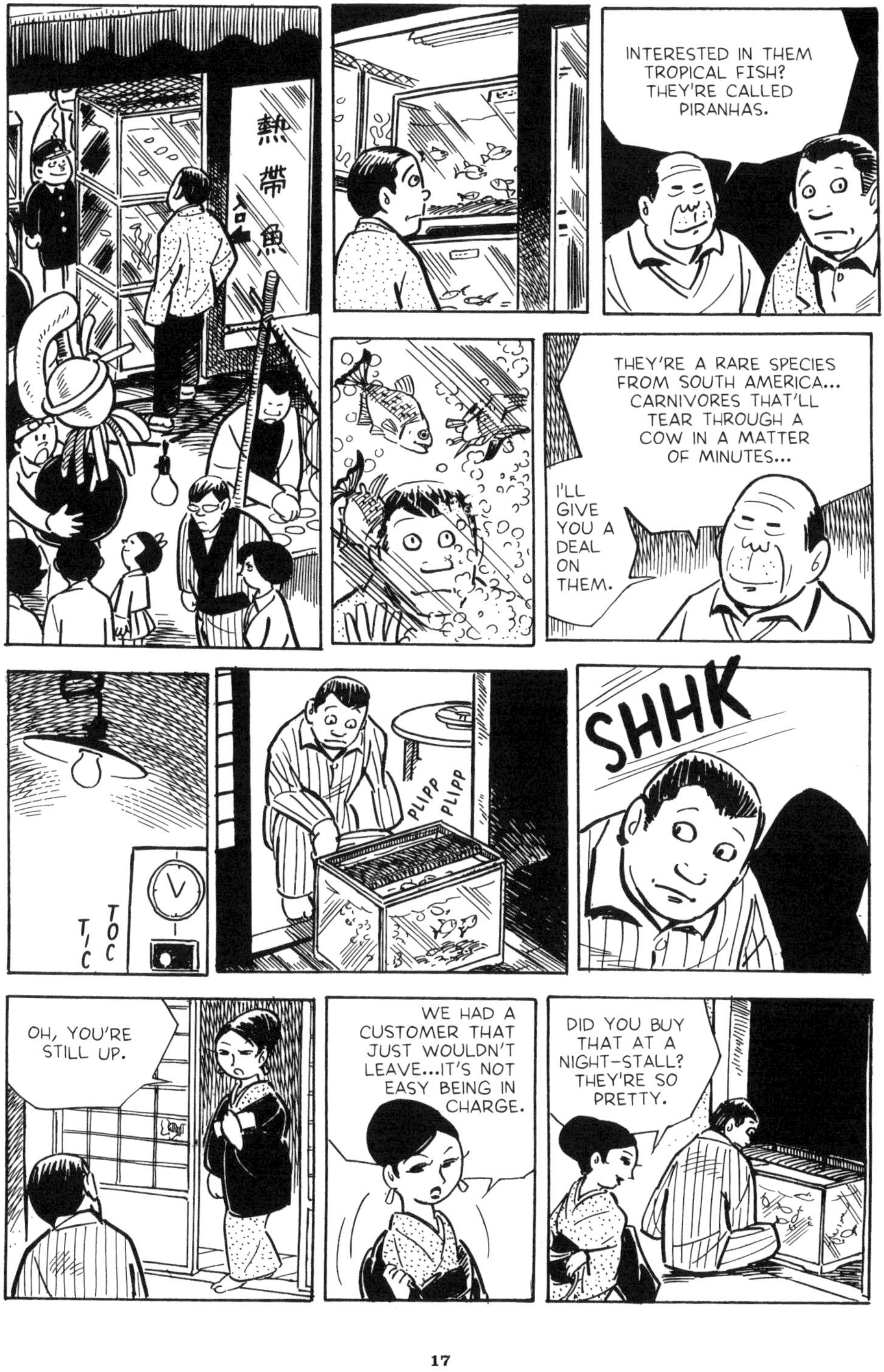
INTERESTED IN THEM TROPICAL FISH? THEY'RE CALLED PIRANHAS.
THEY'RE A RARE SPECIES FROM SOUTH AMERICA... CARNIVORES THAT'LL TEAR THROUGH A COW IN A MATTER OF MINUTES...
I'LL GIVE YOU A DEAL ON THEM.
TIC TOC
PLIPP PLIPP
SHHK
OH, YOU'RE STILL UP.
WE HAD A CUSTOMER THAT JUST WOULDN'T LEAVE...IT'S NOT EASY BEING IN CHARGE.
DID YOU BUY THAT AT A NIGHT-STALL? THEY'RE SO PRETTY.

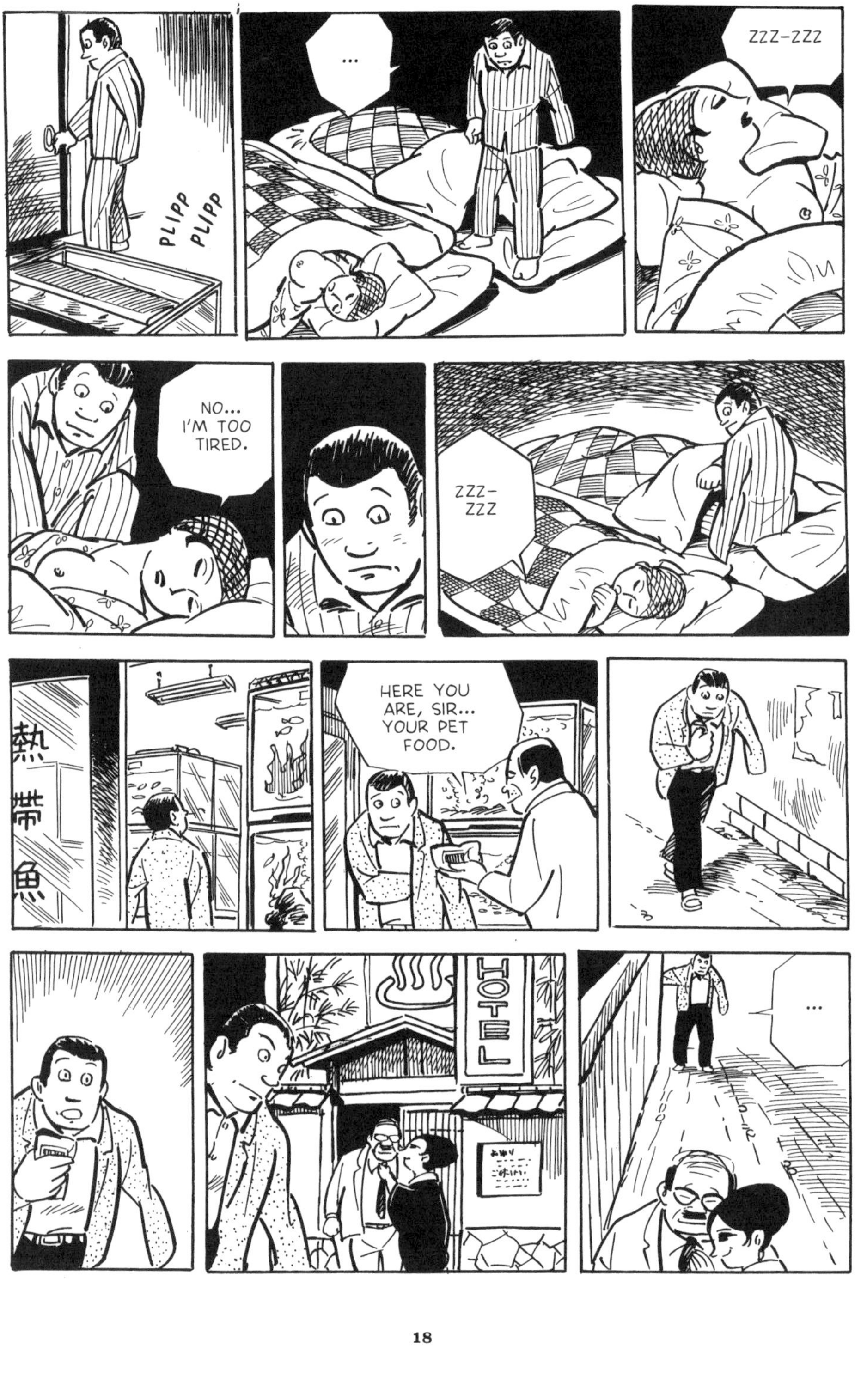
PLIPP PLIPP
...
ZZZ-ZZZ
NO... I'M TOO TIRED.
ZZZ-ZZZ
熱帯魚
HERE YOU ARE, SIR... YOUR PET FOOD.
HOTEL
...

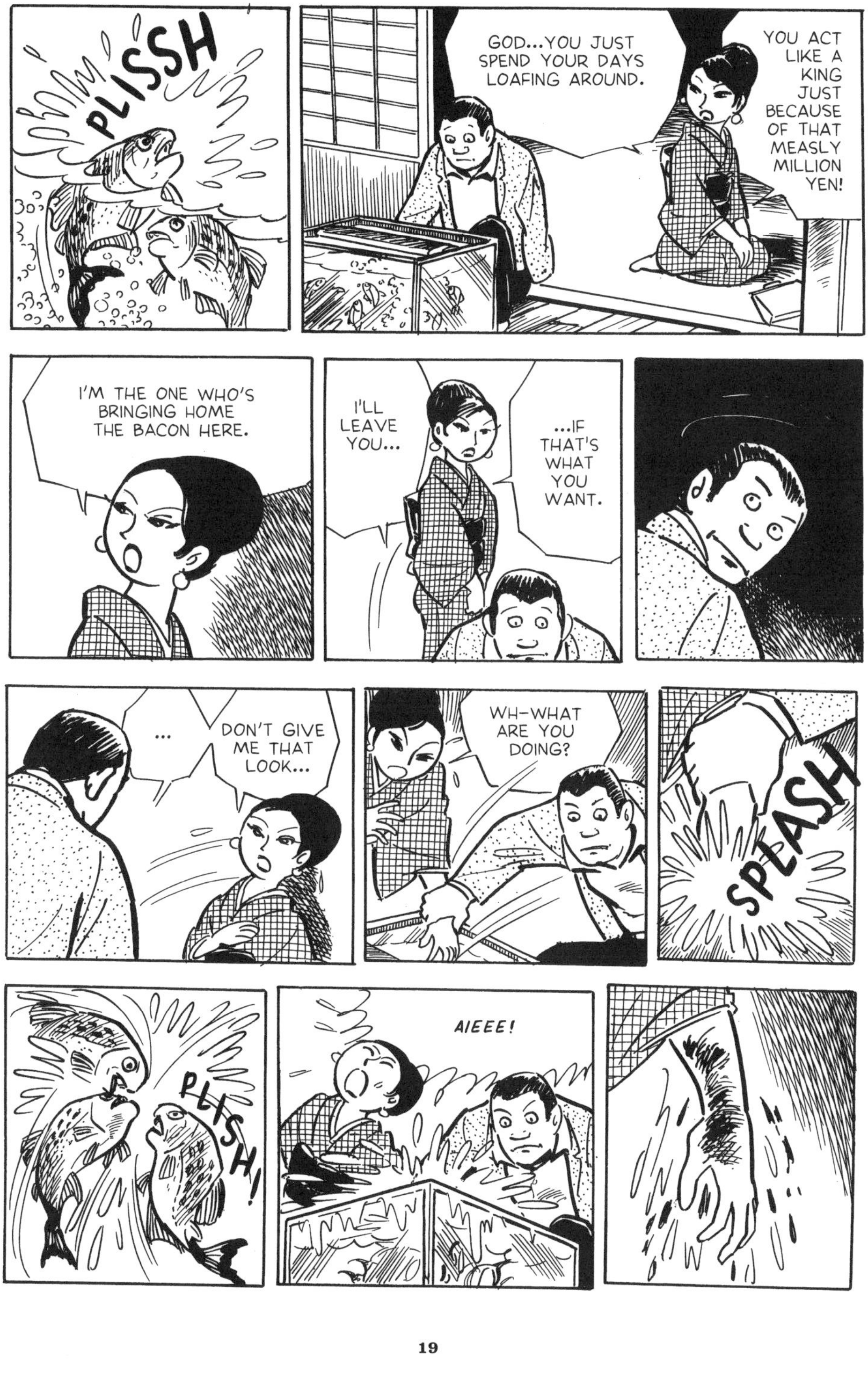
PLISSH
GOD...YOU JUST SPEND YOUR DAYS LOAFING AROUND.
YOU ACT LIKE A KING JUST BECAUSE OF THAT MEASLY MILLION YEN!
I'M THE ONE WHO'S BRINGING HOME THE BACON HERE.
I'LL LEAVE YOU...
...IF THAT'S WHAT YOU WANT.
...
DON'T GIVE ME THAT LOOK...
WH-WHAT ARE YOU DOING?
SPLASH
PLISH!
AIEEE!

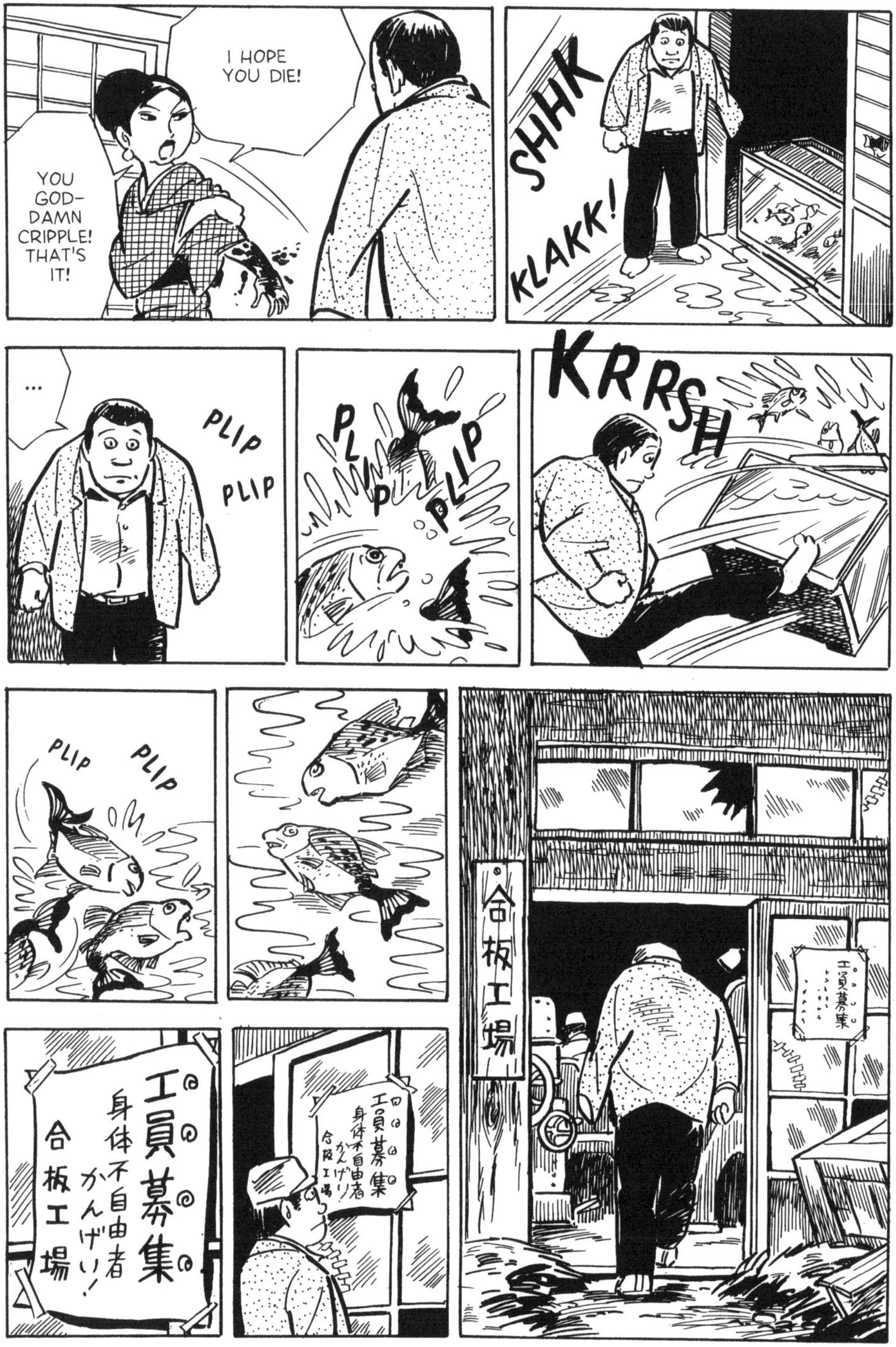
YOU GOD-DAMN CRIPPLE! THAT'S IT!
I HOPE YOU DIE!
SHHK
KLAKK!
...
PLIP
PLIP
PLIP
PLIP
PLIP
KRRSH
PLIP
PLIP
合板工場
工員募集
身体不自由者
かんげい!
合板工場
工員募集
身体不自由者
かんげい!
合板工場

SIGN: WORKERS WANTED / SHEET METAL PLANT / WE WELCOME THE DISABLED

PROJECTIONIST

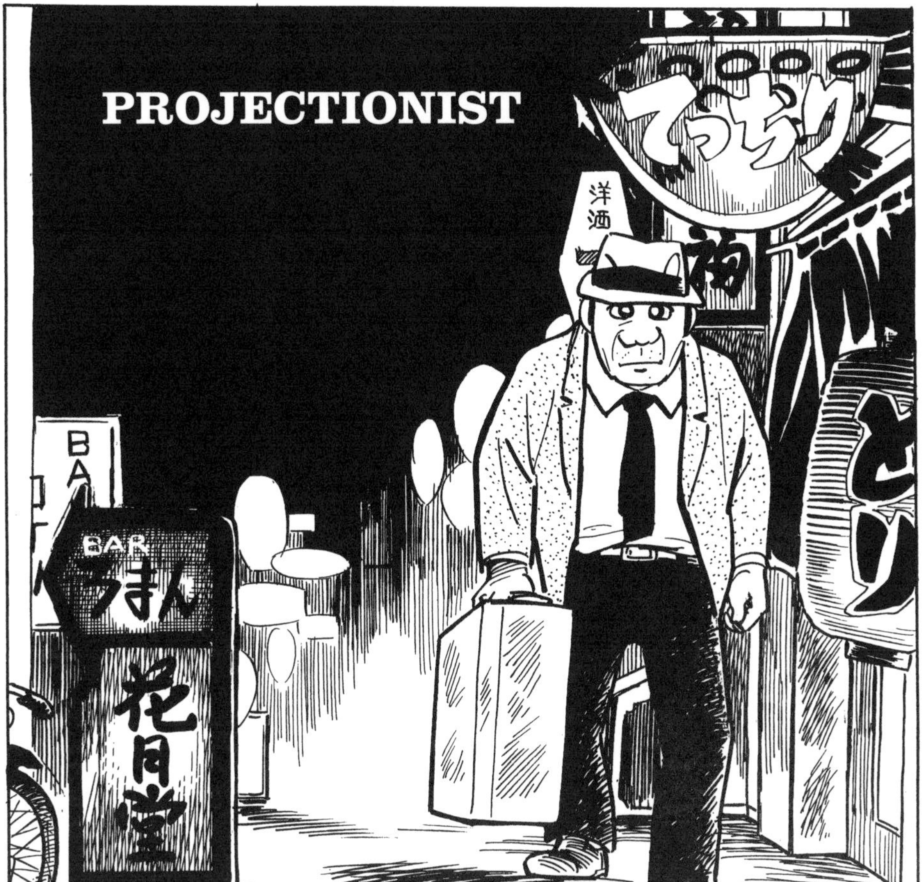

てっちり
洋酒
BAR
花月堂

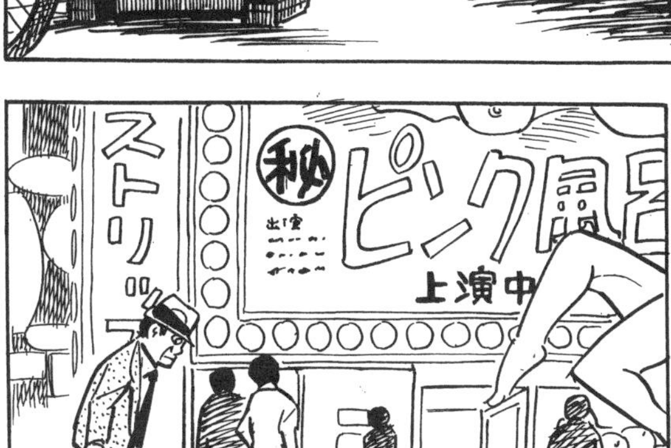

ピンク風呂
上演中

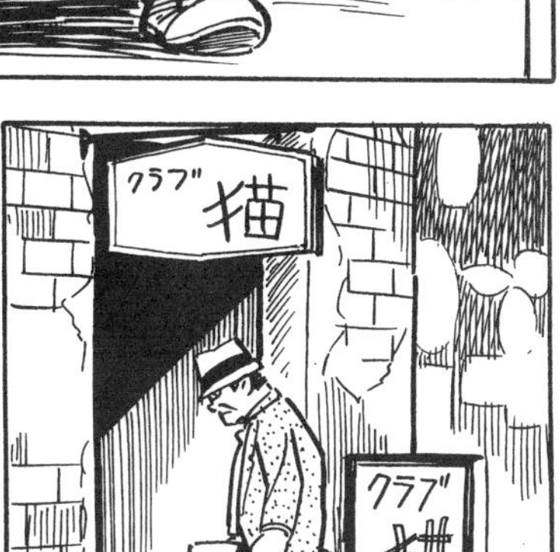

クラブ 猫
クラブ 猫

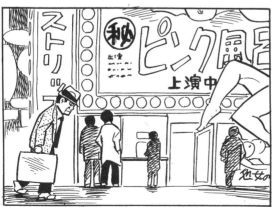

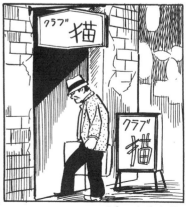

SIGN: CAT CLUB

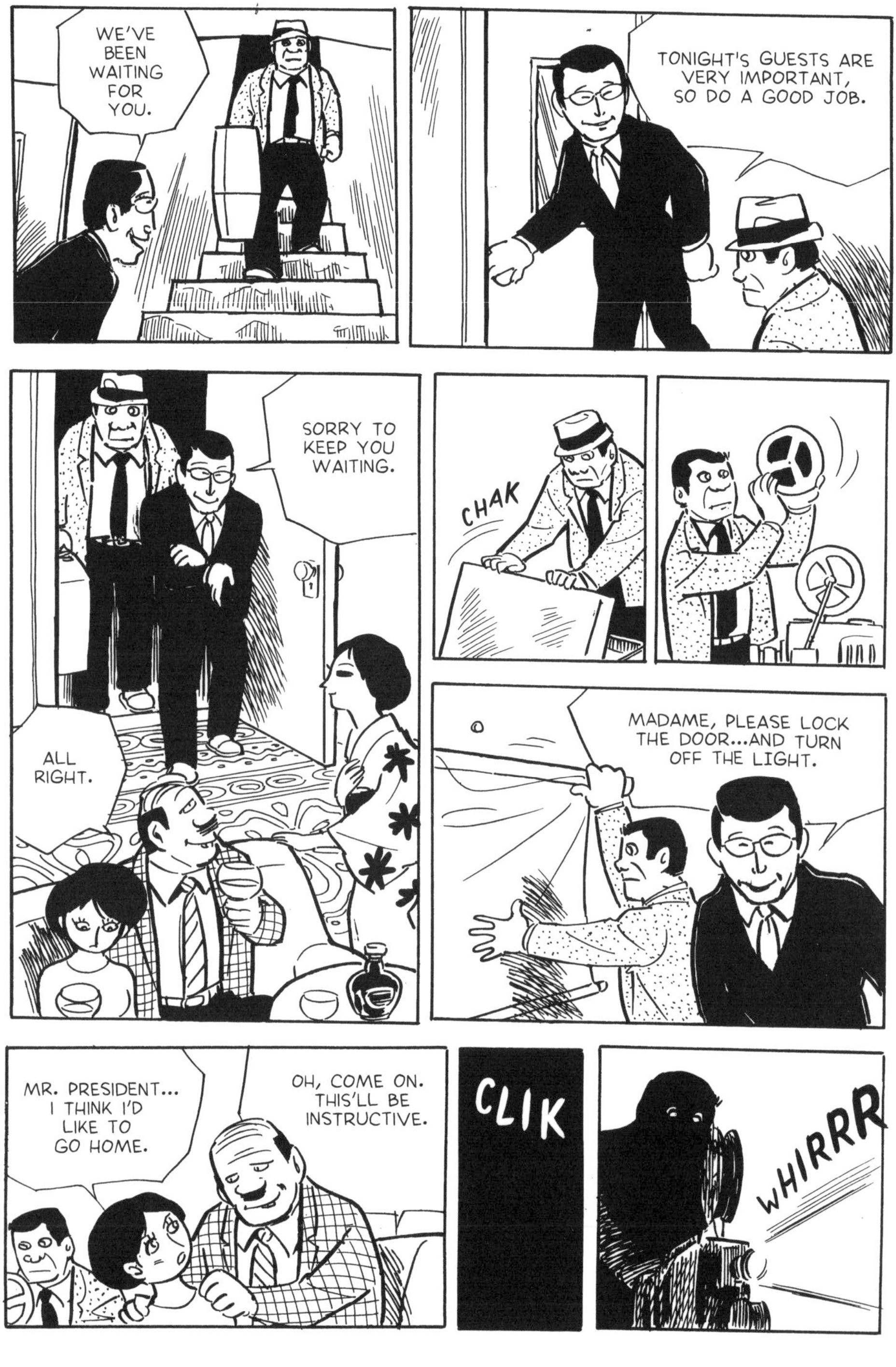
WE'VE BEEN WAITING FOR YOU.
TONIGHT'S GUESTS ARE VERY IMPORTANT, SO DO A GOOD JOB.
SORRY TO KEEP YOU WAITING.
ALL RIGHT.
CHAK
MADAME, PLEASE LOCK THE DOOR...AND TURN OFF THE LIGHT.
MR. PRESIDENT... I THINK I'D LIKE TO GO HOME.
OH, COME ON. THIS'LL BE INSTRUCTIVE.
CLIK
WHIRRR

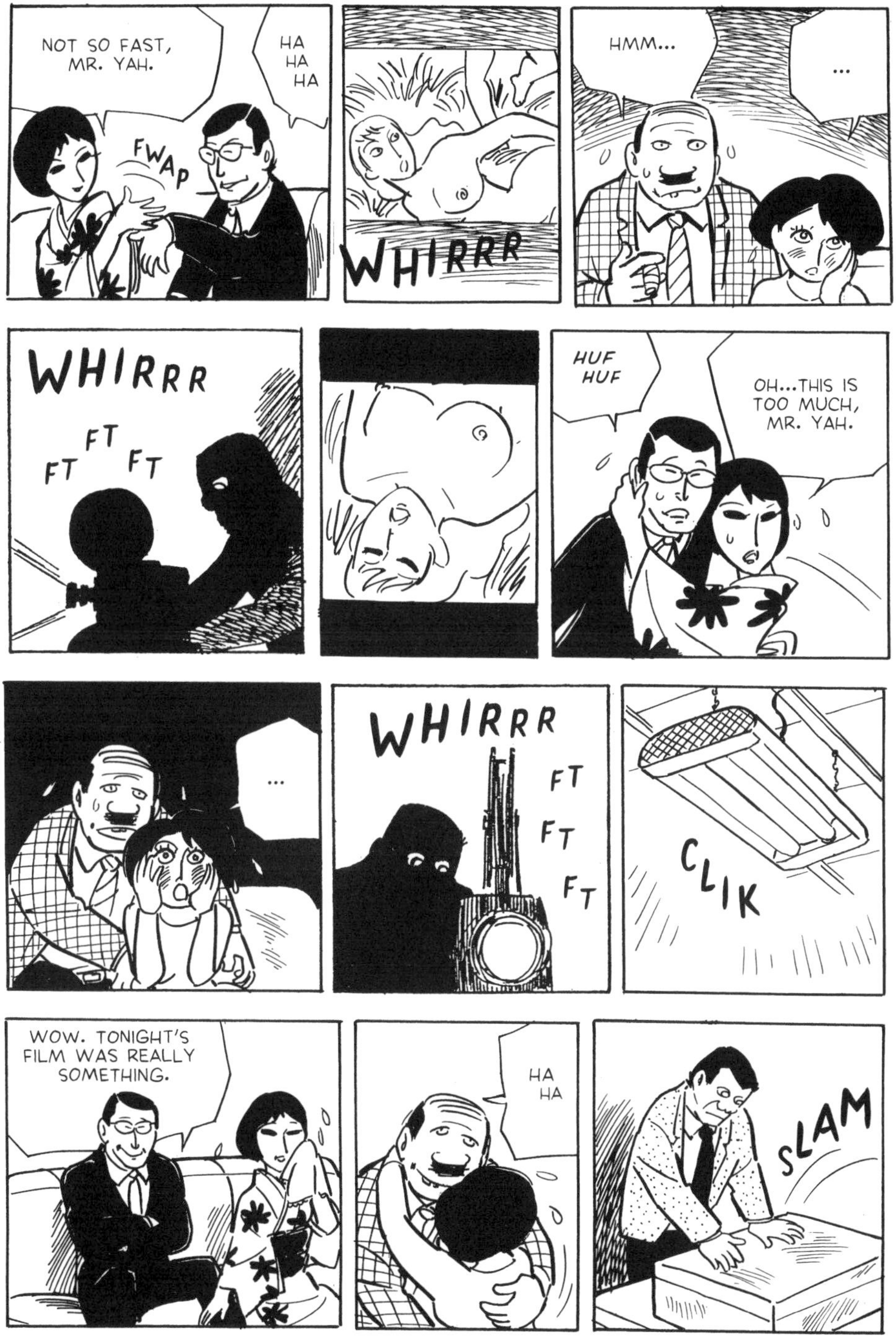
NOT SO FAST, MR. YAH.
HA HA HA
FWAP
WHIRRR
HMM...
...
WHIRRR
FT FT FT
HUF HUF
OH...THIS IS TOO MUCH, MR. YAH.
...
WHIRRR
FT FT FT
CLIK
WOW. TONIGHT'S FILM WAS REALLY SOMETHING.
HA HA
SLAM

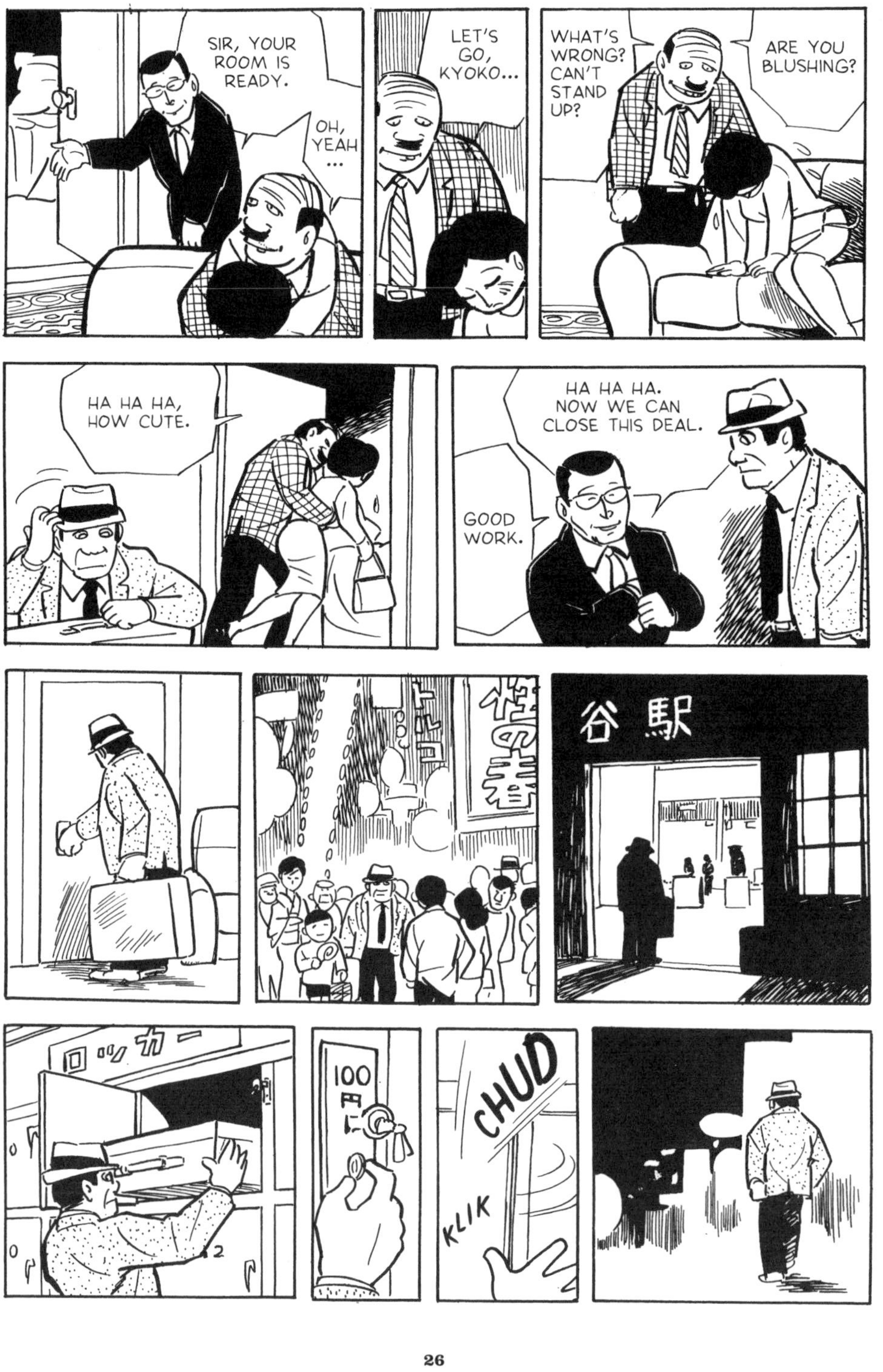
SIR, YOUR ROOM IS READY.
OH, YEAH ...
LET'S GO, KYOKO...
WHAT'S WRONG? CAN'T STAND UP?
ARE YOU BLUSHING?
HA HA HA, HOW CUTE.
HA HA HA. NOW WE CAN CLOSE THIS DEAL.
GOOD WORK.
谷駅
ロッカー
100
円に
CHUD
KLIK

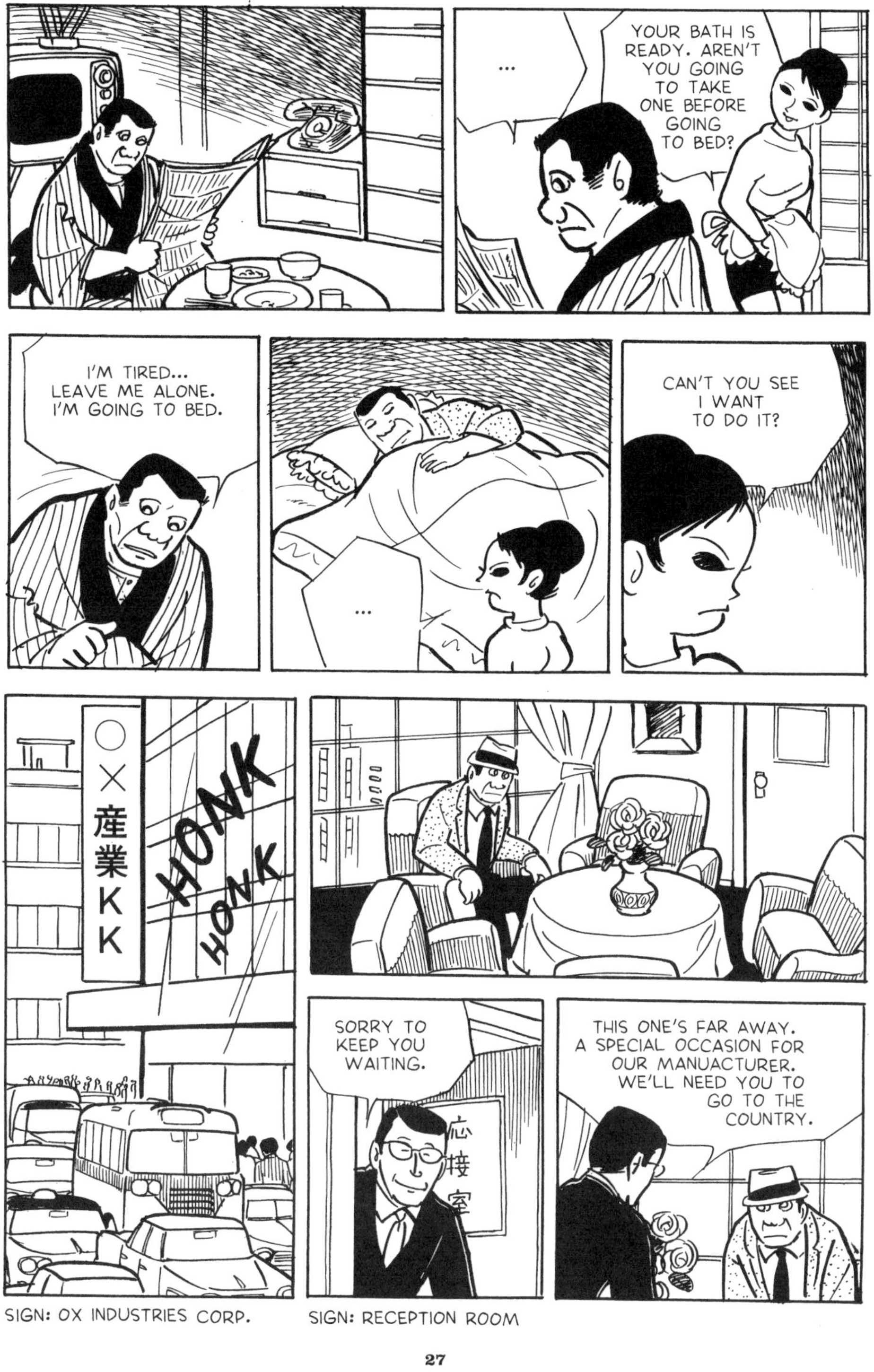
...
YOUR BATH IS READY. AREN'T YOU GOING TO TAKE ONE BEFORE GOING TO BED?
I'M TIRED... LEAVE ME ALONE. I'M GOING TO BED.
...
CAN'T YOU SEE I WANT TO DO IT?
○×産業KK
HONK
HONK
SORRY TO KEEP YOU WAITING.
応接室
THIS ONE'S FAR AWAY. A SPECIAL OCCASION FOR OUR MANUACTURER. WE'LL NEED YOU TO GO TO THE COUNTRY.

SIGN: OX INDUSTRIES CORP.

SIGN: RECEPTION ROOM

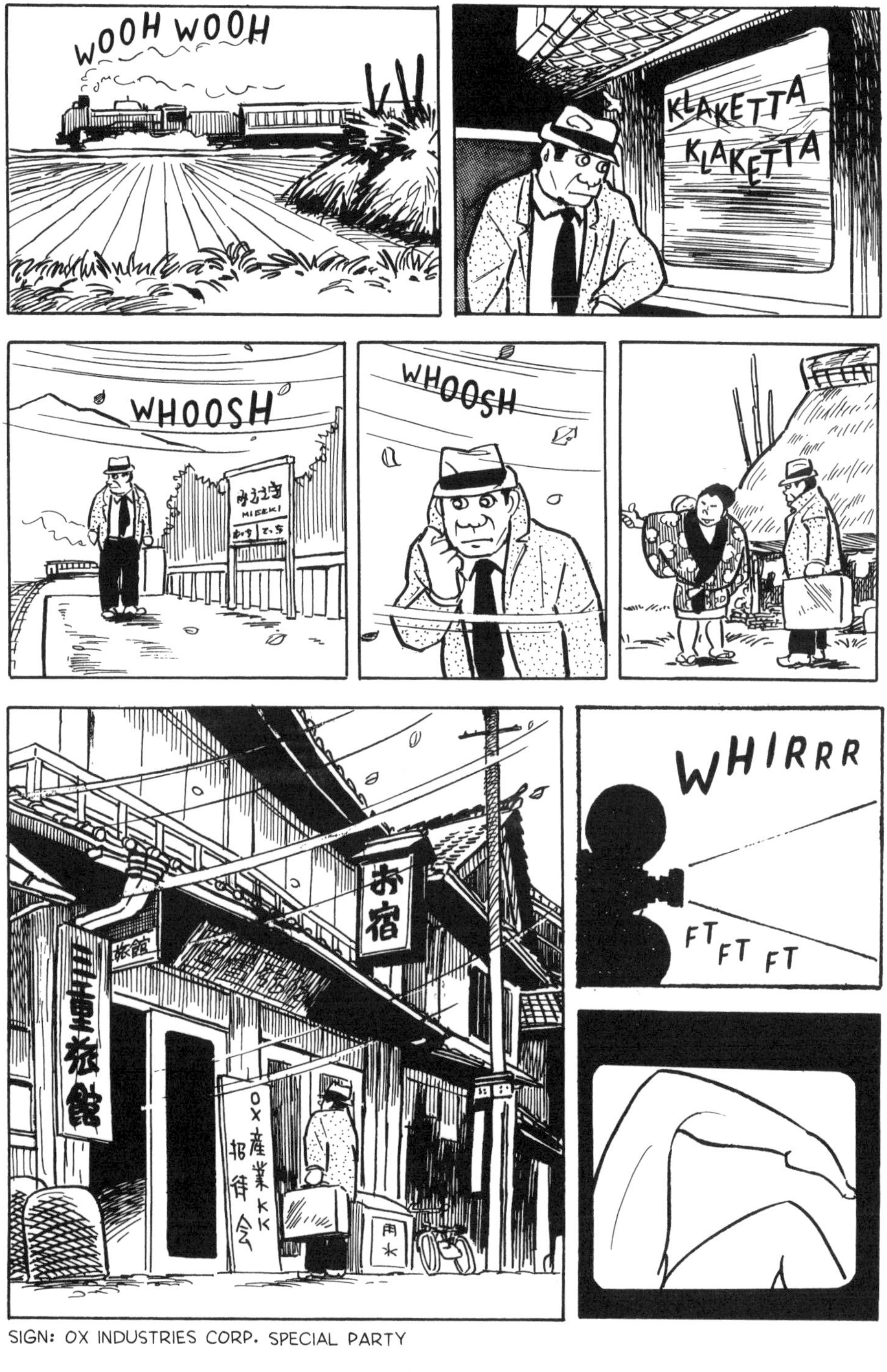
WOOH WOOH
KLAKETTA KLAKETTA
WHOOSH
WHOOSH
三重旅館
旅館
お宿
OX産業KK招待会
WHIRRR
FT FT FT

SIGN: OX INDUSTRIES CORP. SPECIAL PARTY

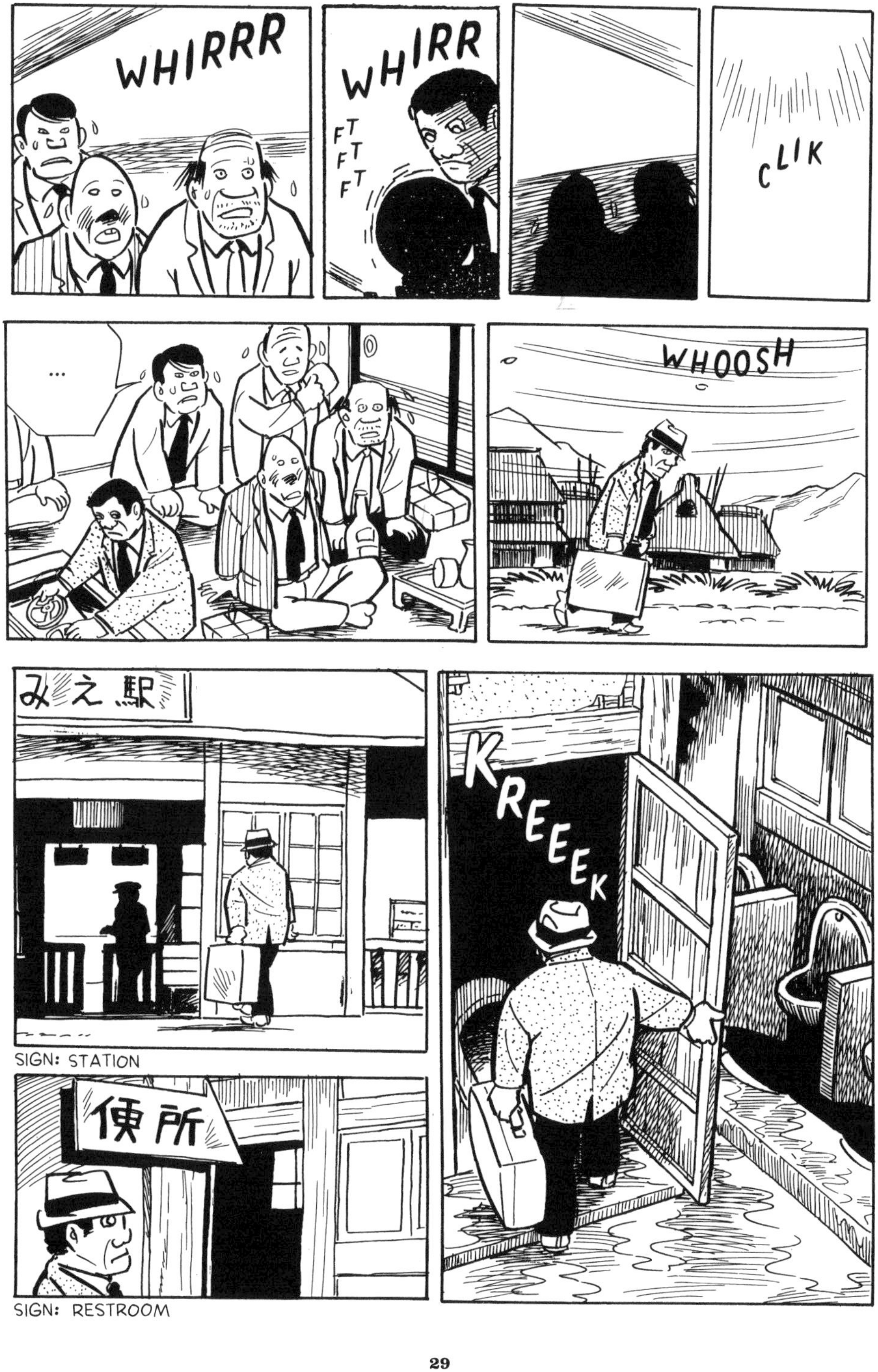
WHIRRR
WHIRR
FT FT FT
CLIK
...
WHOOSH
みえ駅
SIGN: STATION
KREEEEK
便所
SIGN: RESTROOM

GRAFFITI: I WANT TO FUCK PUSSY

...

WOOH WOOH

YOU WERE AMAZING TONIGHT.

IT'S BEEN SO LONG.

ANOTHER JOB, HUH?

BRRRING BRRRING

BRRRING

30

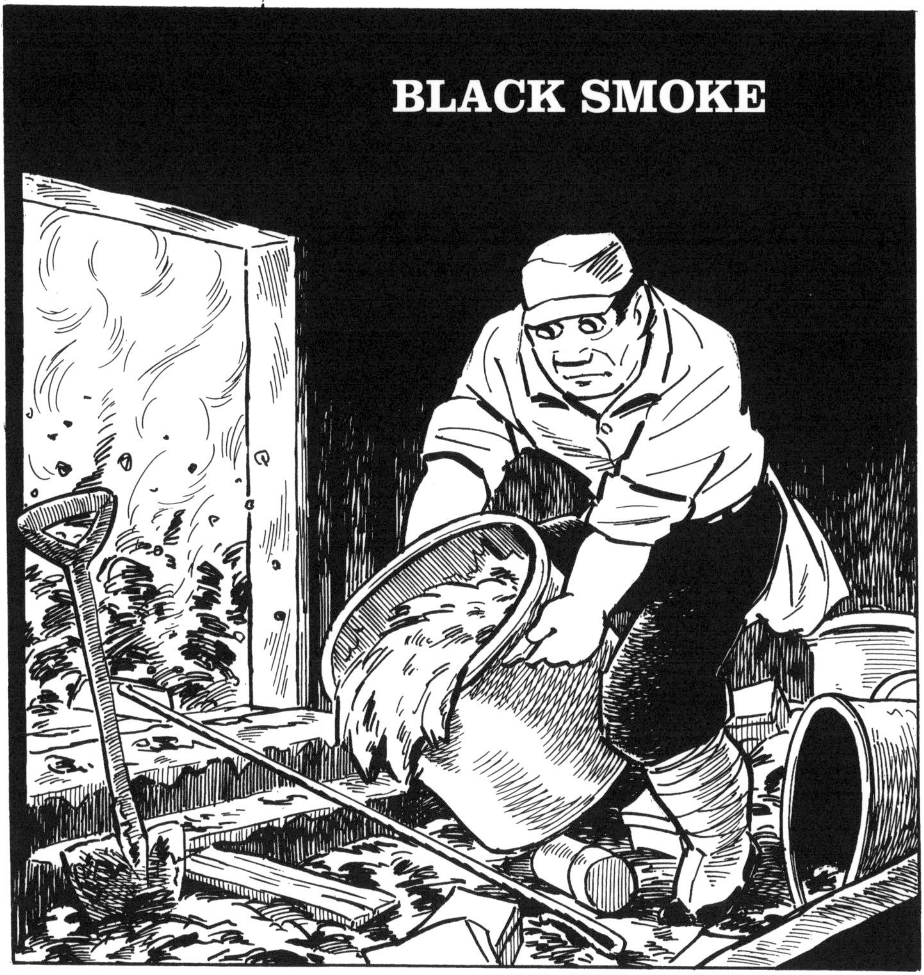
BLACK SMOKE

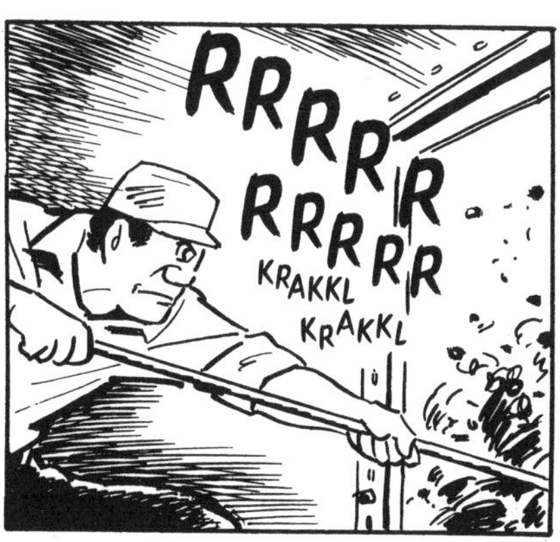
RRRRR
RRRRRR
KRAKKL
KRAKKL

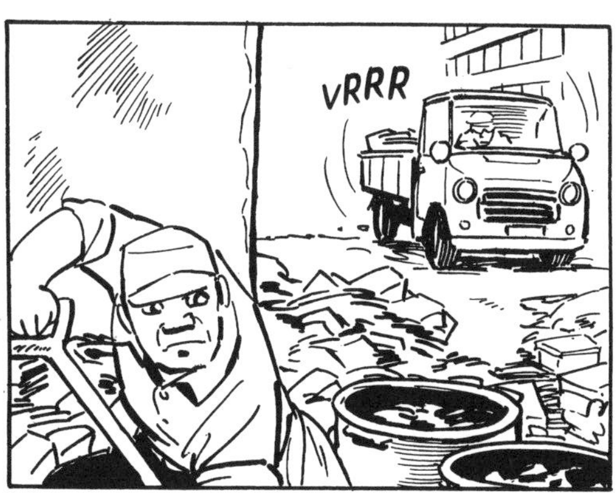
VRRR

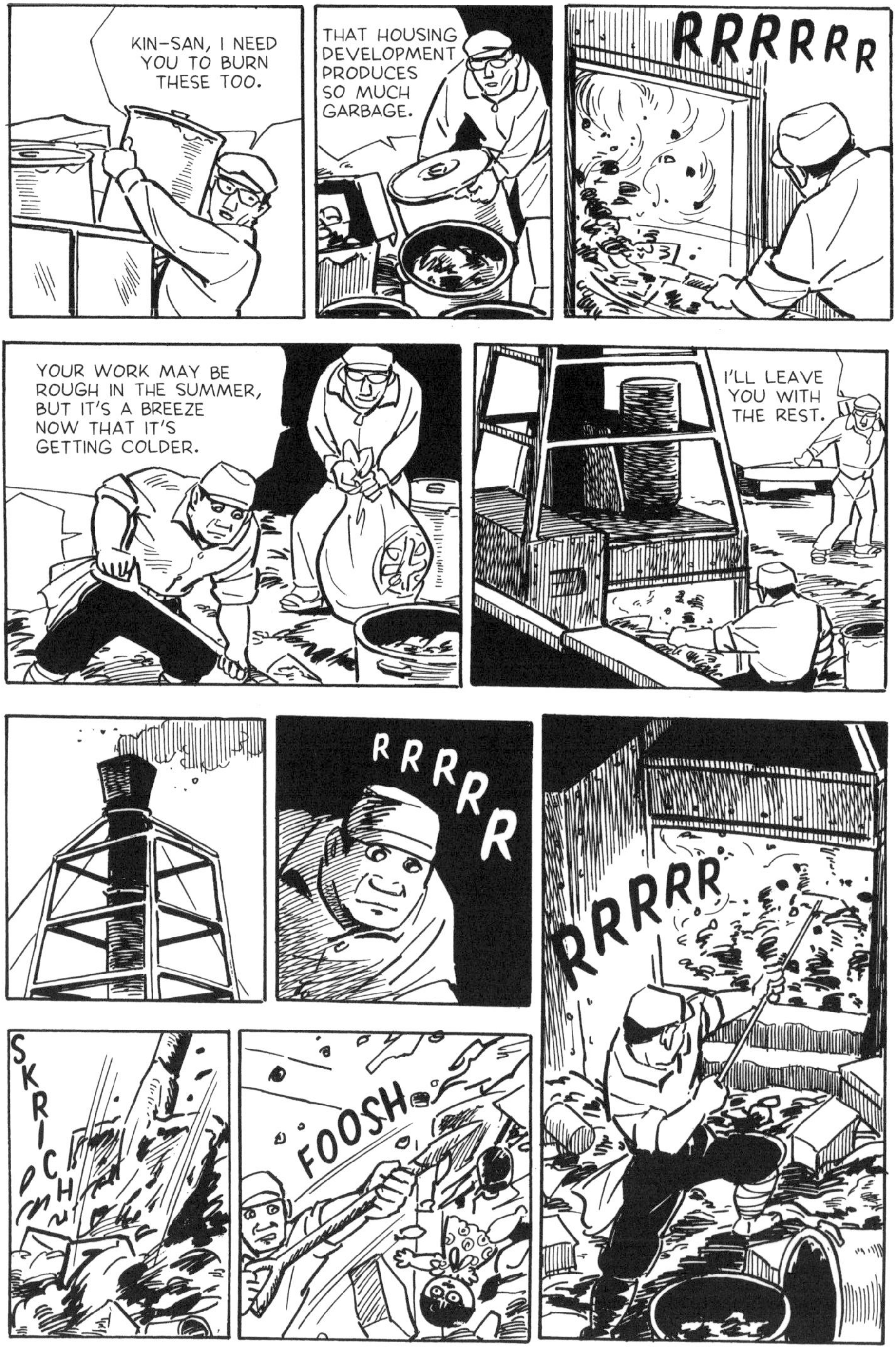
KIN-SAN, I NEED YOU TO BURN THESE TOO.
THAT HOUSING DEVELOPMENT PRODUCES SO MUCH GARBAGE.
RRRRRR
YOUR WORK MAY BE ROUGH IN THE SUMMER, BUT IT'S A BREEZE NOW THAT IT'S GETTING COLDER.
I'LL LEAVE YOU WITH THE REST.
RRRRRR
RRRRRR
SKRICH
FOOSH

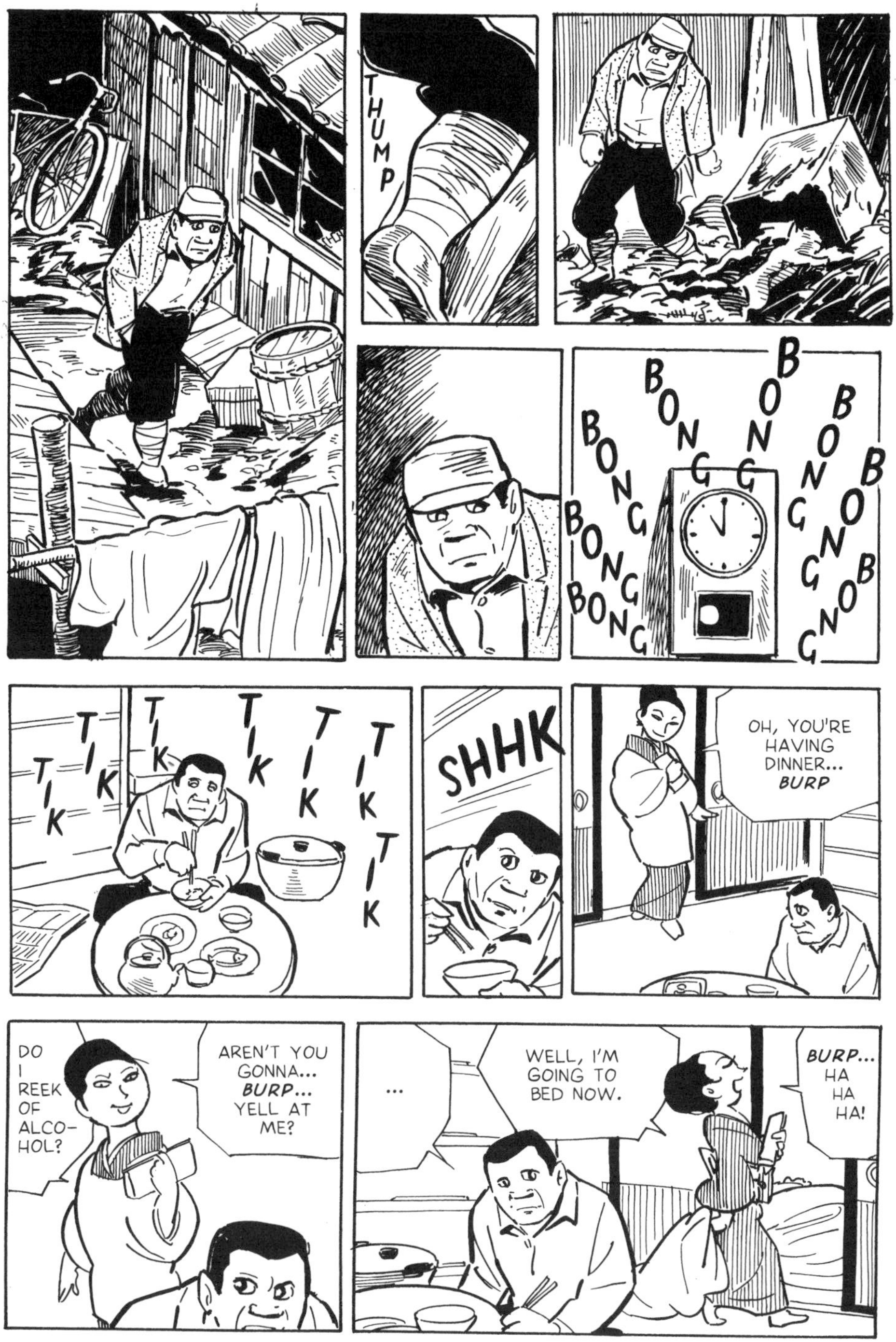
THUMP
BONG BONG BONG BONG
BONG BONG BONG BONG
TIK TIK TIK TIK TIK TIK TIK
SHHK
OH, YOU'RE HAVING DINNER... BURP
DO I REEK OF ALCO-HOL?
AREN'T YOU GONNA... BURP... YELL AT ME?
...
WELL, I'M GOING TO BED NOW.
BURP... HA HA HA!

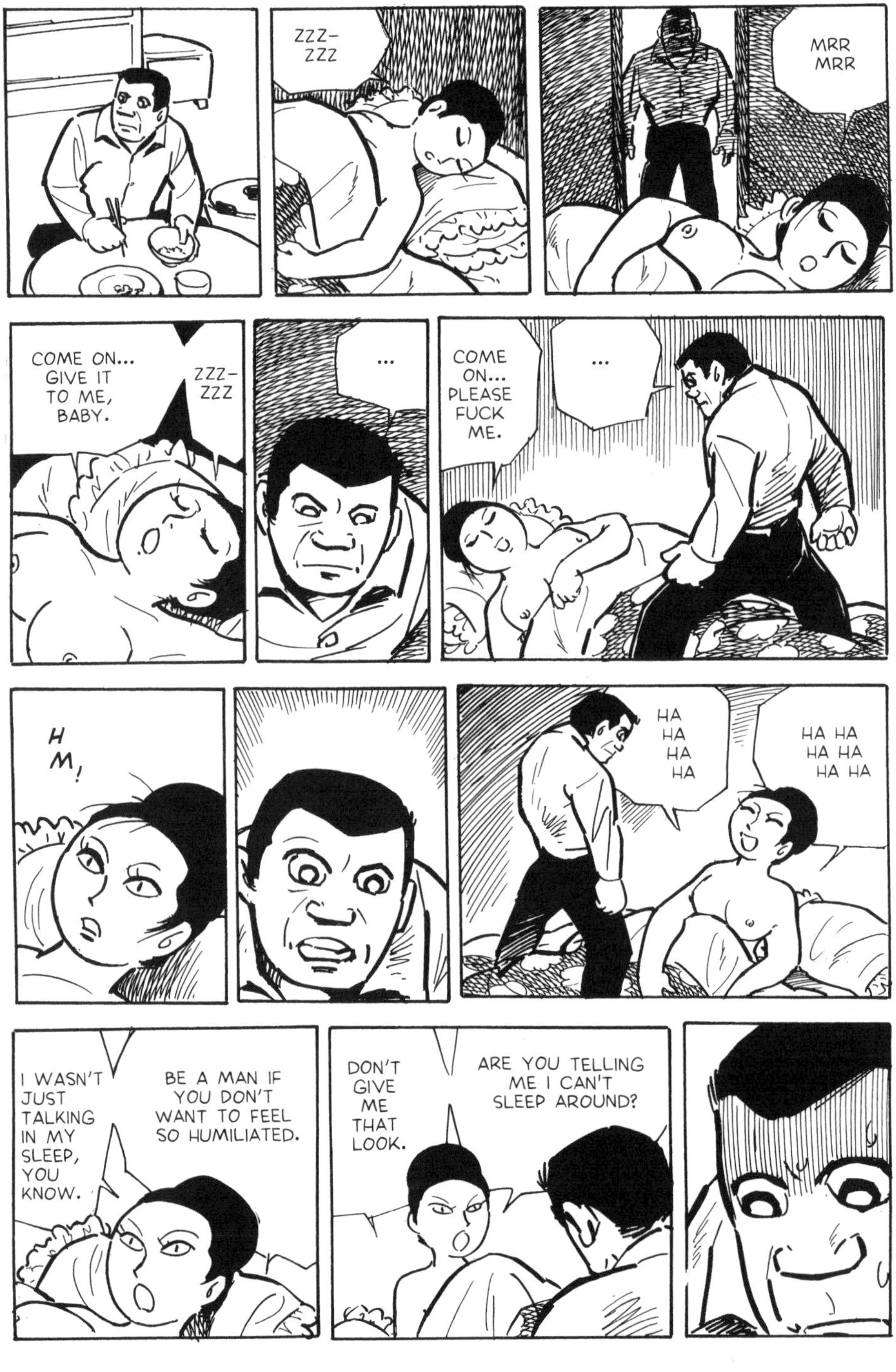
ZZZ-ZZZ
MRR MRR
COME ON... GIVE IT TO ME, BABY.
ZZZ-ZZZ
...
COME ON... PLEASE FUCK ME.
...
HM!
HA HA HA HA
HA HA HA HA HA HA
I WASN'T JUST TALKING IN MY SLEEP, YOU KNOW.
BE A MAN IF YOU DON'T WANT TO FEEL SO HUMILIATED.
DON'T GIVE ME THAT LOOK.
ARE YOU TELLING ME I CAN'T SLEEP AROUND?

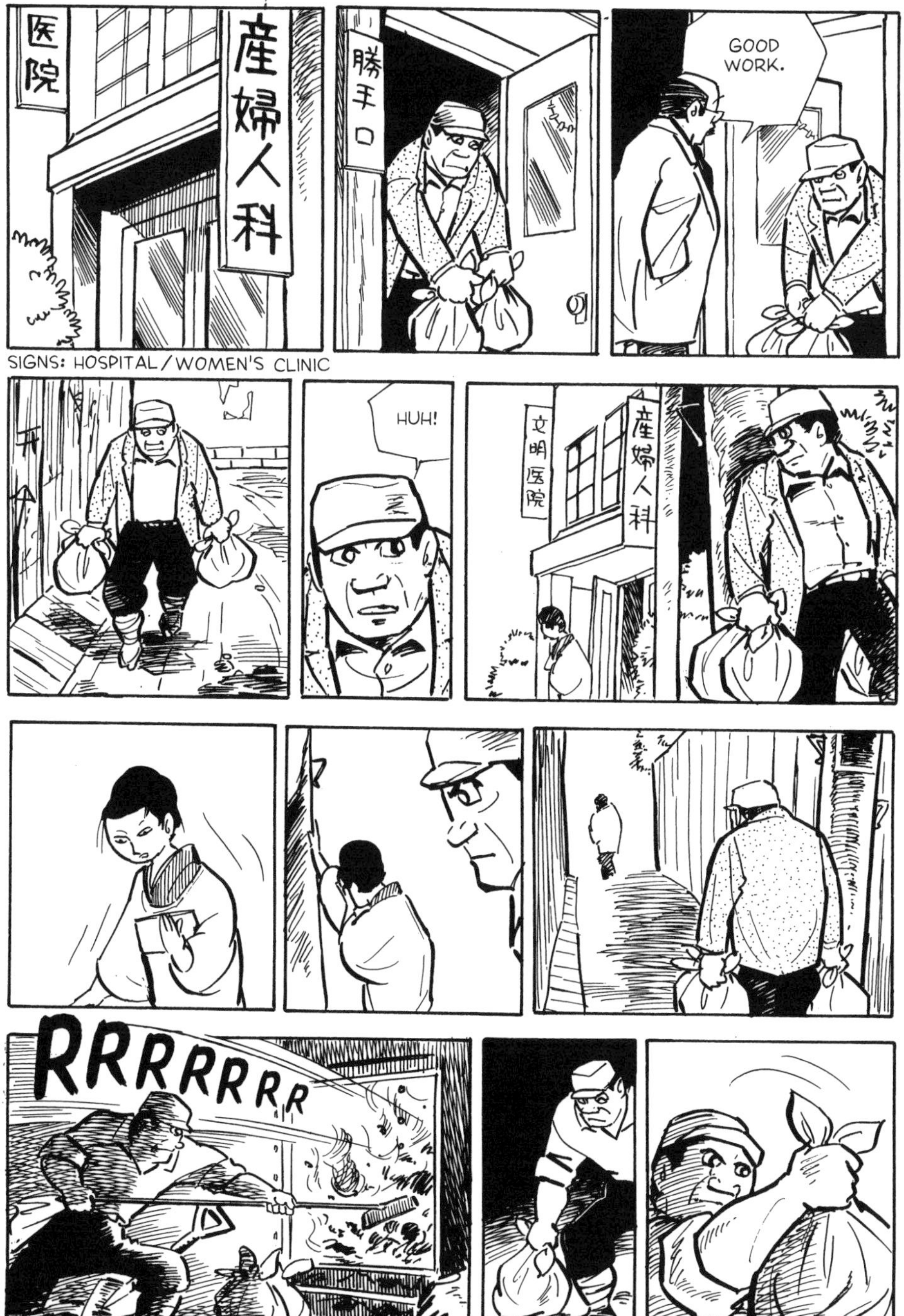
医院
産婦人科
勝手口
GOOD WORK.
SIGNS: HOSPITAL/WOMEN'S CLINIC
HUH!
文明医院
産婦人科
RRRRRRRR

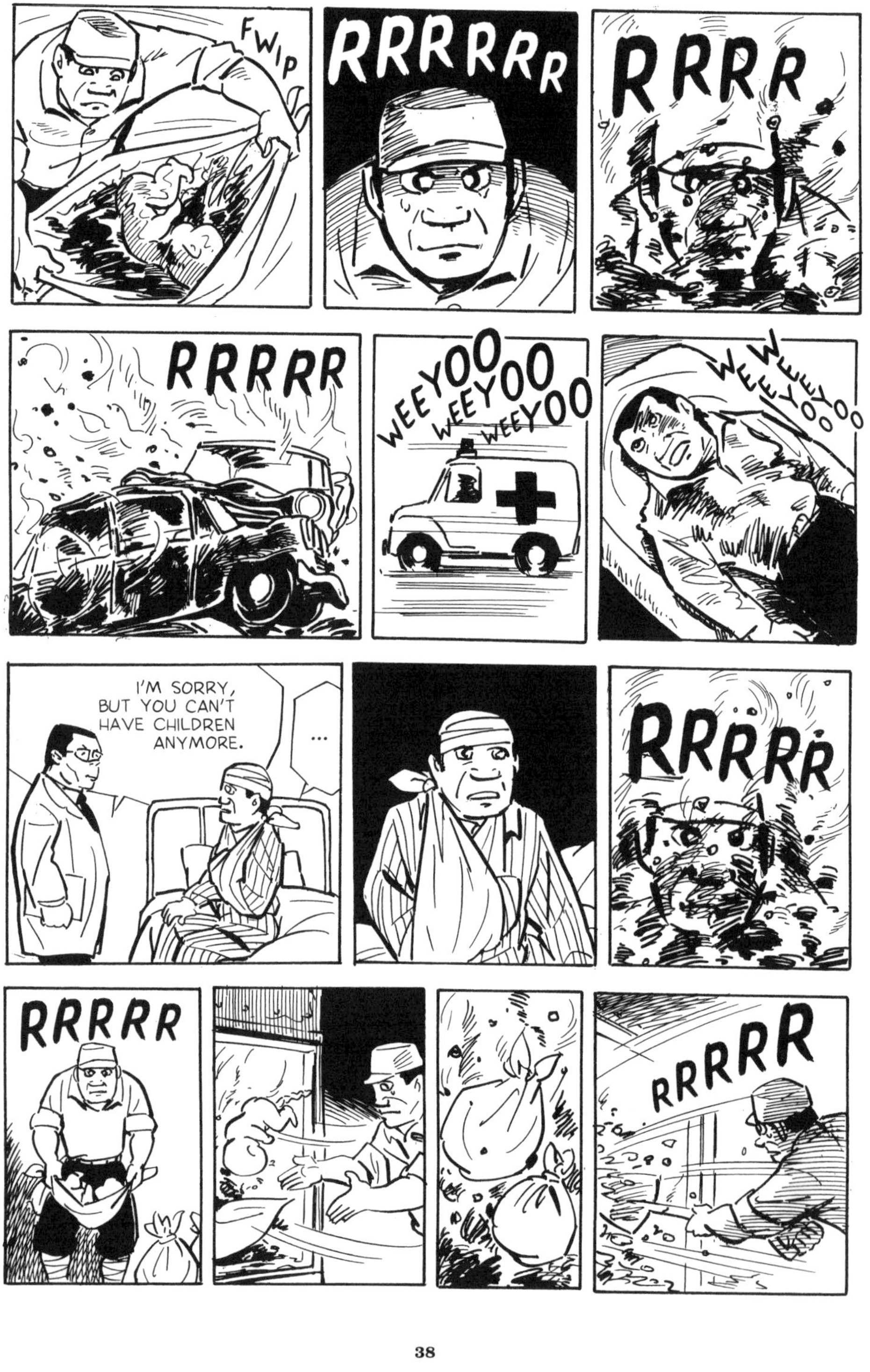
FWIP
RRRRRRR
RRRR
RRRRR
WEEYOO WEEYOO WEEYOO
WWEEYOO WEEYOO
I'M SORRY, BUT YOU CAN'T HAVE CHILDREN ANYMORE.
...
RRRRRR
RRRRR
RRRRR

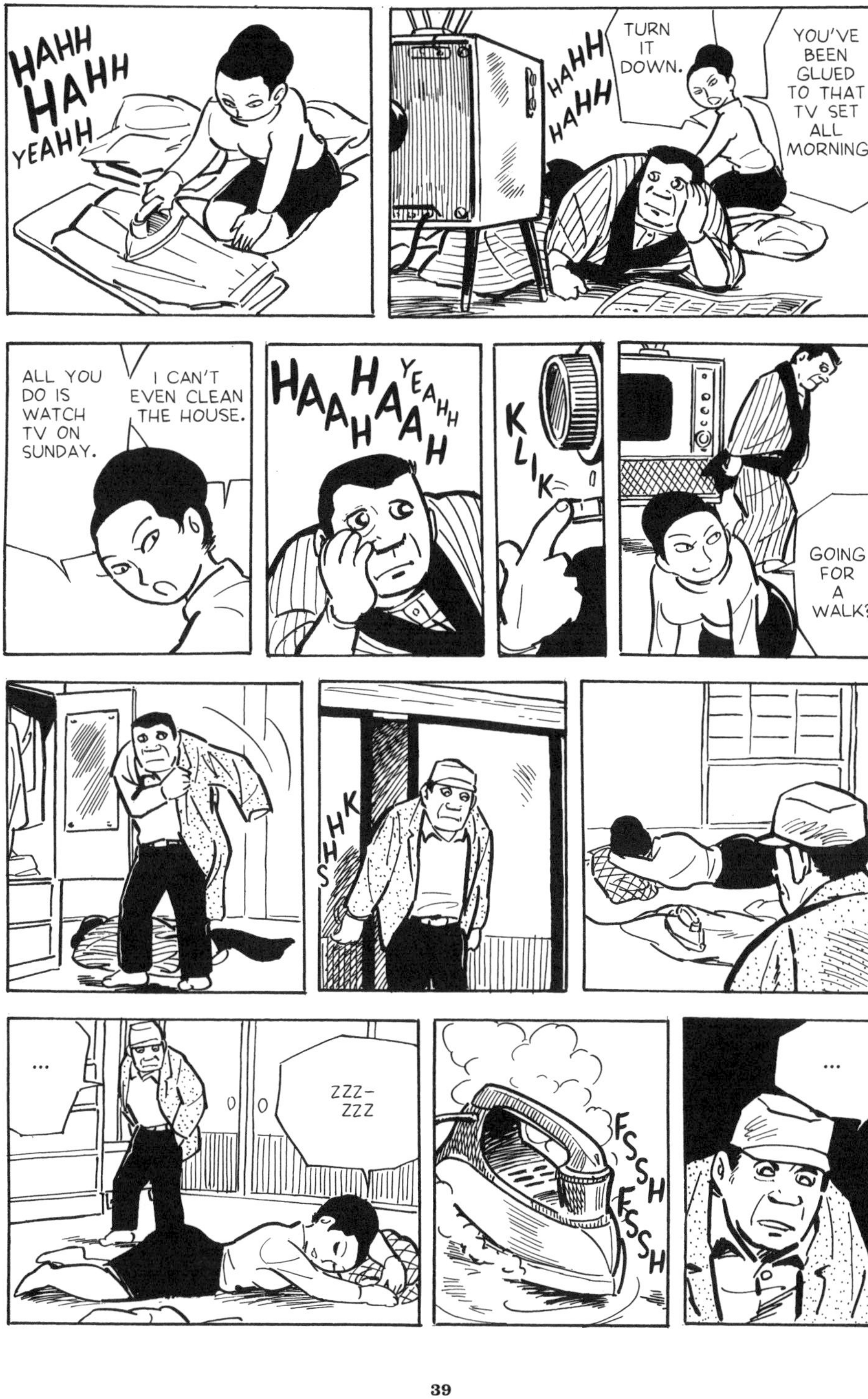
HAHH
HAHH
YEAHH
HAHH
HAHH
TURN IT DOWN.
YOU'VE BEEN GLUED TO THAT TV SET ALL MORNING.
ALL YOU DO IS WATCH TV ON SUNDAY.
I CAN'T EVEN CLEAN THE HOUSE.
HAAHHAAAH
YEAHH
KLIK
GOING FOR A WALK?
SHHK
...
ZZZ-
ZZZ
FSSSH
FSSSH
...

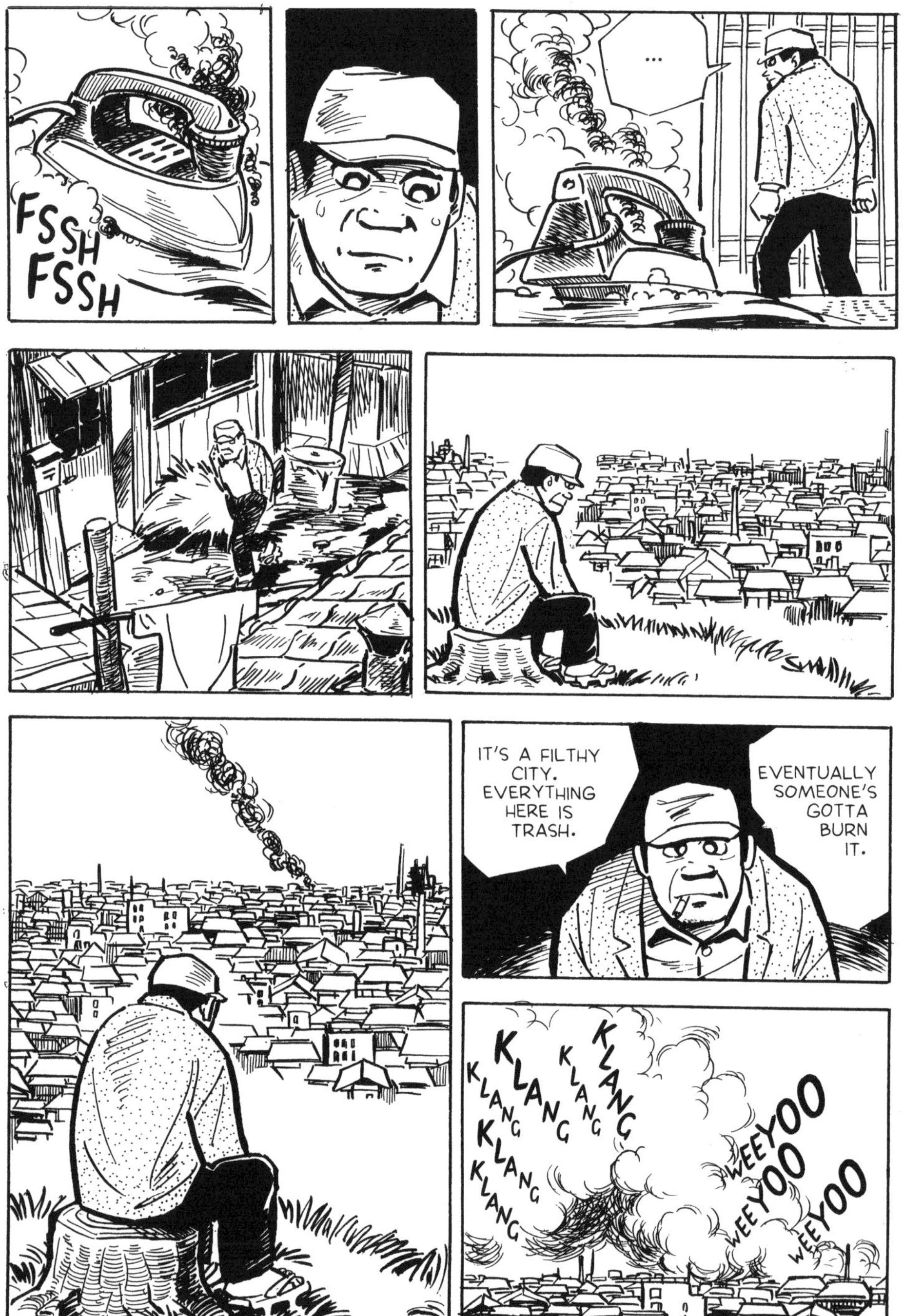
FSSH
FSSH
...
IT'S A FILTHY CITY. EVERYTHING HERE IS TRASH.
EVENTUALLY SOMEONE'S GOTTA BURN IT.
KLANG KLANG KLANG KLANG KLANG KLANG
WEEYOO WEEYOO WEEYOO

THE BURDEN

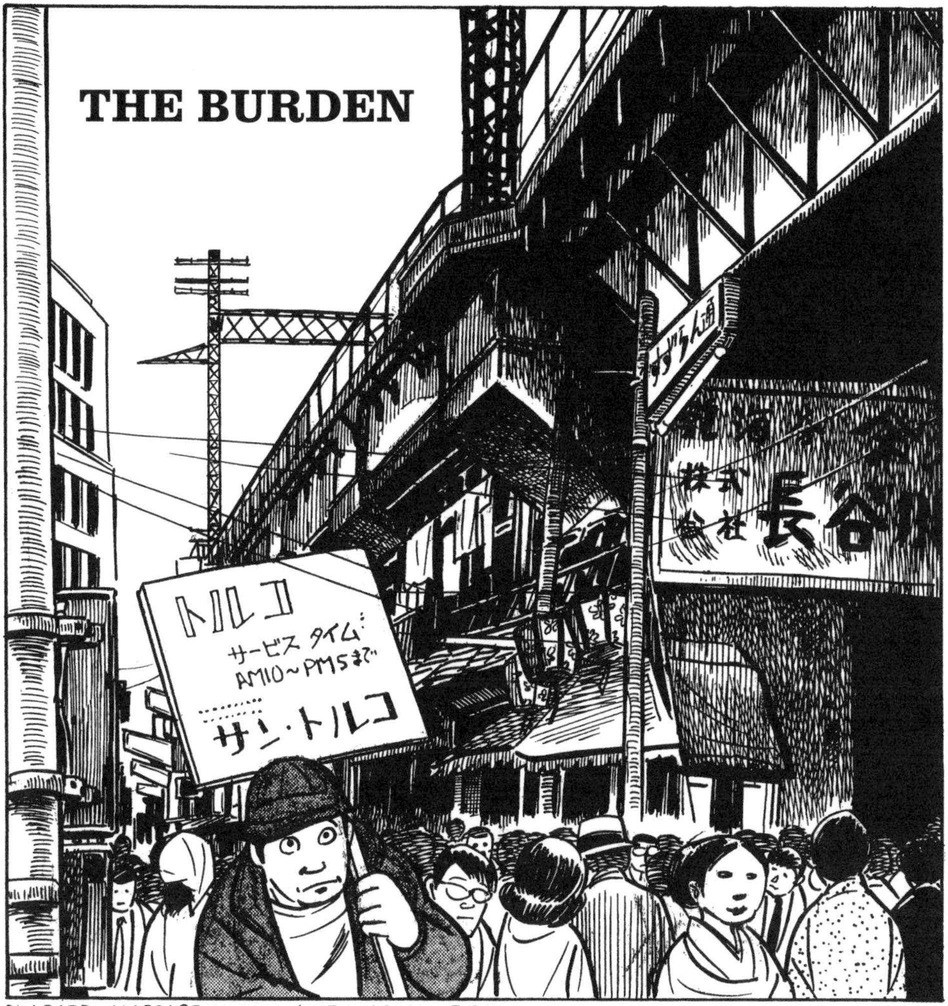
トルコ
サービス タイム
AM10~PM5まで
サン・トルコ
すずらん通
株式会社
長谷

PLACARD: MASSAGE PARLOR / OPEN: 10 AM–5 PM

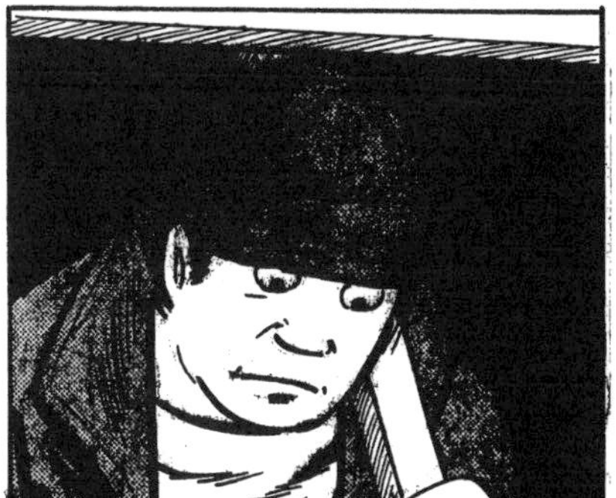

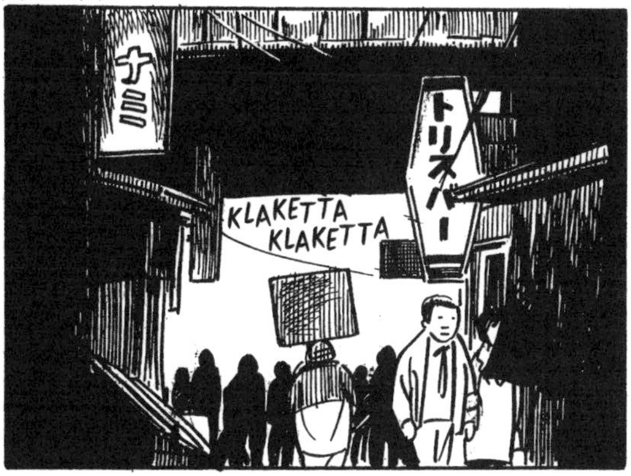
ナミ
トリスバー
KLAKETTA
KLAKETTA

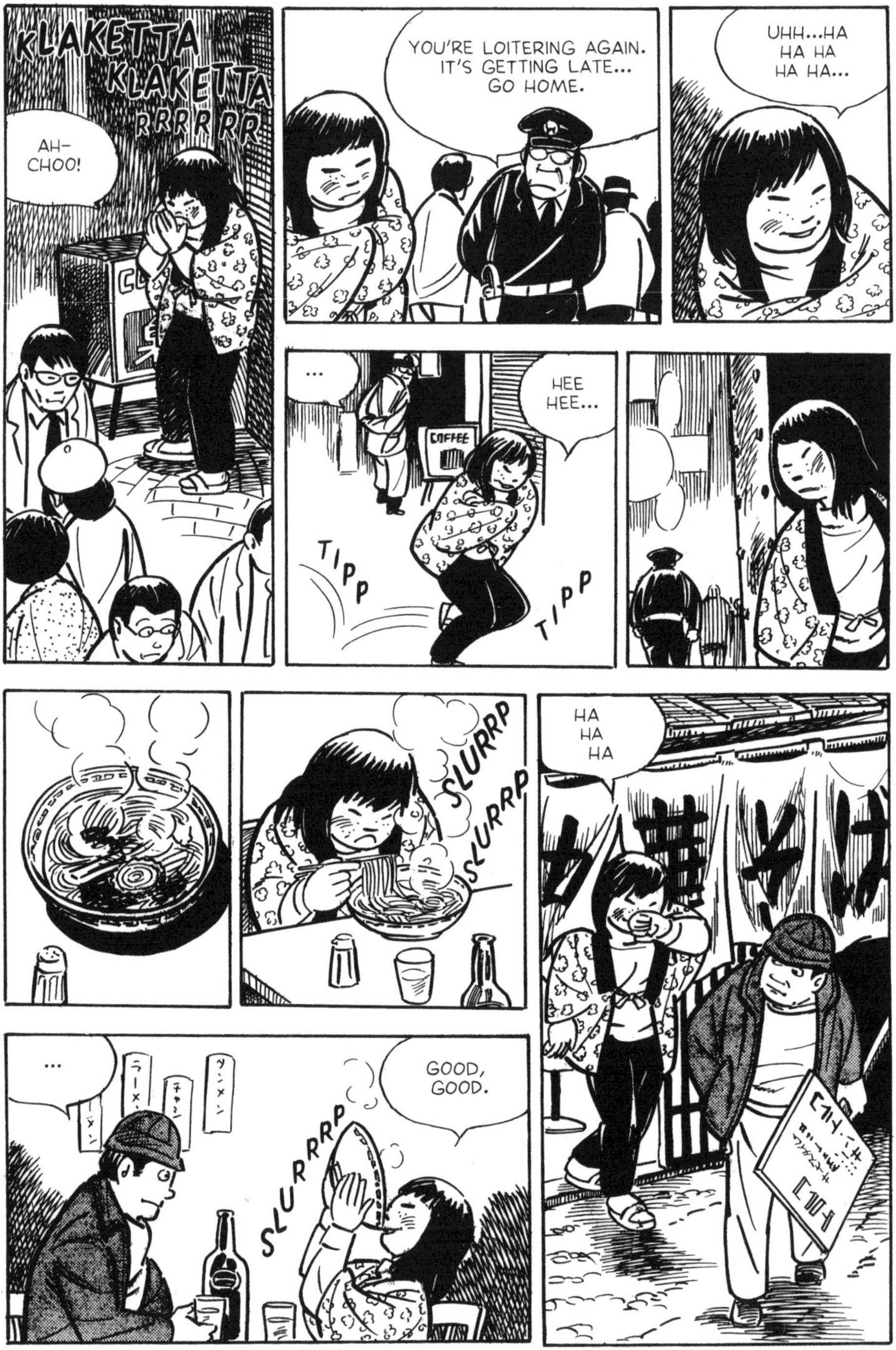
KLAKETTA
KLAKETTA
RRRRRR
AH-CHOO!
YOU'RE LOITERING AGAIN. IT'S GETTING LATE... GO HOME.
UHH...HA HA HA HA HA...
...
HEE HEE...
TIPP
TIPP
SLURRP
SLURRP
HA HA HA
...
GOOD, GOOD.
SLURRRP

STORE SIGN: CHINESE NOODLES

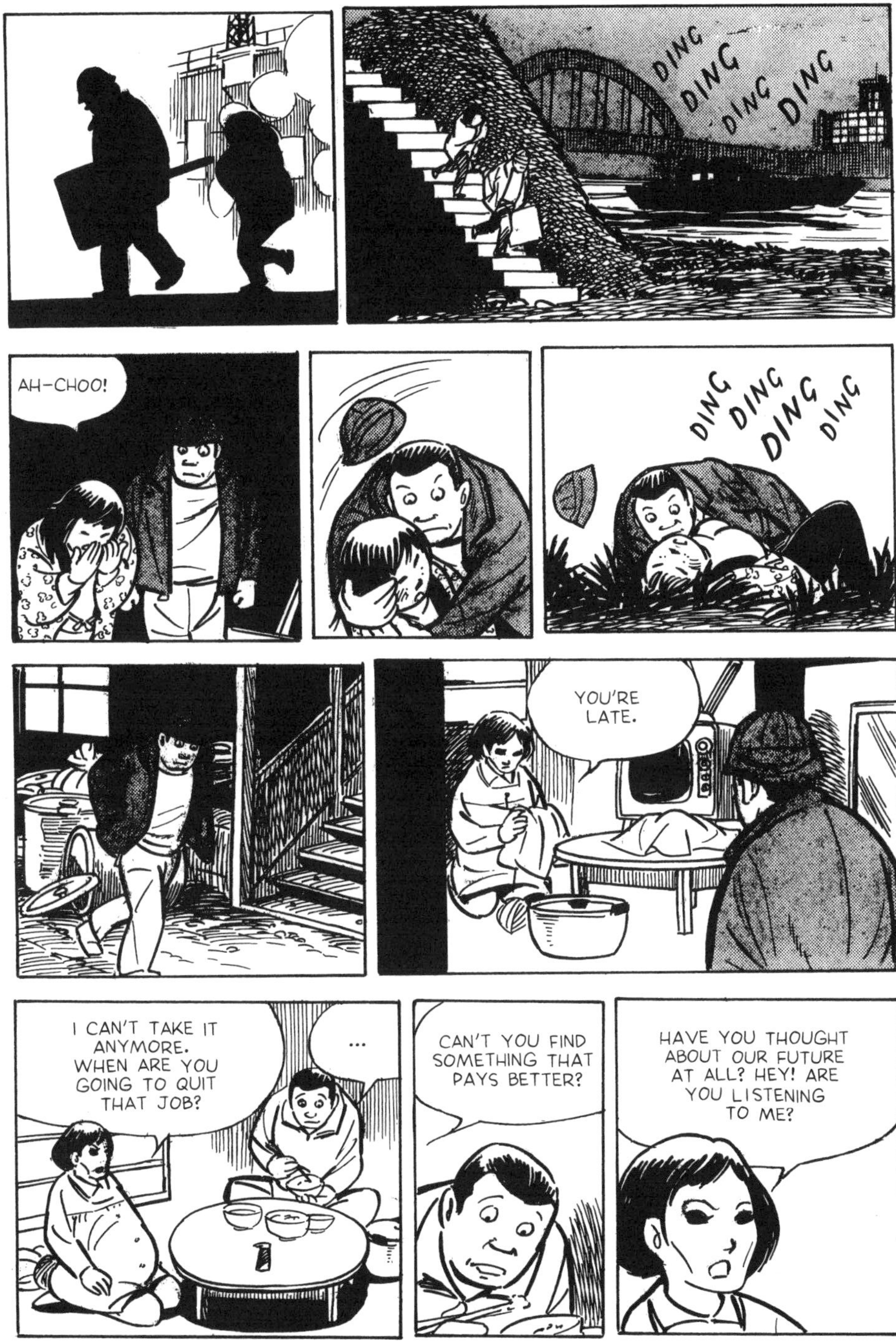
DING DING DING DING
AH-CHOO!
DING DING DING DING
YOU'RE LATE.
I CAN'T TAKE IT ANYMORE. WHEN ARE YOU GOING TO QUIT THAT JOB?
...
CAN'T YOU FIND SOMETHING THAT PAYS BETTER?
HAVE YOU THOUGHT ABOUT OUR FUTURE AT ALL? HEY! ARE YOU LISTENING TO ME?

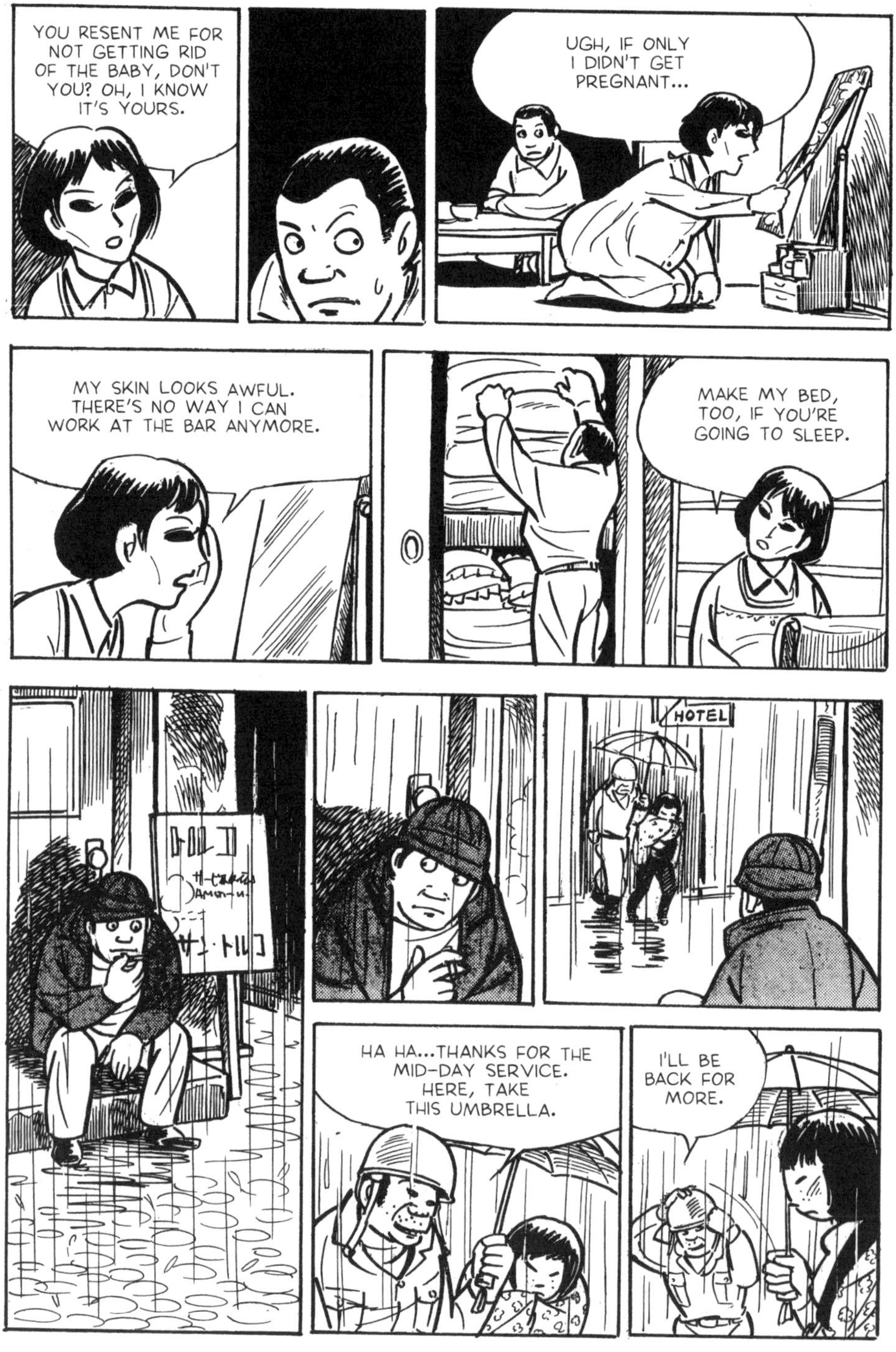
YOU RESENT ME FOR NOT GETTING RID OF THE BABY, DON'T YOU? OH, I KNOW IT'S YOURS.
UGH, IF ONLY I DIDN'T GET PREGNANT...
MY SKIN LOOKS AWFUL. THERE'S NO WAY I CAN WORK AT THE BAR ANYMORE.
MAKE MY BED, TOO, IF YOU'RE GOING TO SLEEP.
HOTEL
HA HA...THANKS FOR THE MID-DAY SERVICE. HERE, TAKE THIS UMBRELLA.
I'LL BE BACK FOR MORE.

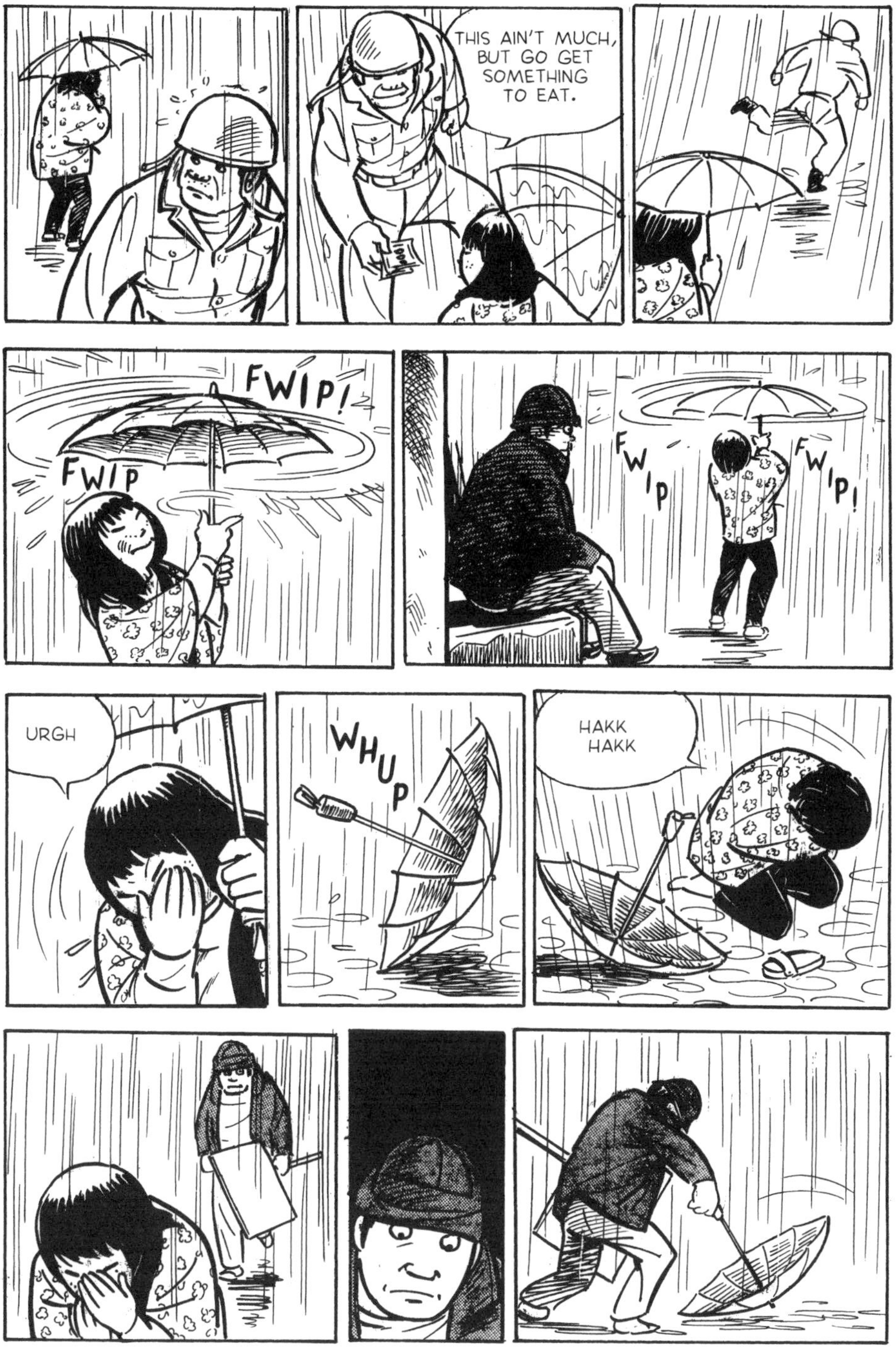
THIS AIN'T MUCH, BUT GO GET SOMETHING TO EAT.
FWIP!
FWIP
FWIP
FWIP!
URGH
WHUP
HAKK HAKK

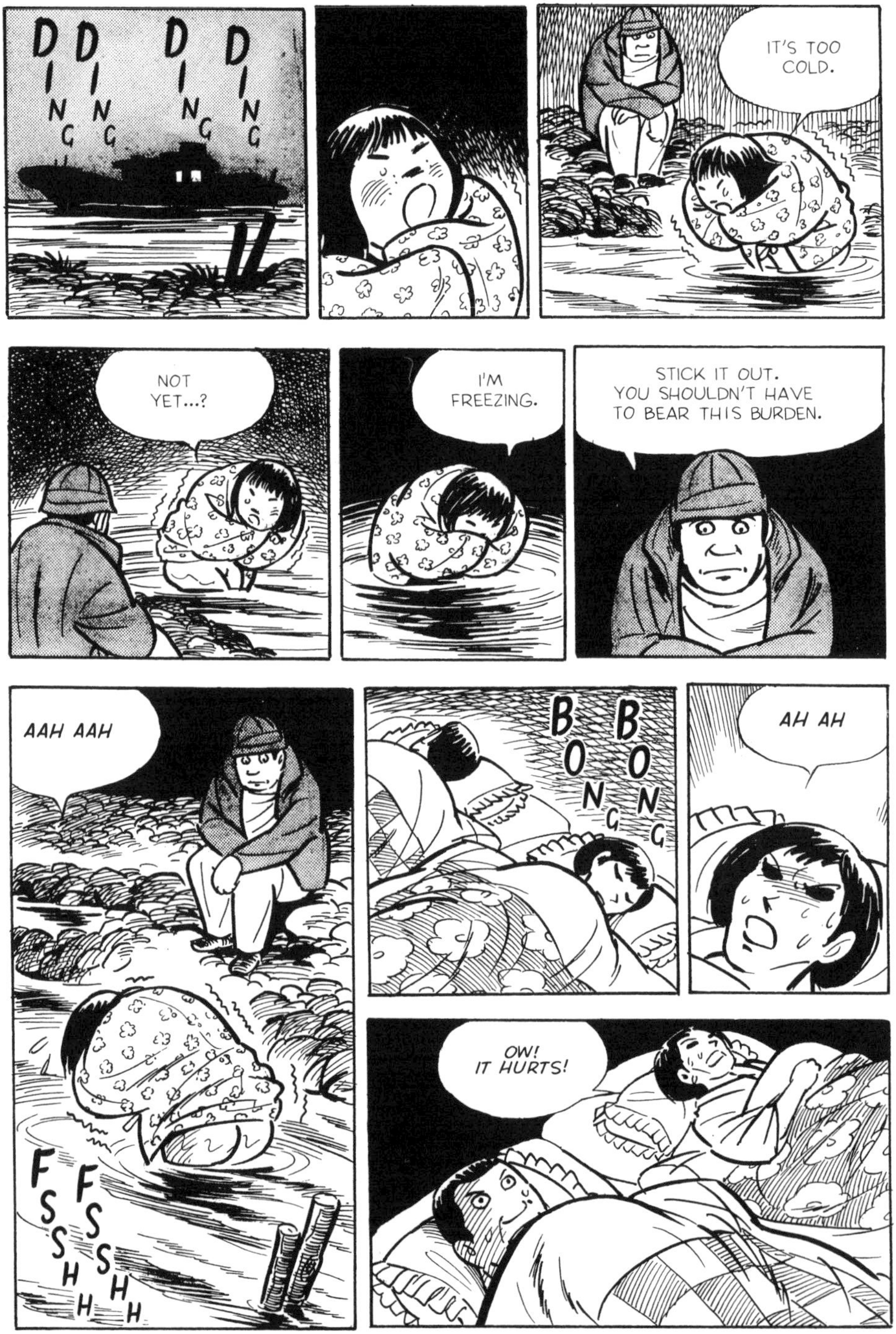
DDING DDING DDING DDING
IT'S TOO COLD.
NOT YET...?
I'M FREEZING.
STICK IT OUT. YOU SHOULDN'T HAVE TO BEAR THIS BURDEN.
AAH AAH
FSSHH FSSHH
BONG BONG
AH AH
OW! IT HURTS!

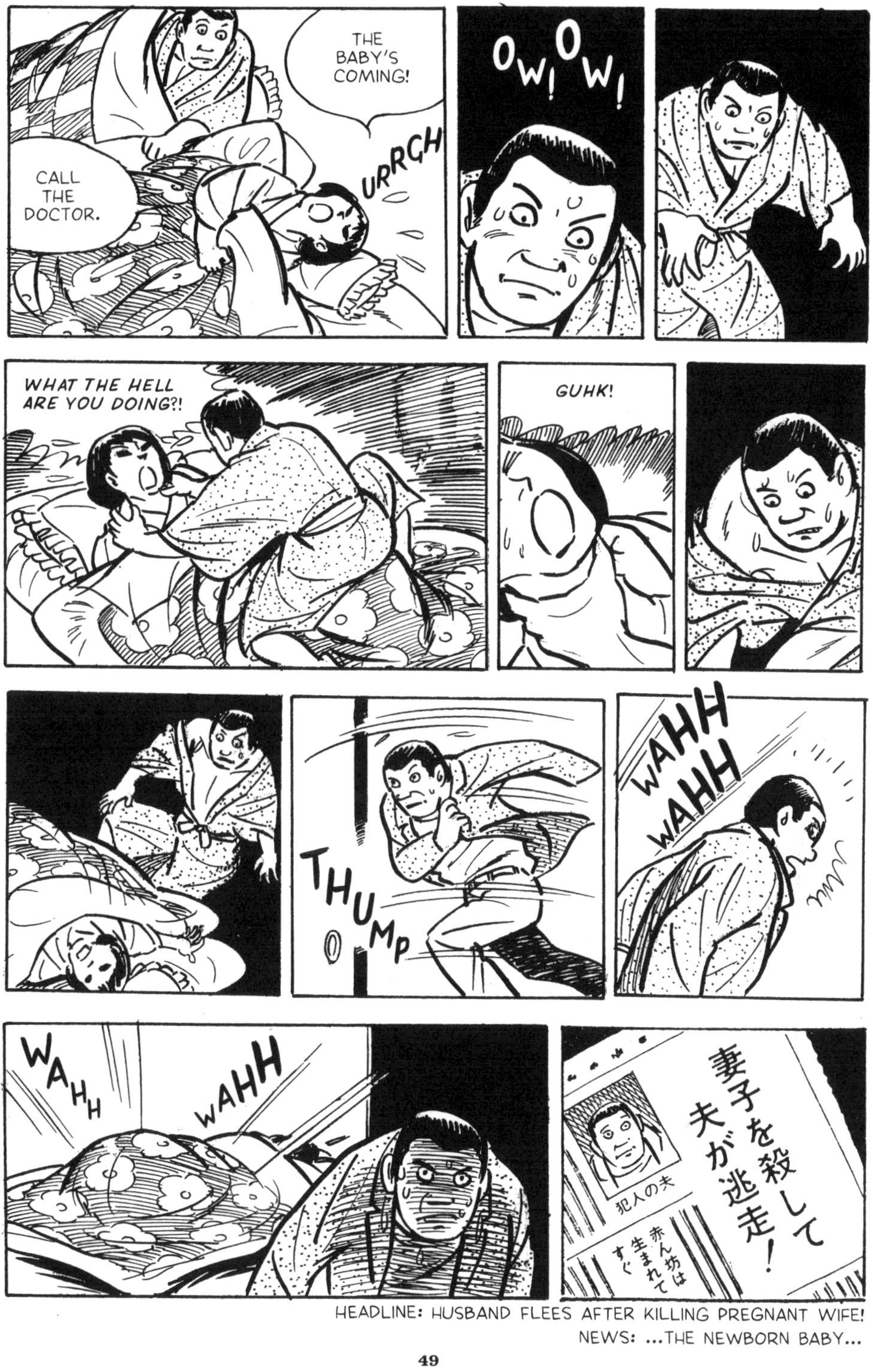
THE BABY'S COMING!
CALL THE DOCTOR.
URRGH
OWOW!
WHAT THE HELL ARE YOU DOING?!
GUHK!
THUMP
WAHH WAHH
WAHH
WAHH
妻子を殺して夫が逃走！
犯人の夫
赤ん坊は生まれてすぐ

HEADLINE: HUSBAND FLEES AFTER KILLING PREGNANT WIFE!
NEWS: ...THE NEWBORN BABY...

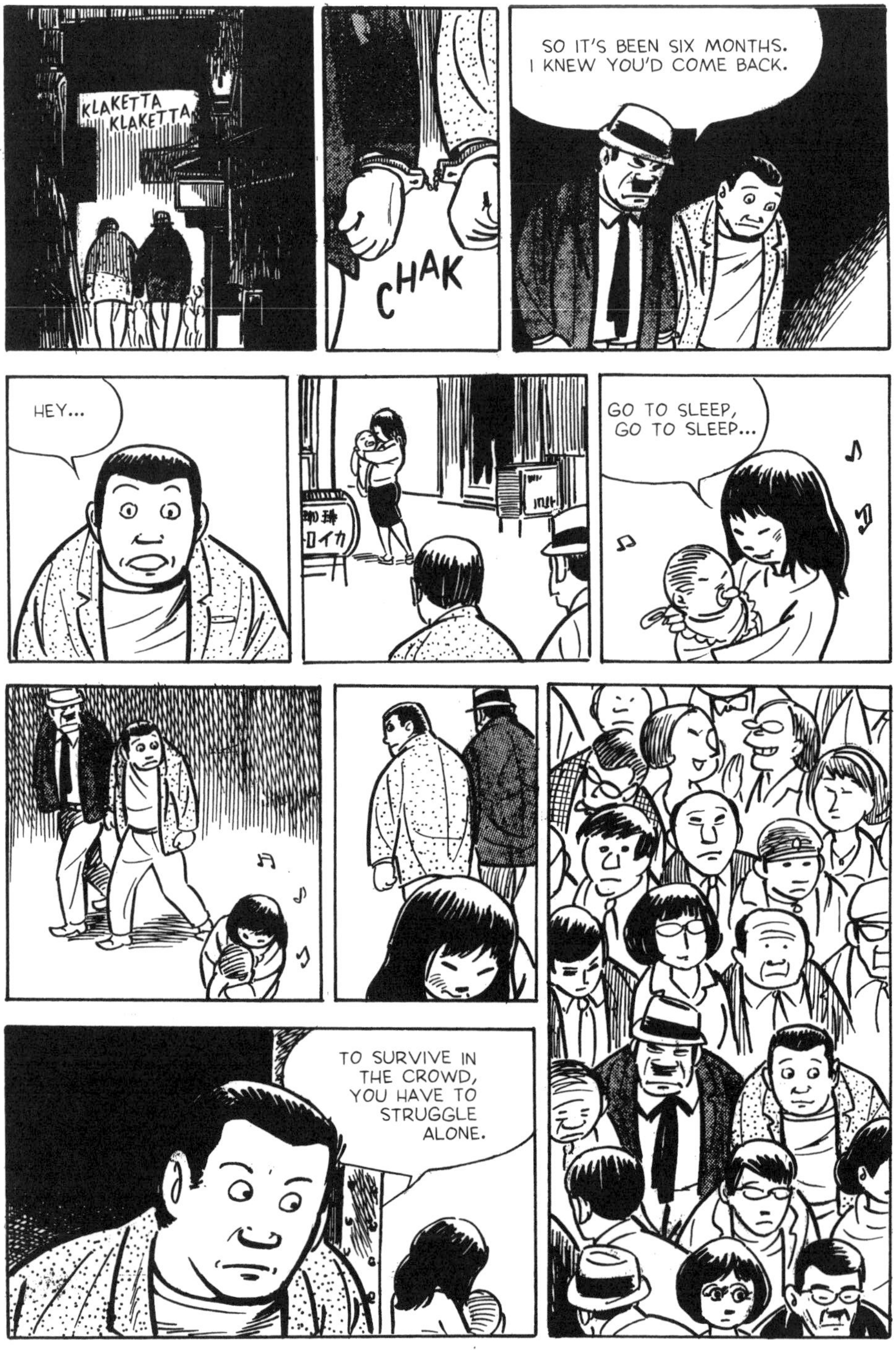
KLAKETTA KLAKETTA
CHAK
SO IT'S BEEN SIX MONTHS. I KNEW YOU'D COME BACK.
HEY...
GO TO SLEEP, GO TO SLEEP...
TO SURVIVE IN THE CROWD, YOU HAVE TO STRUGGLE ALONE.

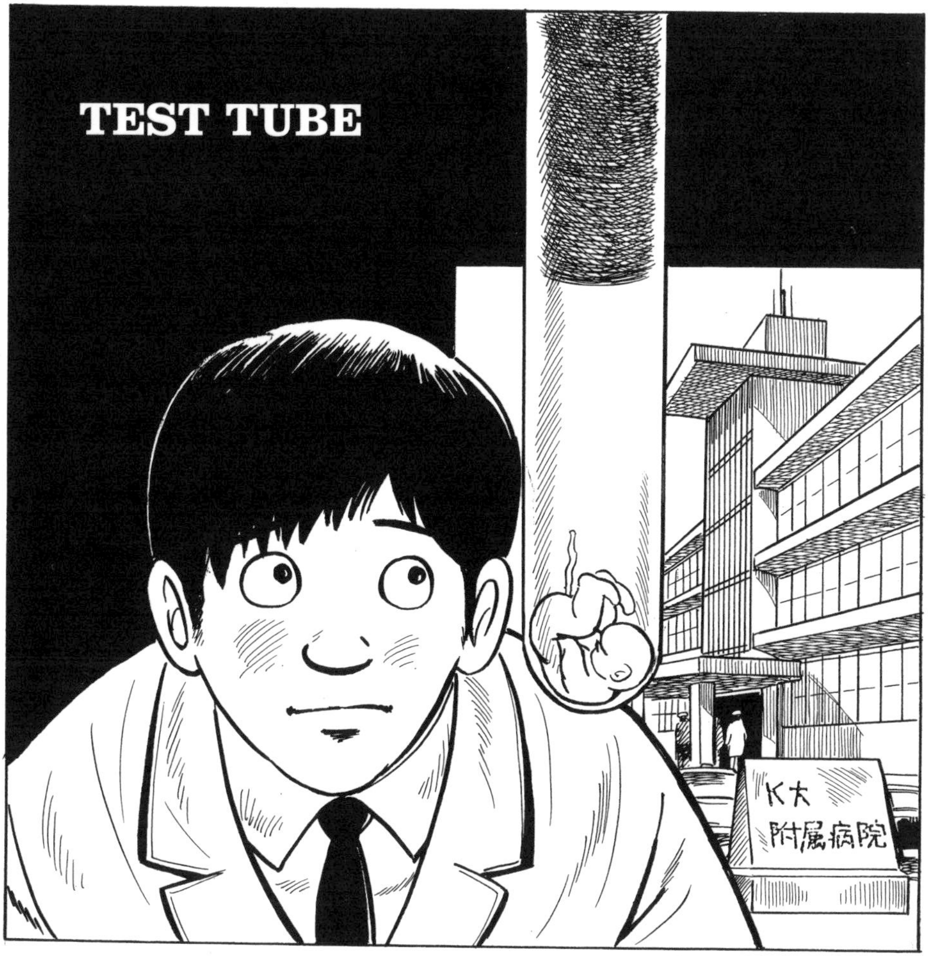
TEST TUBE
K大
附属病院
SIGN: UNIVERSITY HOSPITAL

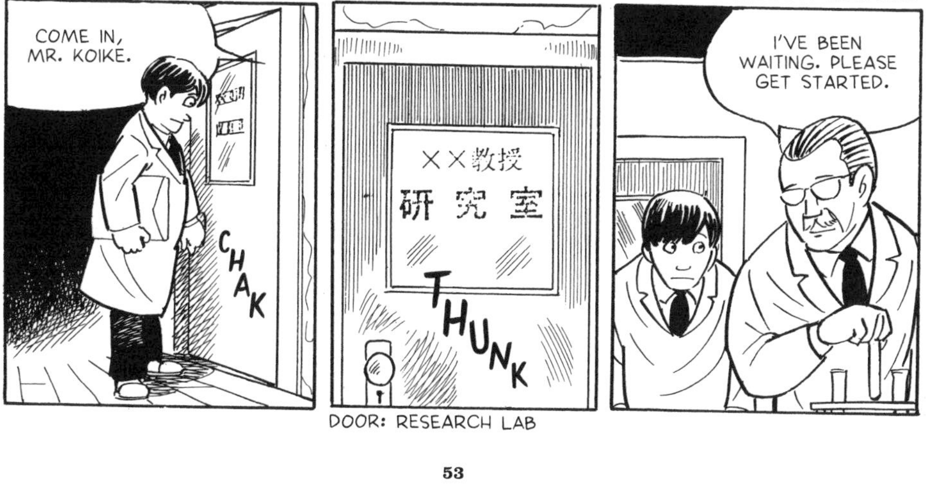
COME IN, MR. KOIKE.
CHAK
××教授
研究室
THUNK
I'VE BEEN WAITING. PLEASE GET STARTED.
DOOR: RESEARCH LAB

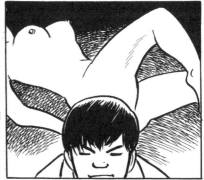

GOOD WORK. I KNOW IT'S NOT EASY DOING IT THIS WAY... WITH NO PASSION INVOLVED.

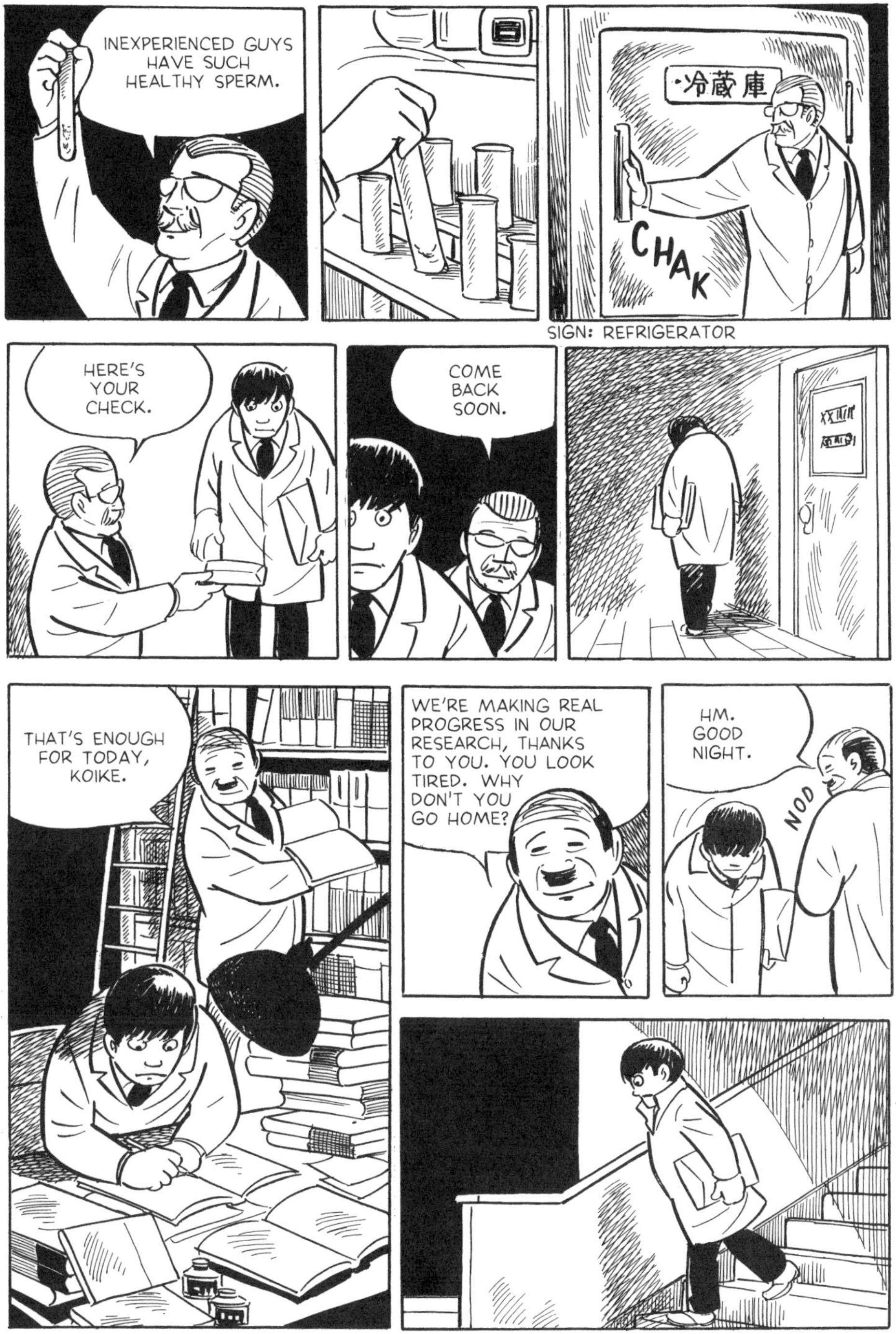
INEXPERIENCED GUYS HAVE SUCH HEALTHY SPERM.
冷蔵庫
CHAK
SIGN: REFRIGERATOR
HERE'S YOUR CHECK.
COME BACK SOON.
THAT'S ENOUGH FOR TODAY, KOIKE.
WE'RE MAKING REAL PROGRESS IN OUR RESEARCH, THANKS TO YOU. YOU LOOK TIRED. WHY DON'T YOU GO HOME?
HM. GOOD NIGHT.
NOD

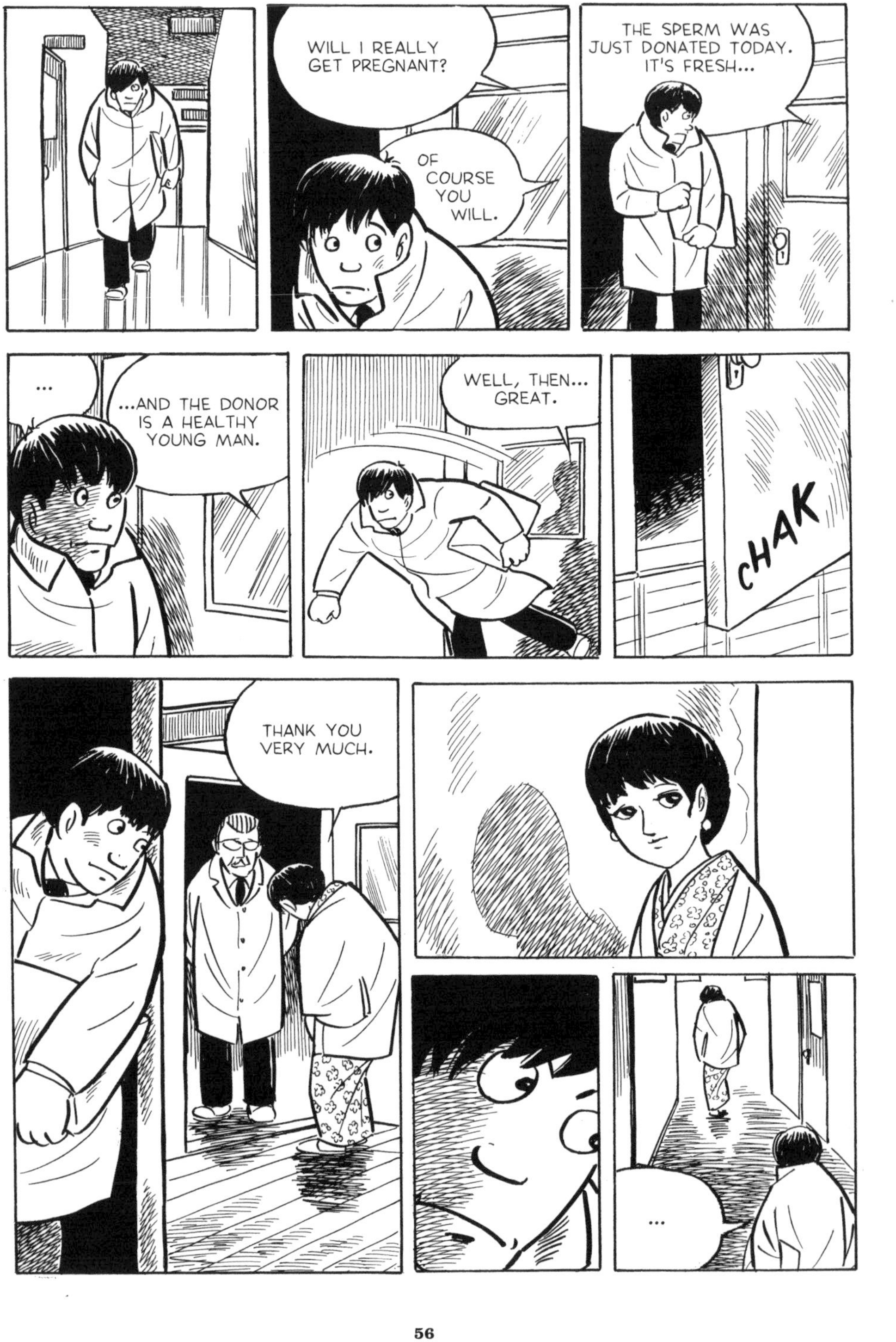
WILL I REALLY GET PREGNANT?
OF COURSE YOU WILL.
THE SPERM WAS JUST DONATED TODAY. IT'S FRESH...
...
...AND THE DONOR IS A HEALTHY YOUNG MAN.
WELL, THEN... GREAT.
CHAK
THANK YOU VERY MUCH.
...

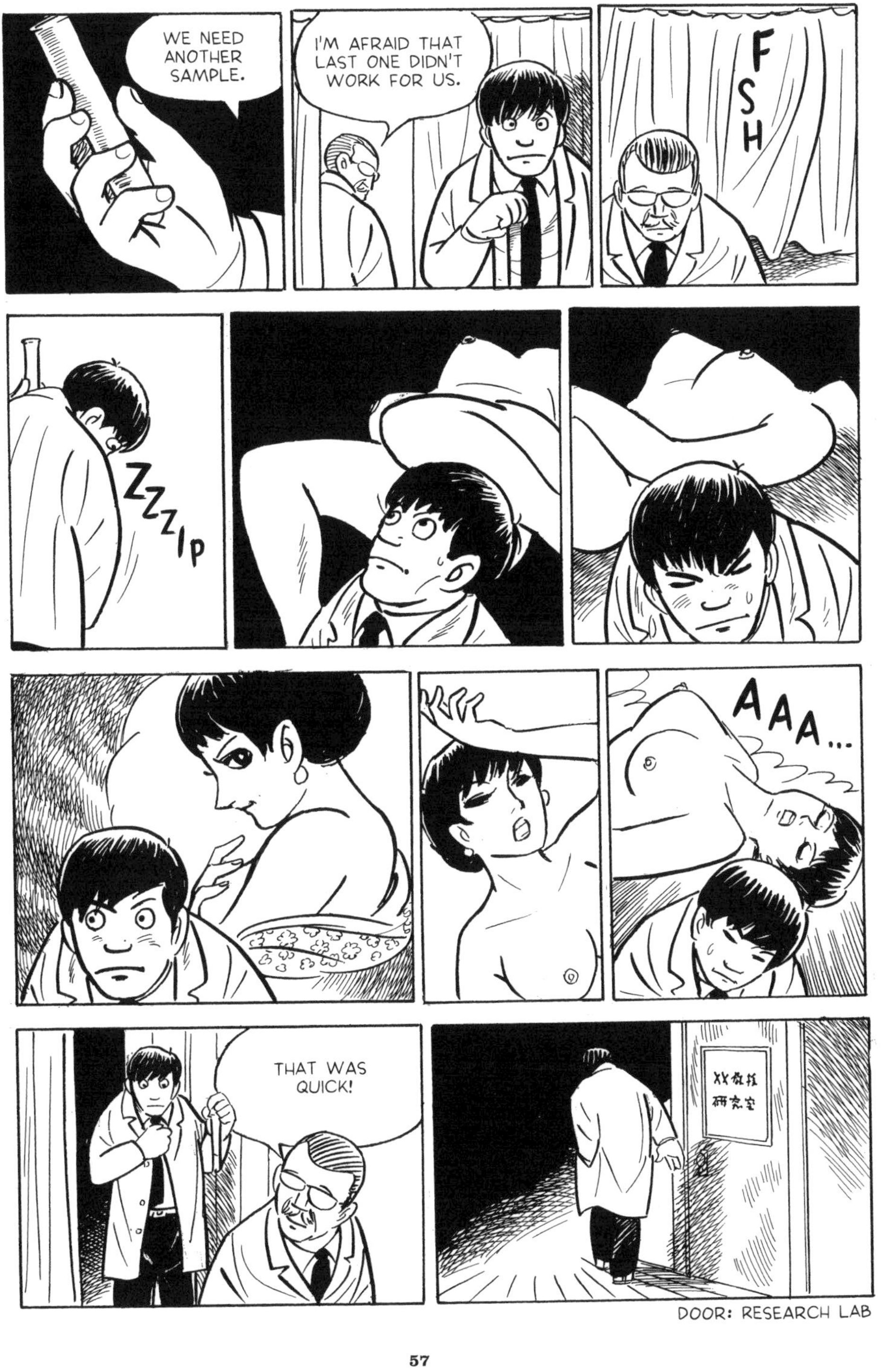
WE NEED ANOTHER SAMPLE.
I'M AFRAID THAT LAST ONE DIDN'T WORK FOR US.
FSH
ZZZIp
AAA...
THAT WAS QUICK!
DOOR: RESEARCH LAB

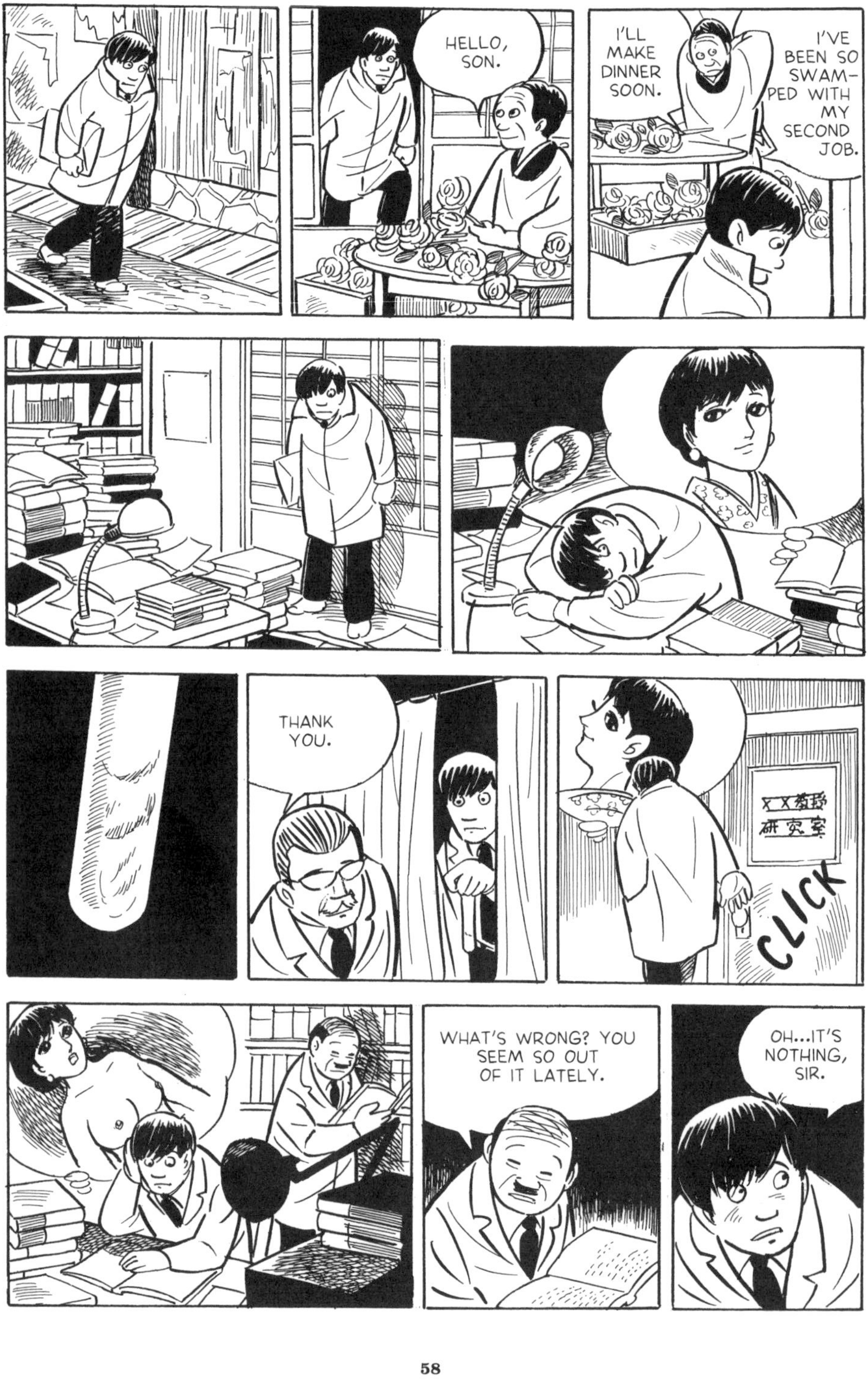
HELLO, SON.
I'LL MAKE DINNER SOON.
I'VE BEEN SO SWAM-PED WITH MY SECOND JOB.
THANK YOU.
CLICK
WHAT'S WRONG? YOU SEEM SO OUT OF IT LATELY.
OH...IT'S NOTHING, SIR.

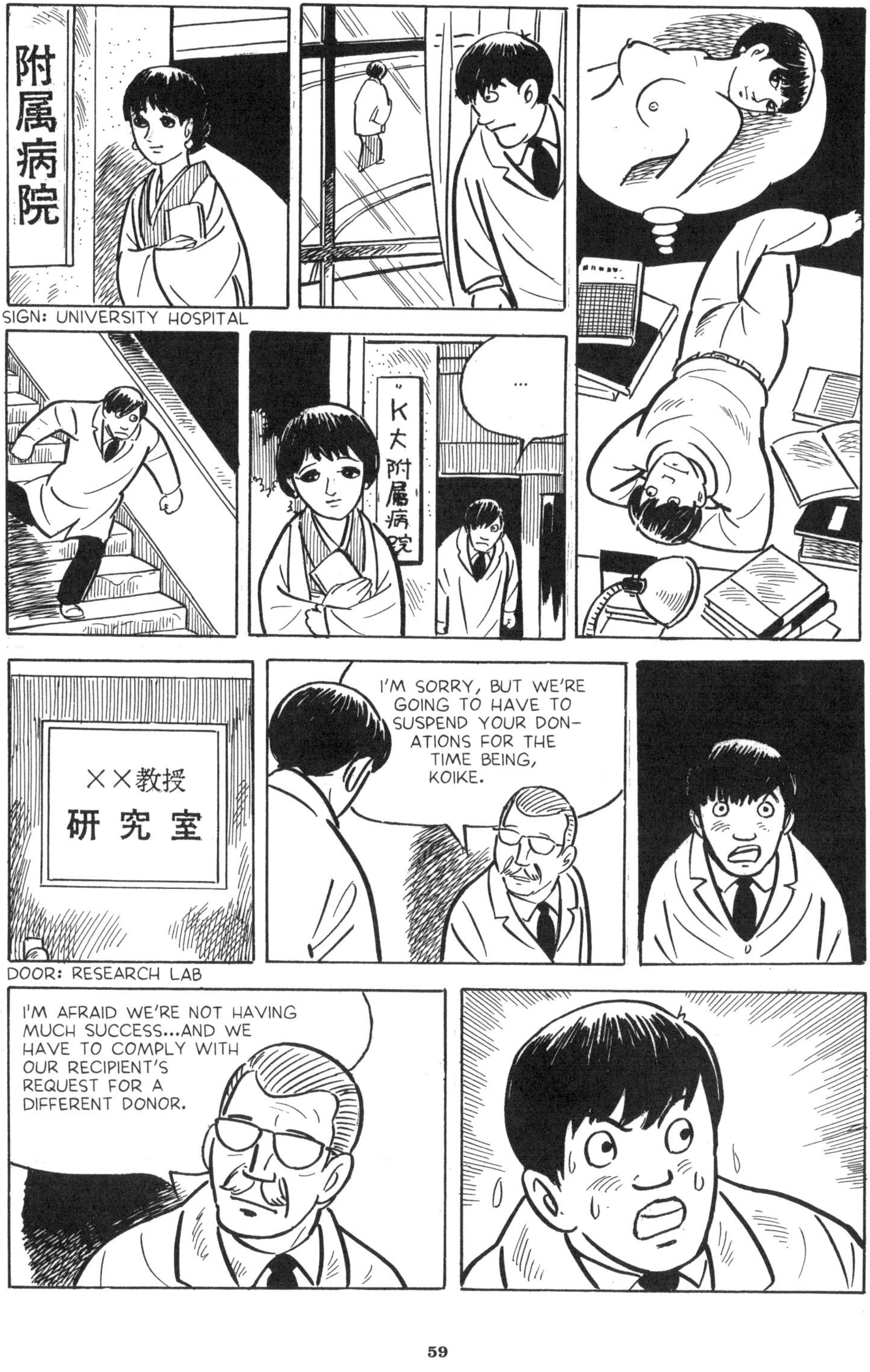
附属病院
SIGN: UNIVERSITY HOSPITAL
...
K大附属病院
××教授
研究室
DOOR: RESEARCH LAB
I'M SORRY, BUT WE'RE GOING TO HAVE TO SUSPEND YOUR DON-ATIONS FOR THE TIME BEING, KOIKE.
I'M AFRAID WE'RE NOT HAVING MUCH SUCCESS...AND WE HAVE TO COMPLY WITH OUR RECIPIENT'S REQUEST FOR A DIFFERENT DONOR.

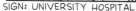

WHO ARE YOU?
WHAT DO YOU WANT?

WHAT DO
YOU MEAN,
"WHO AM I"?

PLEASE...DON'T
DO THIS TO ME.

HOW COULD
THIS HAVE
HAPPENED?

AAAHH!

インターン生が

婦女暴行未遂

HEADLINE: INTERN CHARGED WITH ATTEMPTED RAPE

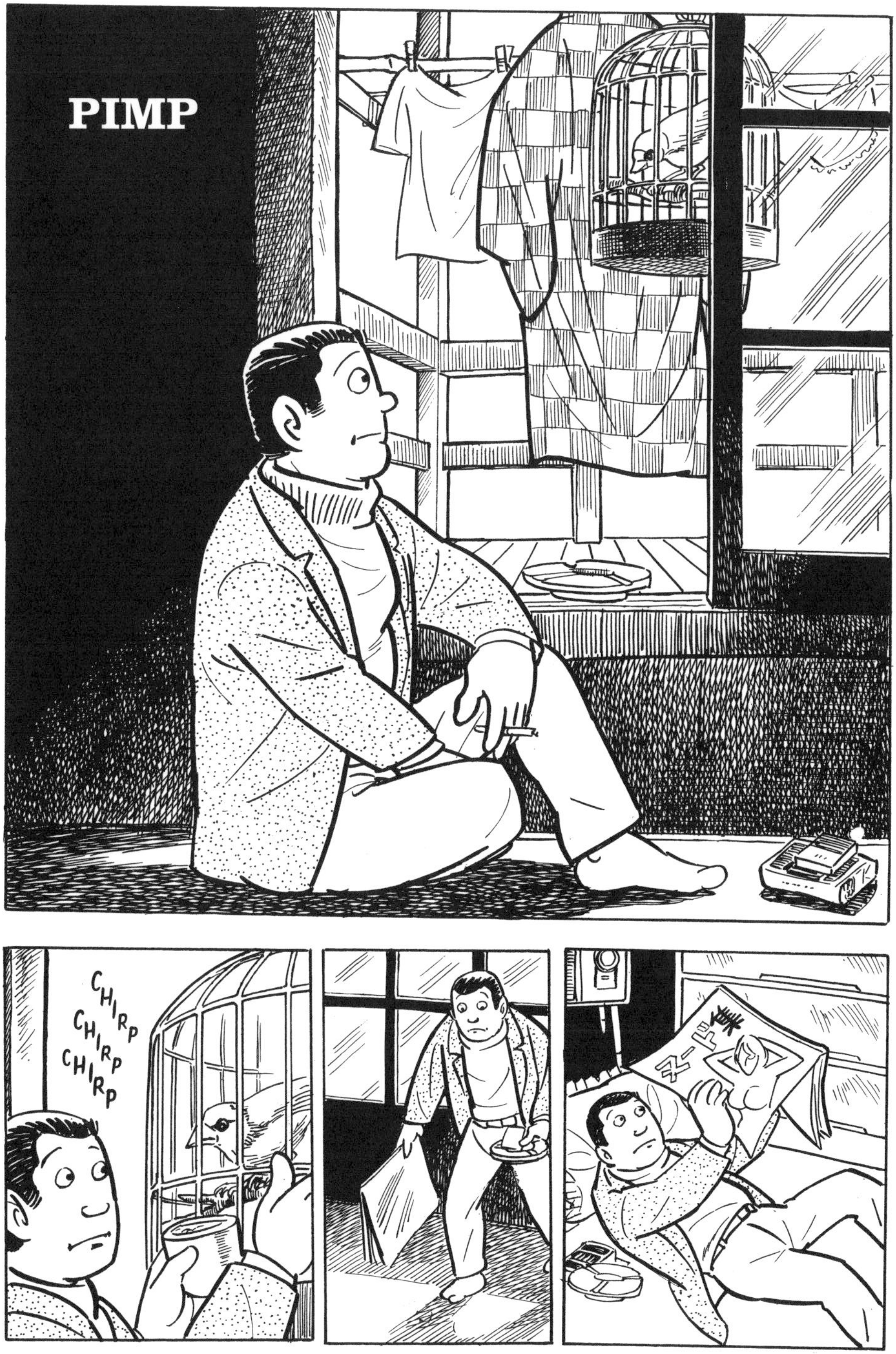
PIMP
CHIRP
CHIRP
CHIRP
ヌード集

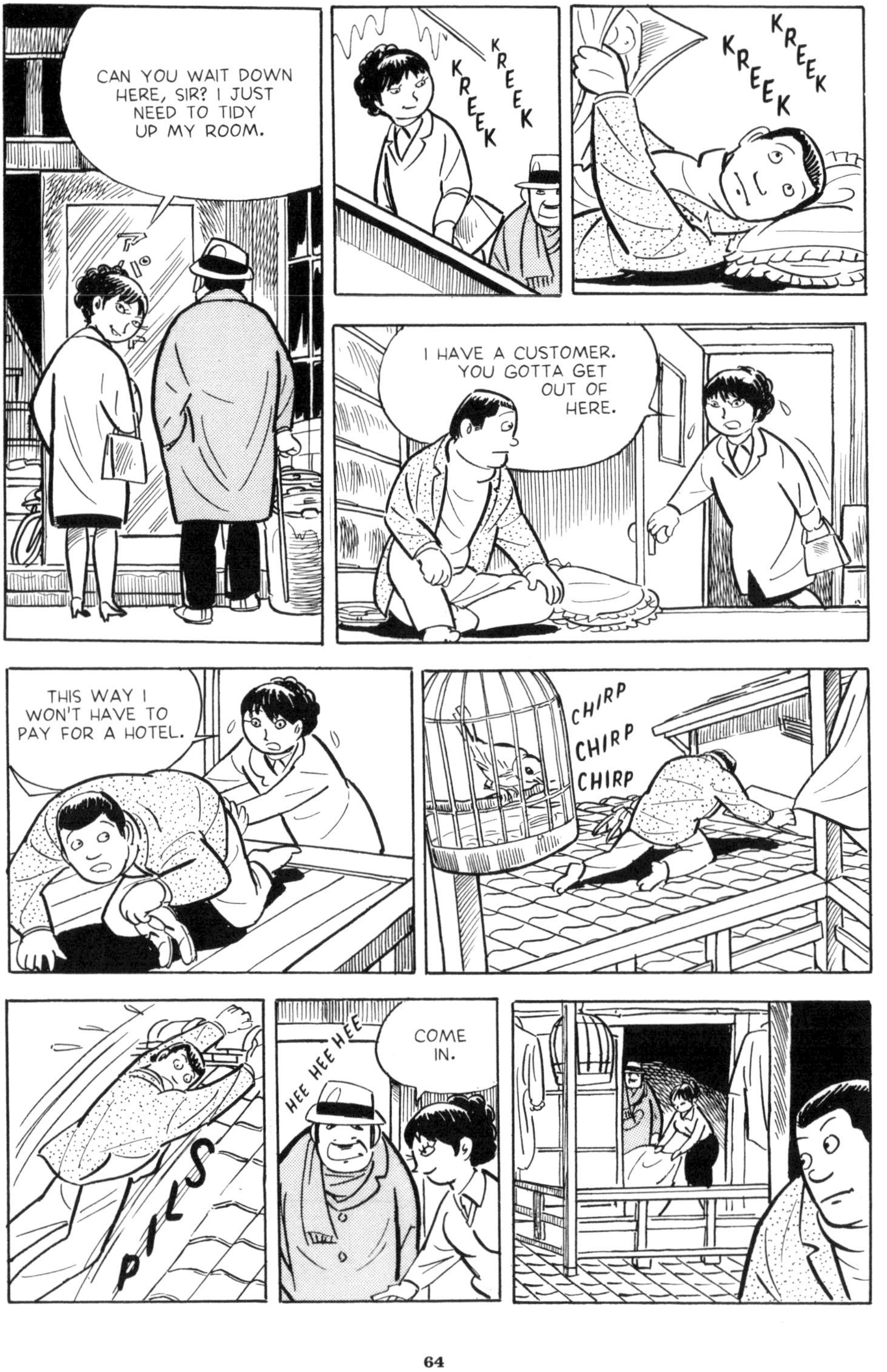
CAN YOU WAIT DOWN HERE, SIR? I JUST NEED TO TIDY UP MY ROOM.
KREEK KREEK
KREEK KREEK
I HAVE A CUSTOMER. YOU GOTTA GET OUT OF HERE.
THIS WAY I WON'T HAVE TO PAY FOR A HOTEL.
CHIRP
CHIRP
CHIRP
HEE HEE HEE
COME IN.

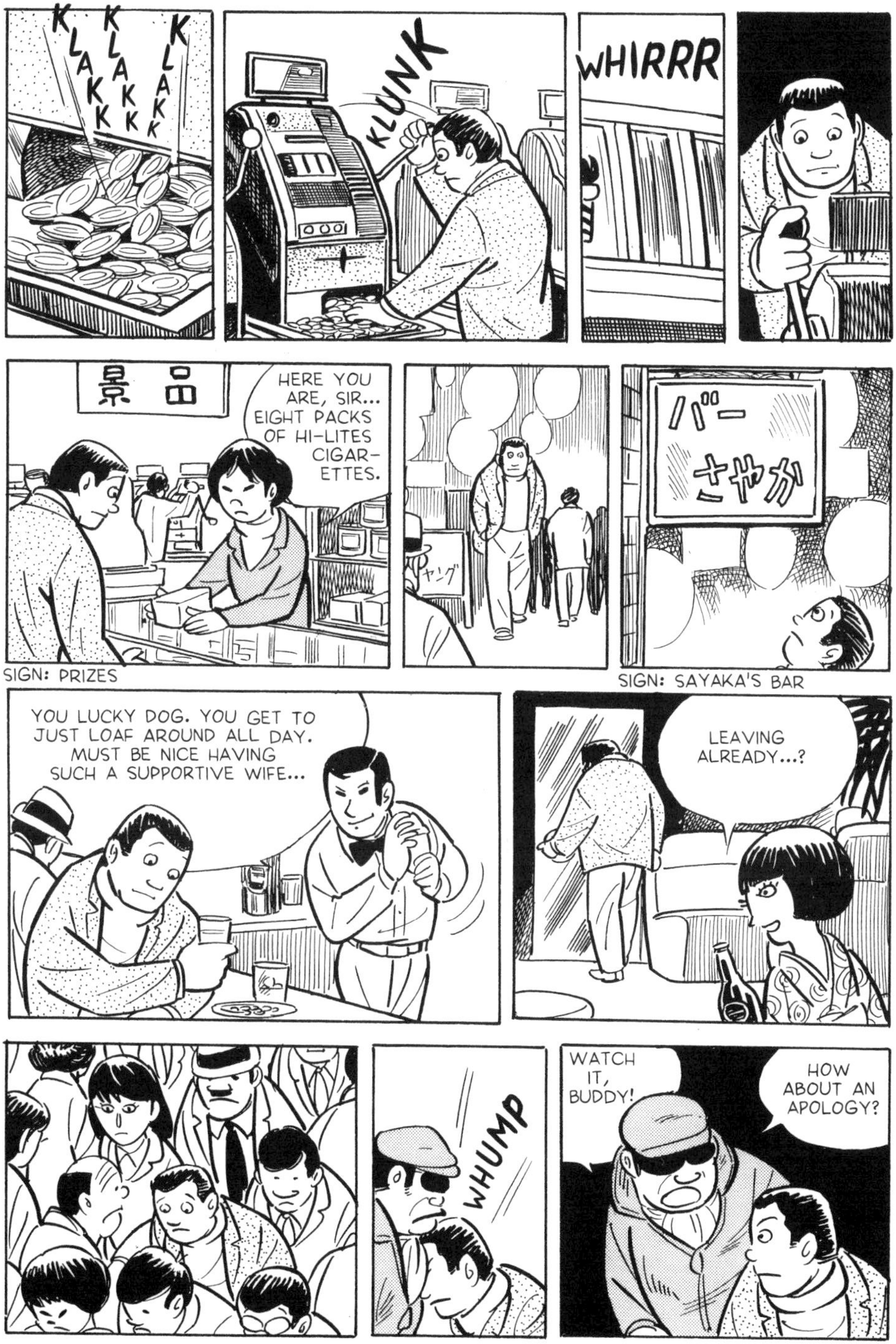
K
LAKK
K
LAKK
K
LAKK
KLUNK
WHIRRR
景品
HERE YOU ARE, SIR... EIGHT PACKS OF HI-LITES CIGAR-ETTES.
バー
さやか
SIGN: PRIZES
SIGN: SAYAKA'S BAR
YOU LUCKY DOG. YOU GET TO JUST LOAF AROUND ALL DAY. MUST BE NICE HAVING SUCH A SUPPORTIVE WIFE...
LEAVING ALREADY...?
WHUMP
WATCH IT, BUDDY!
HOW ABOUT AN APOLOGY?

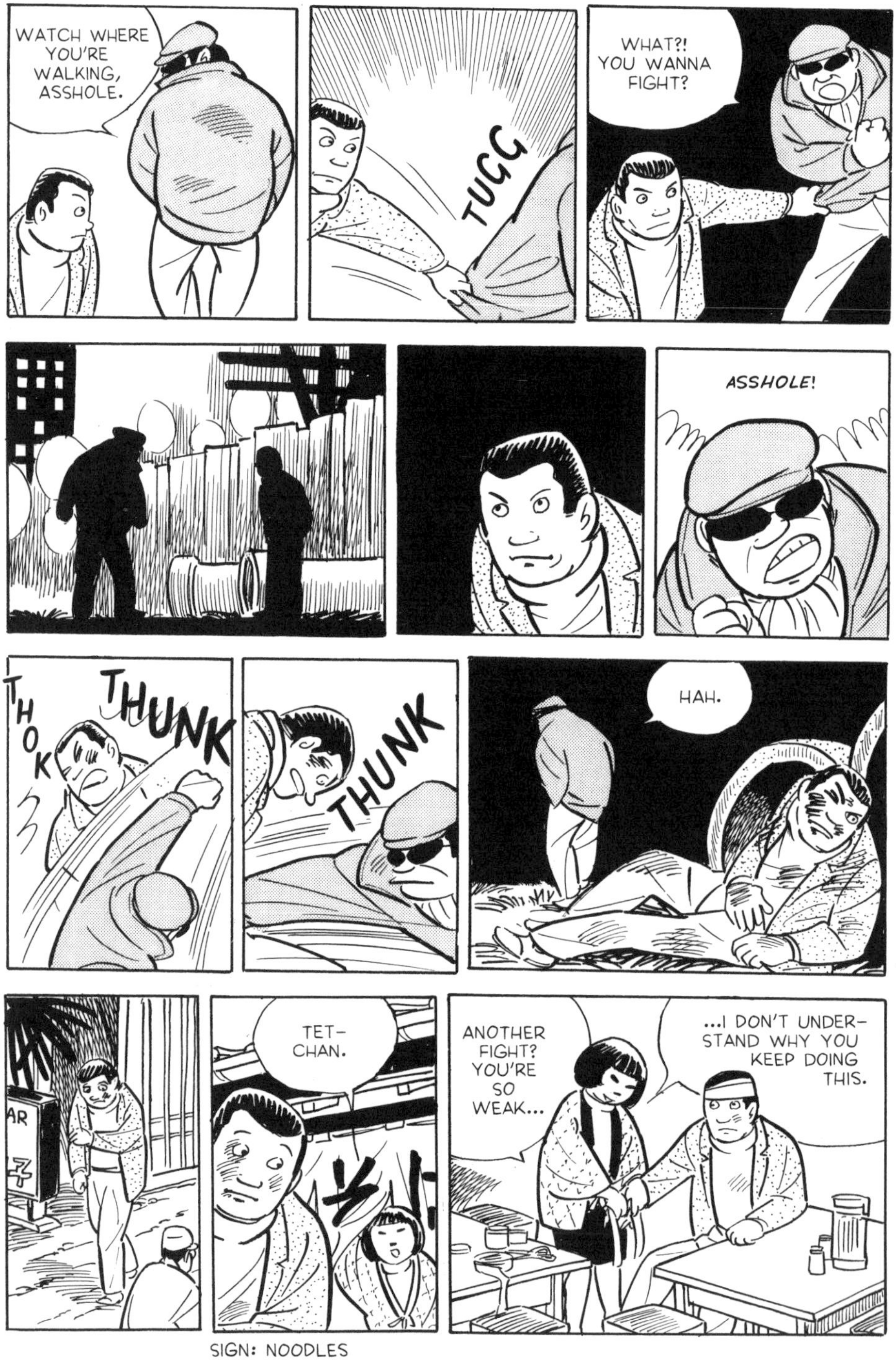
WATCH WHERE YOU'RE WALKING, ASSHOLE.
TUGG
WHAT?! YOU WANNA FIGHT?
ASSHOLE!
THOK
THUNK
THUNK
HAH.
TET-CHAN.
ANOTHER FIGHT? YOU'RE SO WEAK...
...I DON'T UNDERSTAND WHY YOU KEEP DOING THIS.

SIGN: NOODLES

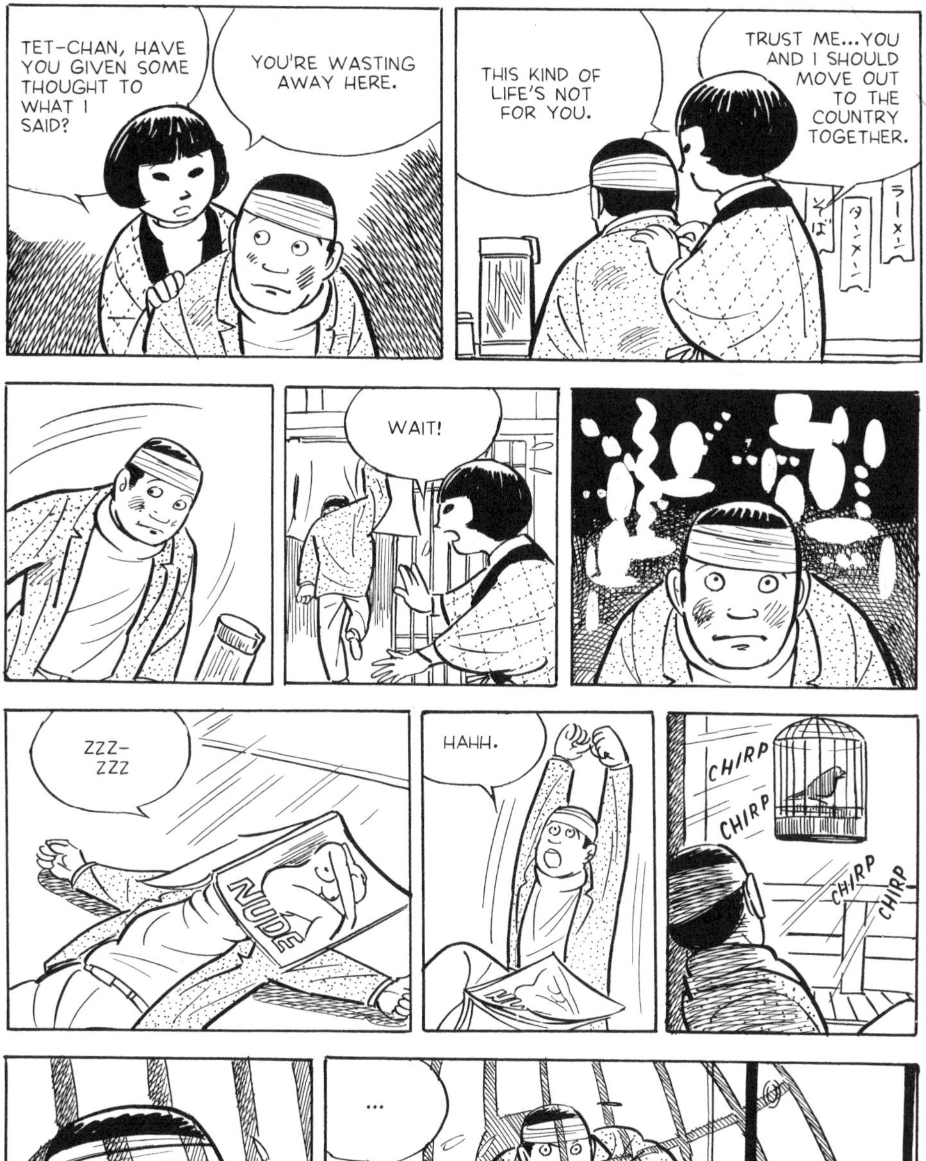
TET-CHAN, HAVE YOU GIVEN SOME THOUGHT TO WHAT I SAID?
YOU'RE WASTING AWAY HERE.
THIS KIND OF LIFE'S NOT FOR YOU.
TRUST ME...YOU AND I SHOULD MOVE OUT TO THE COUNTRY TOGETHER.
ラーメン
タンメン
そば
WAIT!
ZZZ-ZZZ
NUDE
HAHH.
CHIRP
CHIRP
CHIRP
CHIRP
...

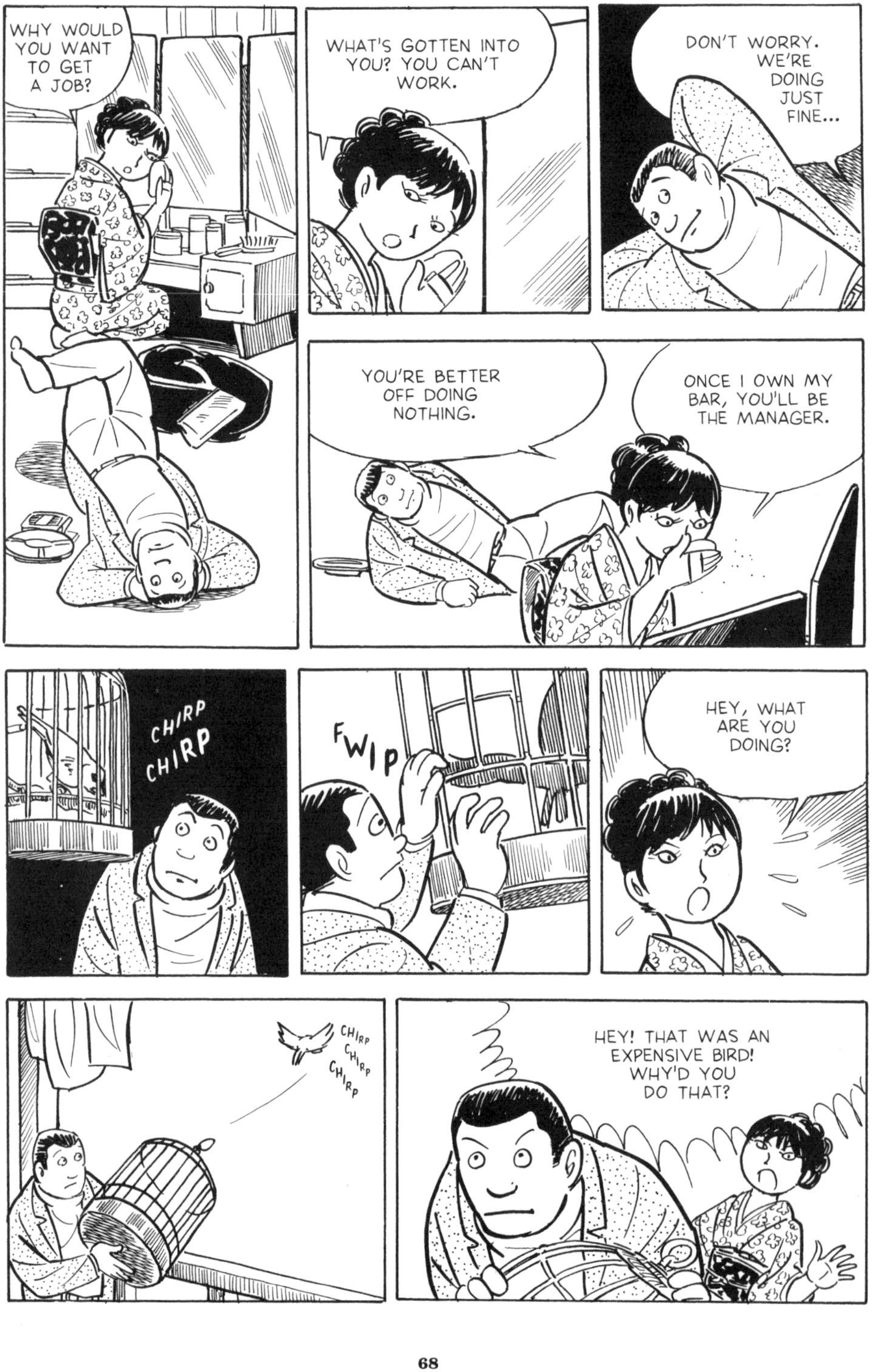
WHY WOULD YOU WANT TO GET A JOB?
WHAT'S GOTTEN INTO YOU? YOU CAN'T WORK.
DON'T WORRY. WE'RE DOING JUST FINE...
YOU'RE BETTER OFF DOING NOTHING.
ONCE I OWN MY BAR, YOU'LL BE THE MANAGER.
CHIRP CHIRP
FWIP
HEY, WHAT ARE YOU DOING?
CHIRP CHIRP CHIRP
HEY! THAT WAS AN EXPENSIVE BIRD! WHY'D YOU DO THAT?

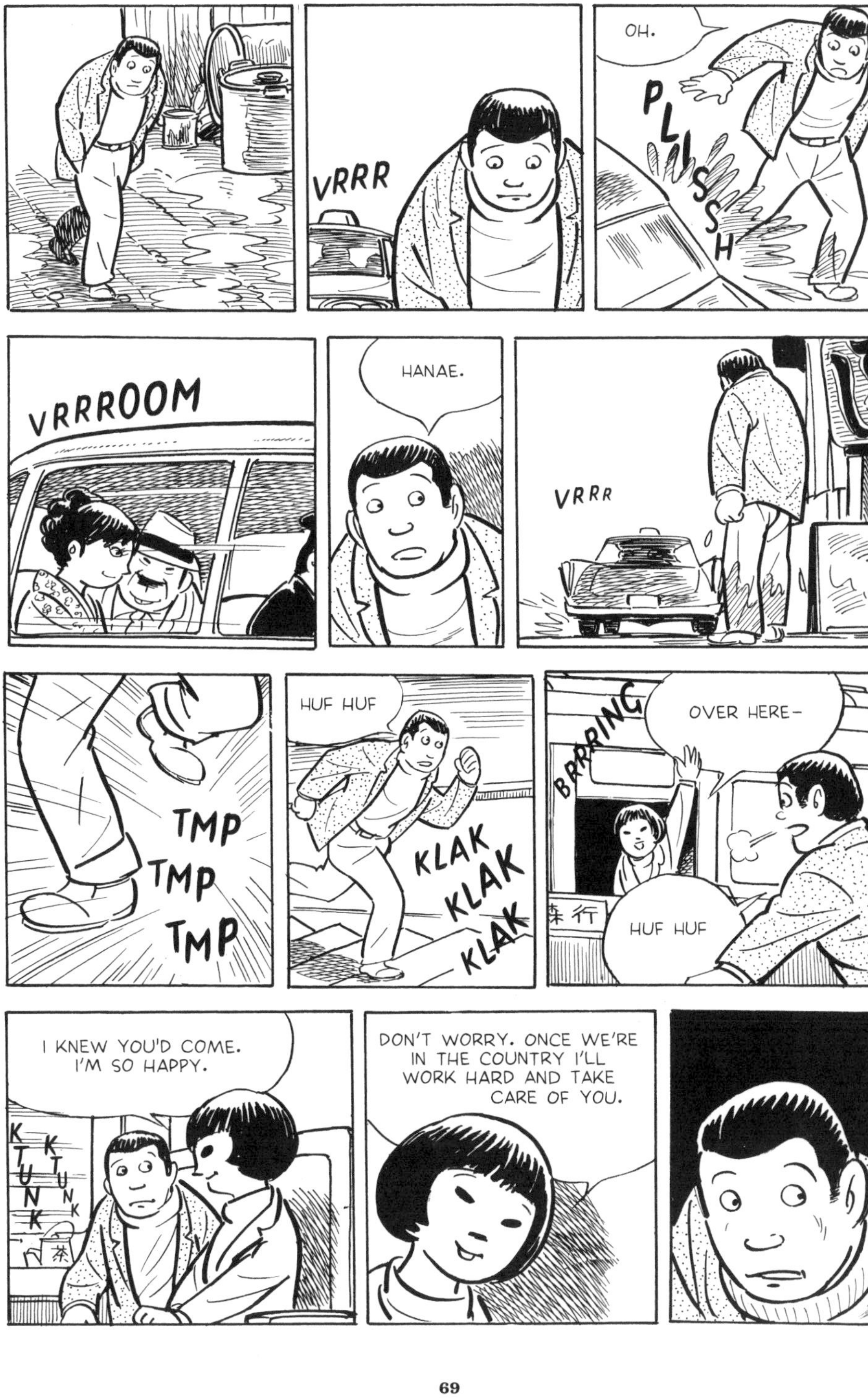
VRRR
OH.
PLISSH
VRRROOM
HANAE.
VRRR
TMP
TMP
TMP
HUF HUF
KLAK
KLAK
KLAK
BRRRING
OVER HERE-
HUF HUF
I KNEW YOU'D COME. I'M SO HAPPY.
KTUNK
KTUNK
DON'T WORRY. ONCE WE'RE IN THE COUNTRY I'LL WORK HARD AND TAKE CARE OF YOU.

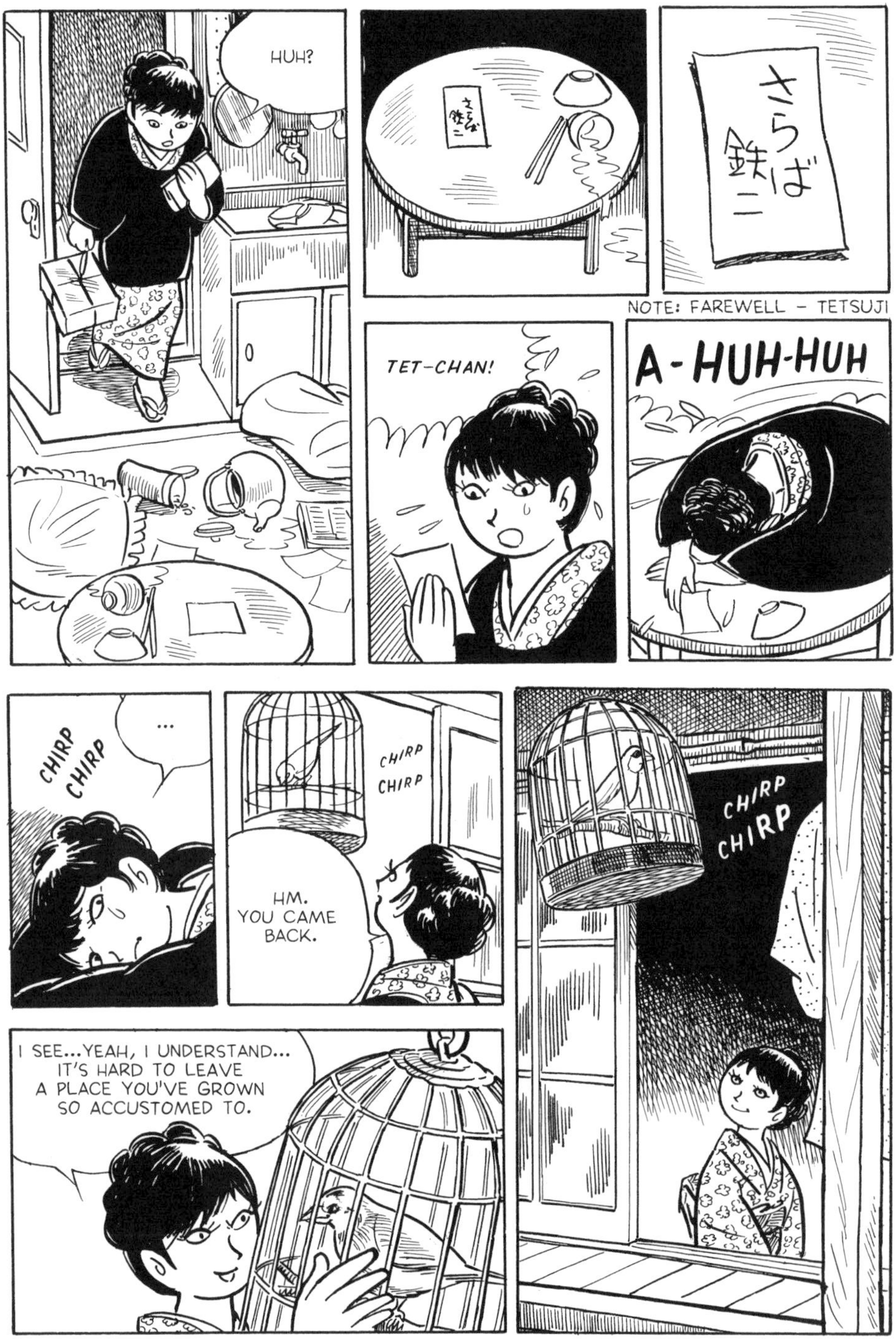
HUH?
さらば
鉄二
NOTE: FAREWELL - TETSUJI
TET-CHAN!
A-HUH-HUH
CHIRP CHIRP
...
CHIRP CHIRP
HM. YOU CAME BACK.
CHIRP CHIRP
I SEE...YEAH, I UNDERSTAND... IT'S HARD TO LEAVE A PLACE YOU'VE GROWN SO ACCUSTOMED TO.

THE PUSH MAN

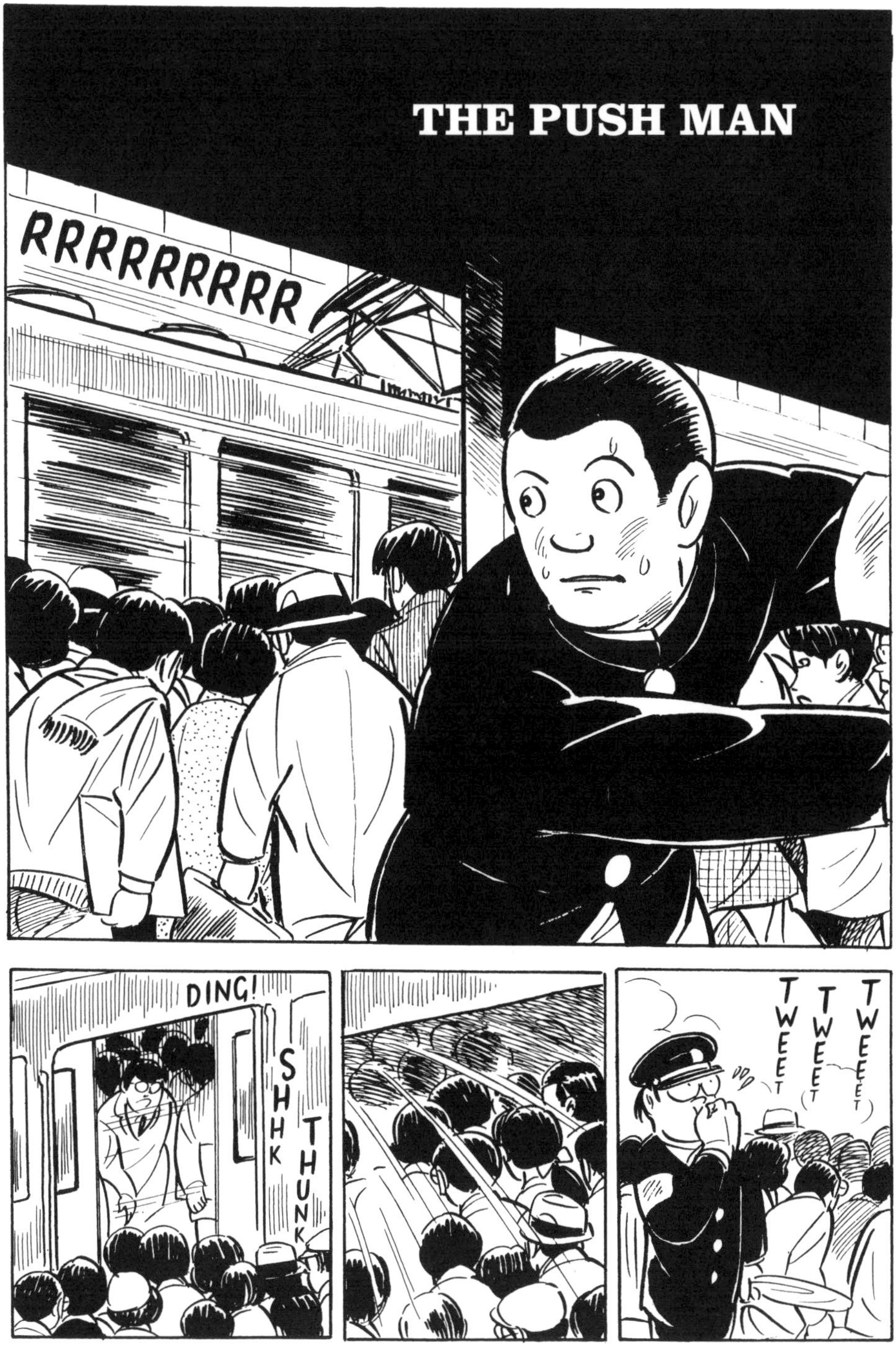
RRRRRRRRRR
DING!
SHHK
THUNK
TWEET
TWEET
TWEEET

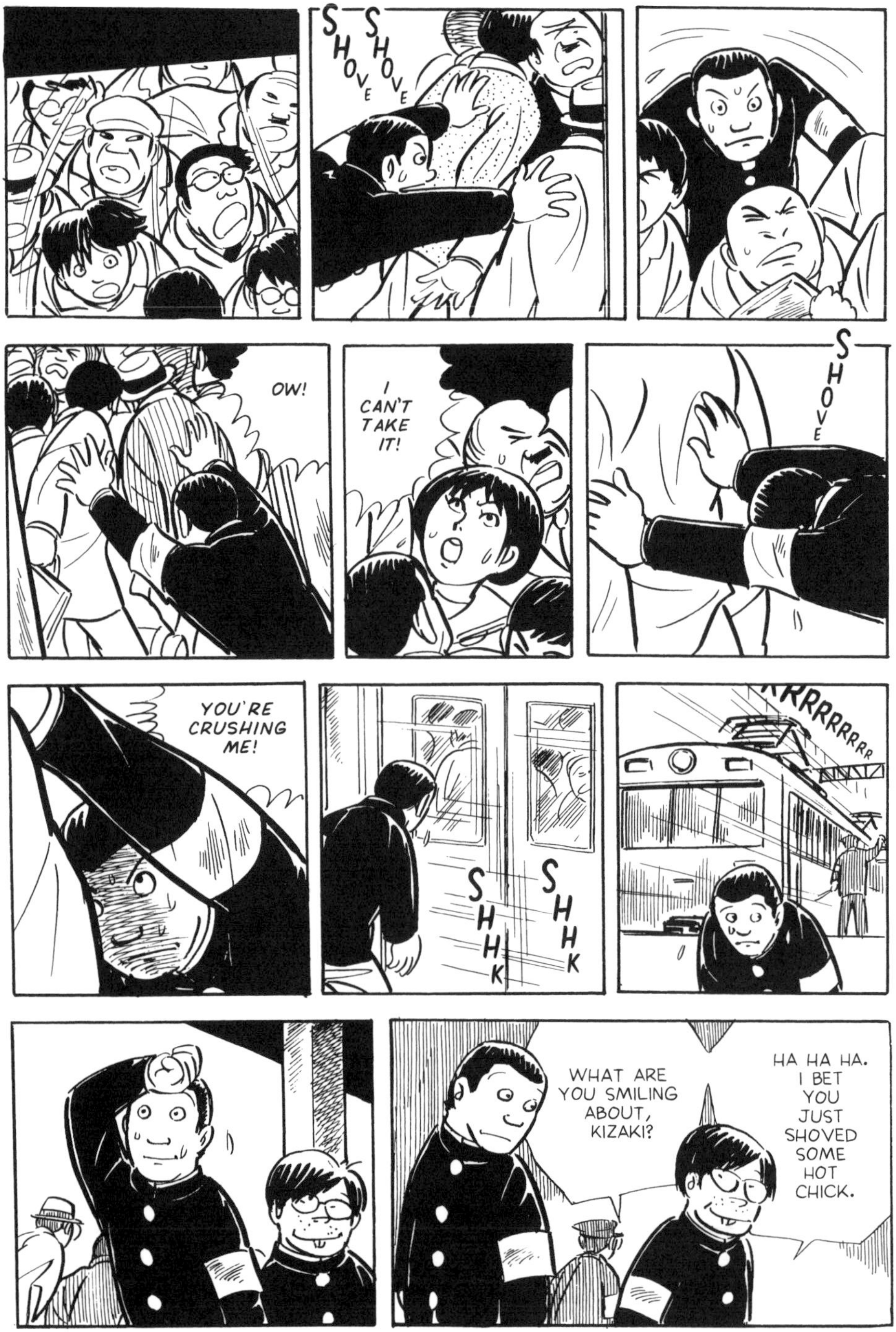
SHOVE SHOVE
OW!
I CAN'T TAKE IT!
SHOVE
YOU'RE CRUSHING ME!
SHHK SHHK
RRRRRRRRR
WHAT ARE YOU SMILING ABOUT, KIZAKI?
HA HA HA. I BET YOU JUST SHOVED SOME HOT CHICK.

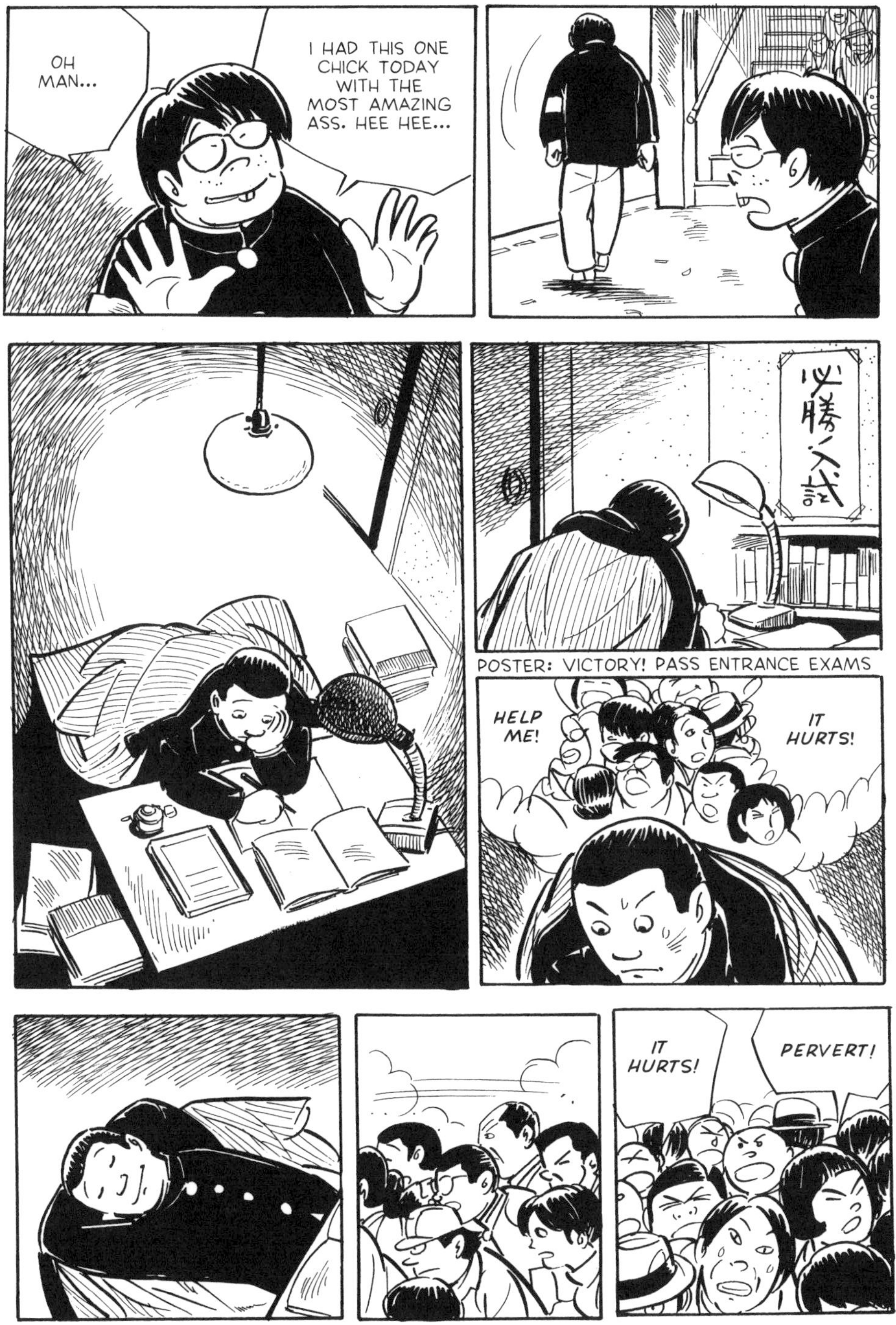

OH MAN...
I HAD THIS ONE CHICK TODAY WITH THE MOST AMAZING ASS. HEE HEE...
POSTER: VICTORY! PASS ENTRANCE EXAMS
HELP ME!
IT HURTS!
IT HURTS!
PERVERT!

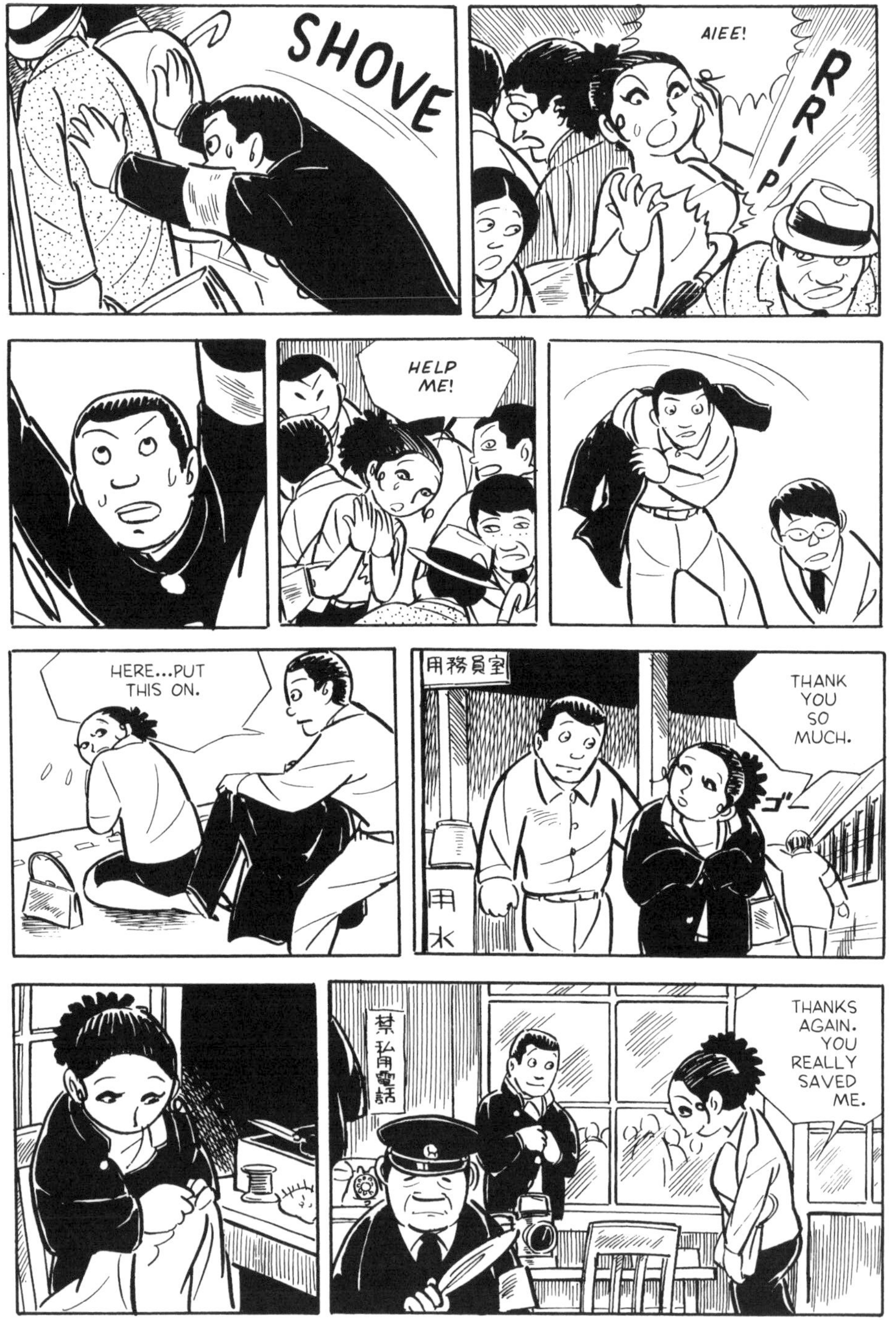
SHOVE
AIEE!
RRIP
HELP ME!
HERE...PUT THIS ON.
用務員室
THANK YOU SO MUCH.
ゴー
用水
禁私用電話
THANKS AGAIN. YOU REALLY SAVED ME.

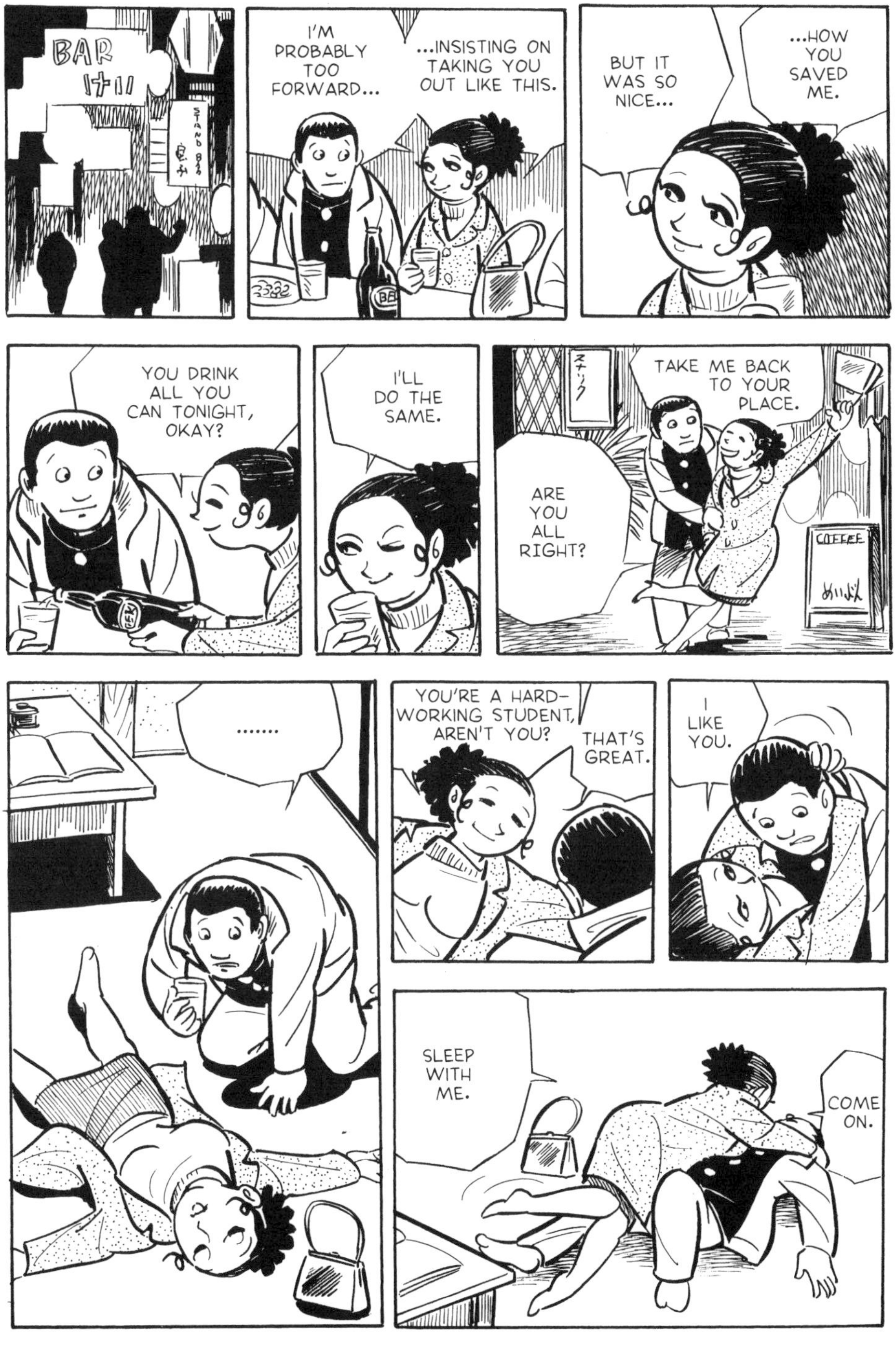
BAR
I'M PROBABLY TOO FORWARD...
...INSISTING ON TAKING YOU OUT LIKE THIS.
BUT IT WAS SO NICE...
...HOW YOU SAVED ME.
YOU DRINK ALL YOU CAN TONIGHT, OKAY?
I'LL DO THE SAME.
TAKE ME BACK TO YOUR PLACE.
ARE YOU ALL RIGHT?
COFFEE
....
YOU'RE A HARD-WORKING STUDENT, AREN'T YOU?
THAT'S GREAT.
I LIKE YOU.
SLEEP WITH ME.
COME ON.

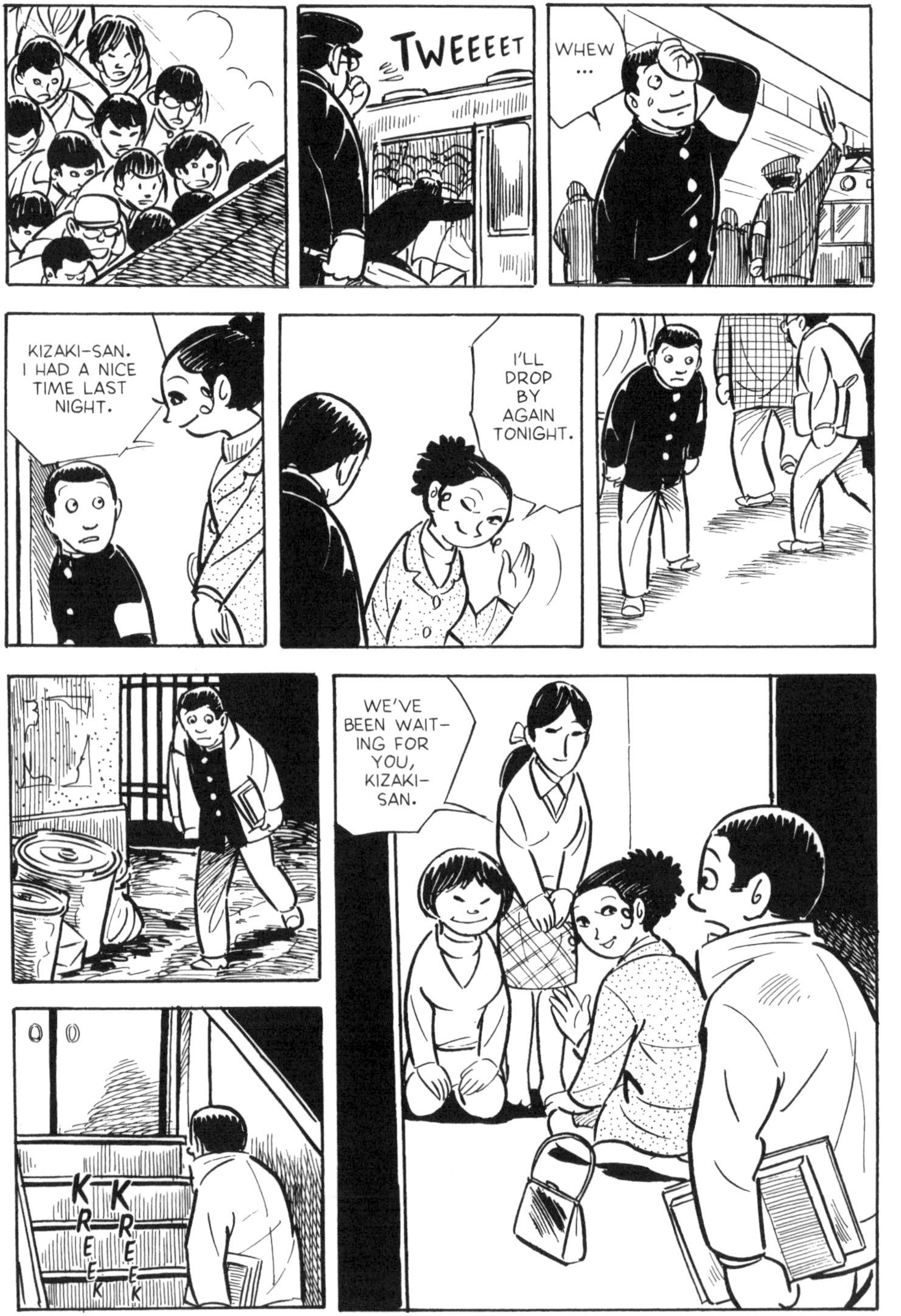
TWEEEEET
WHEW ...
KIZAKI-SAN. I HAD A NICE TIME LAST NIGHT.
I'LL DROP BY AGAIN TONIGHT.
WE'VE BEEN WAITING FOR YOU, KIZAKI-SAN.
KREEK KREEK

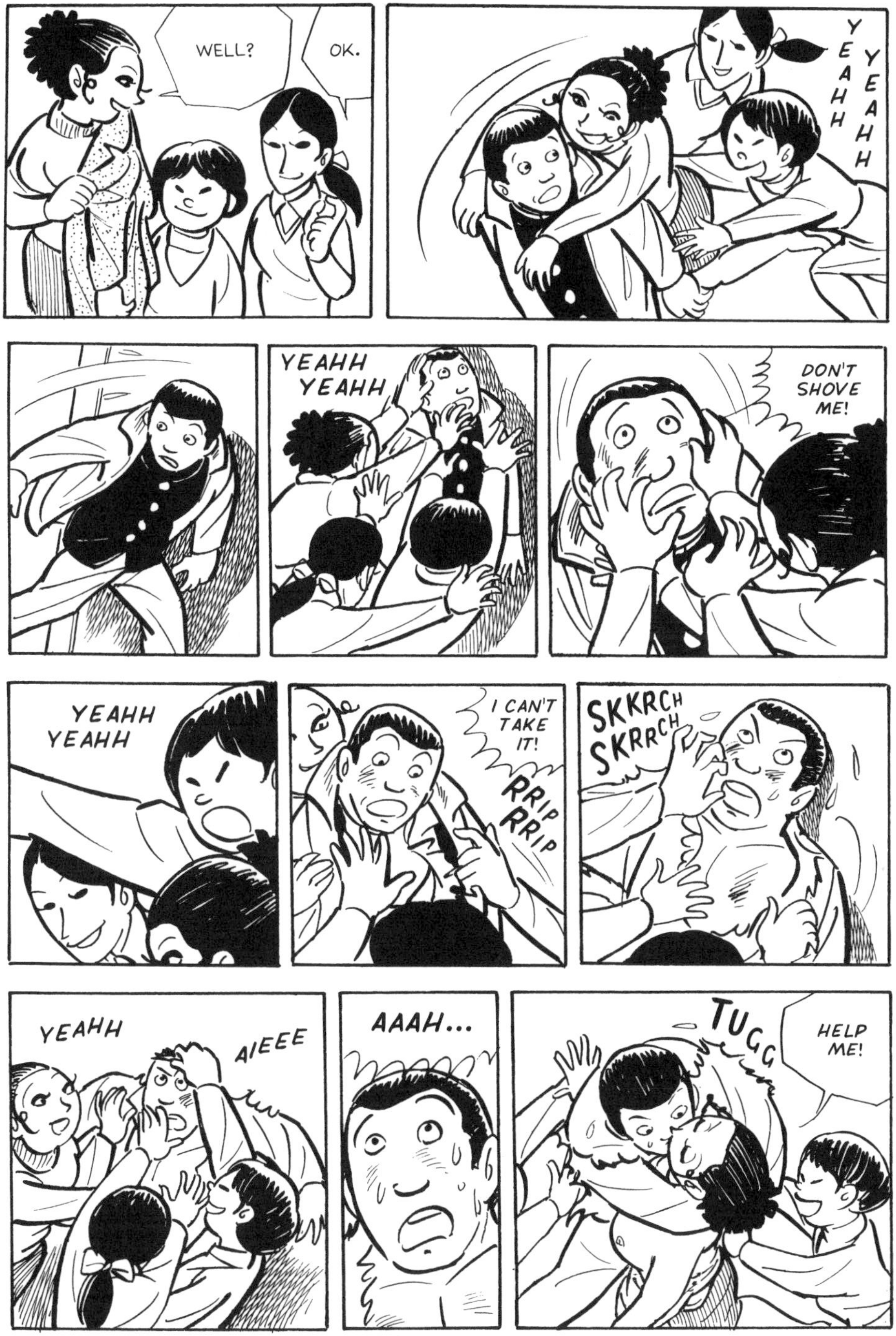
WELL?
OK.
YEAHH YEAHH
YEAHH YEAHH
DON'T SHOVE ME!
YEAHH YEAHH
I CAN'T TAKE IT!
RRIP RRIP
SKKRCH SKRRCH
YEAHH
AIEEE
AAAH...
TUGG
HELP ME!

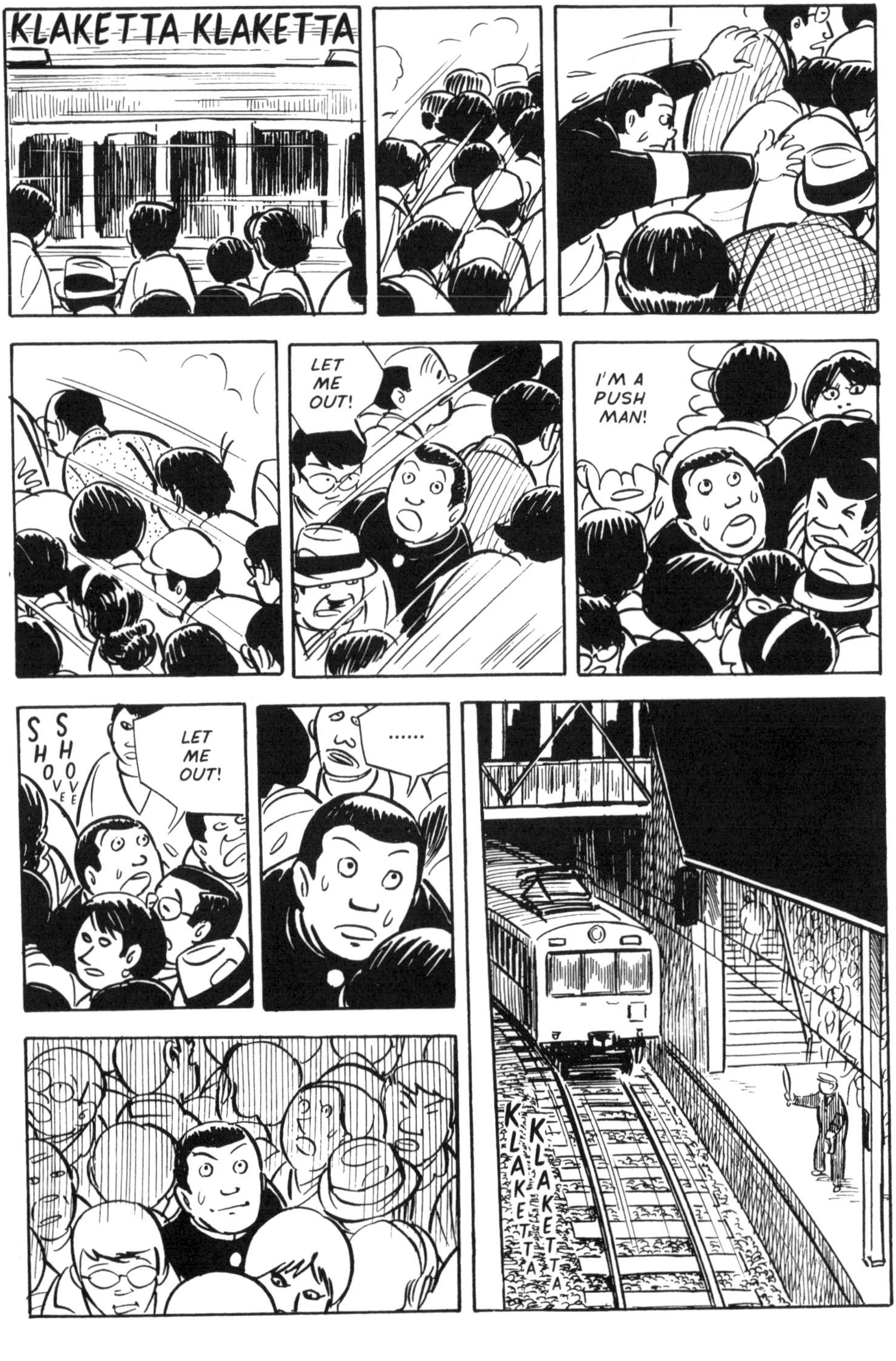
KLAKETTA KLAKETTA
LET ME OUT!
I'M A PUSH MAN!
SHOVE SHOVE
LET ME OUT!
......
KLAKETTA KLAKETTA

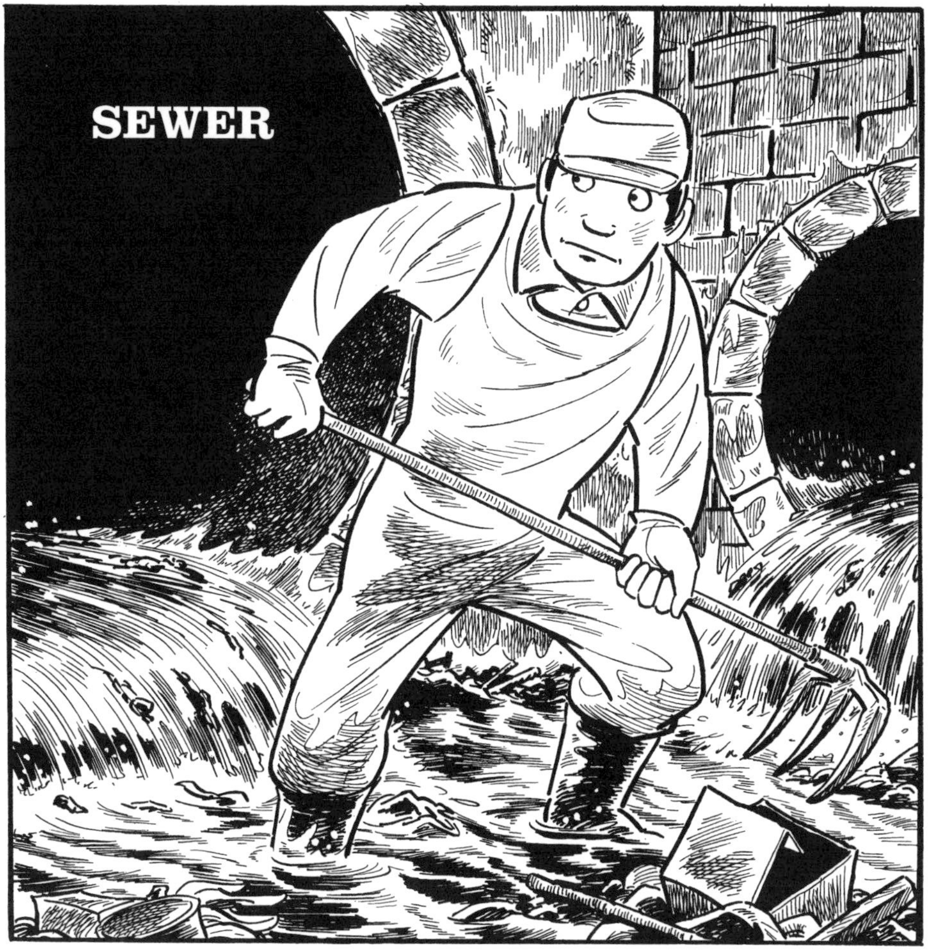
SEWER

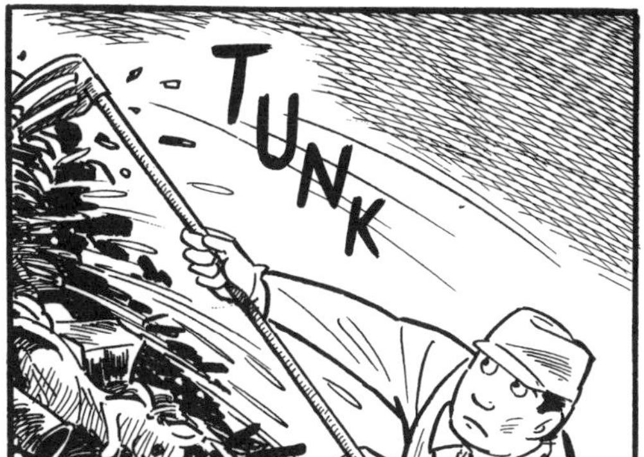
TUNK

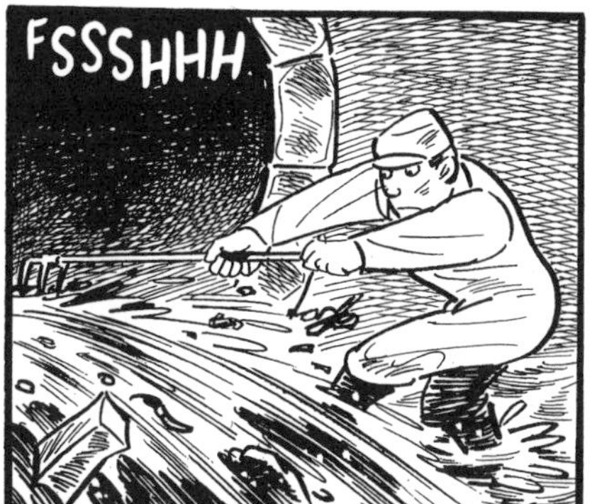
FSSSHHH

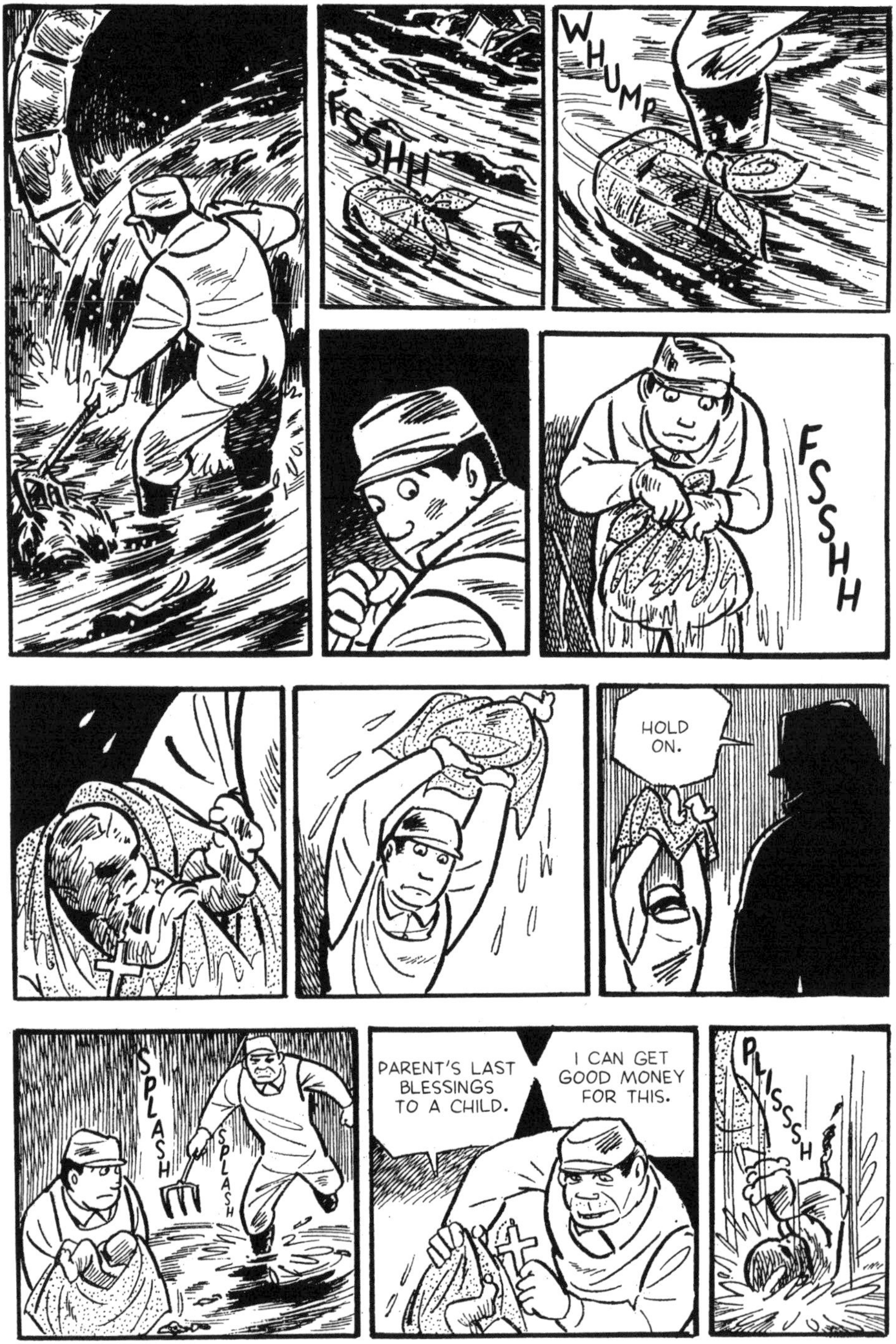
FSSHH
WHUMP
FSSHH
HOLD ON.
SPLASH
SPLASH
PARENT'S LAST BLESSINGS TO A CHILD.
I CAN GET GOOD MONEY FOR THIS.
PLISSSH

LET'S CALL IT A DAY.

KLANG KLANG

職員専用
浴室

SIGN: STAFF SHOWER

FSSHHH

YOU'RE AN ODD ONE.

YOU'RE YOUNG...

I DON'T KNOW WHY YOU'D WANT TO BE A SEWER CLEANER...

WHOOSH

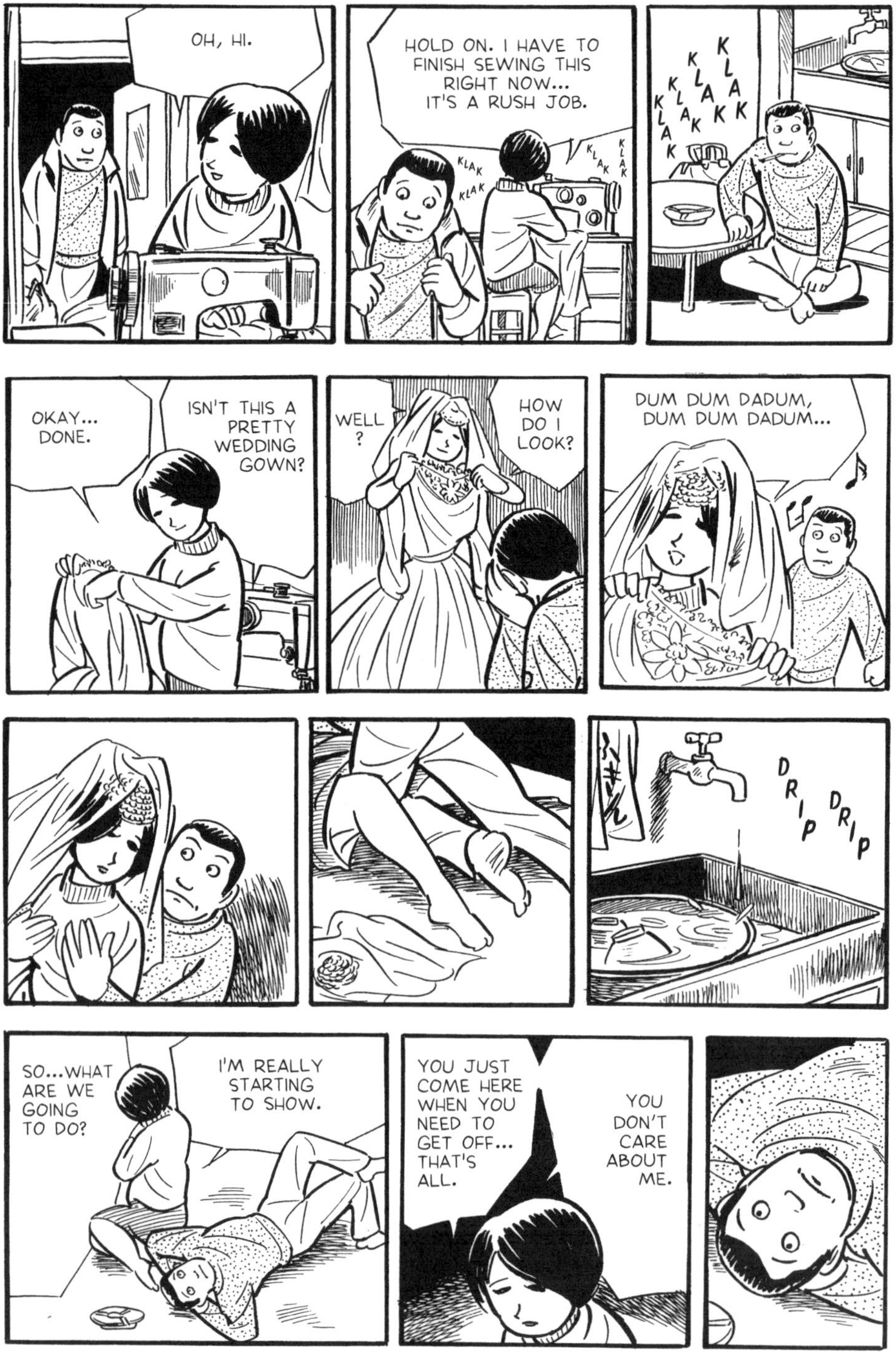
OH, HI.
HOLD ON. I HAVE TO FINISH SEWING THIS RIGHT NOW... IT'S A RUSH JOB.
KLAK KLAK
KLAK KLAK
KLAK KLAK KLAK KLAK KLAK KLAK KLAK
OKAY... DONE.
ISN'T THIS A PRETTY WEDDING GOWN?
WELL?
HOW DO I LOOK?
DUM DUM DADUM, DUM DUM DADUM...
DRIP DRIP
SO...WHAT ARE WE GOING TO DO?
I'M REALLY STARTING TO SHOW.
YOU JUST COME HERE WHEN YOU NEED TO GET OFF... THAT'S ALL.
YOU DON'T CARE ABOUT ME.

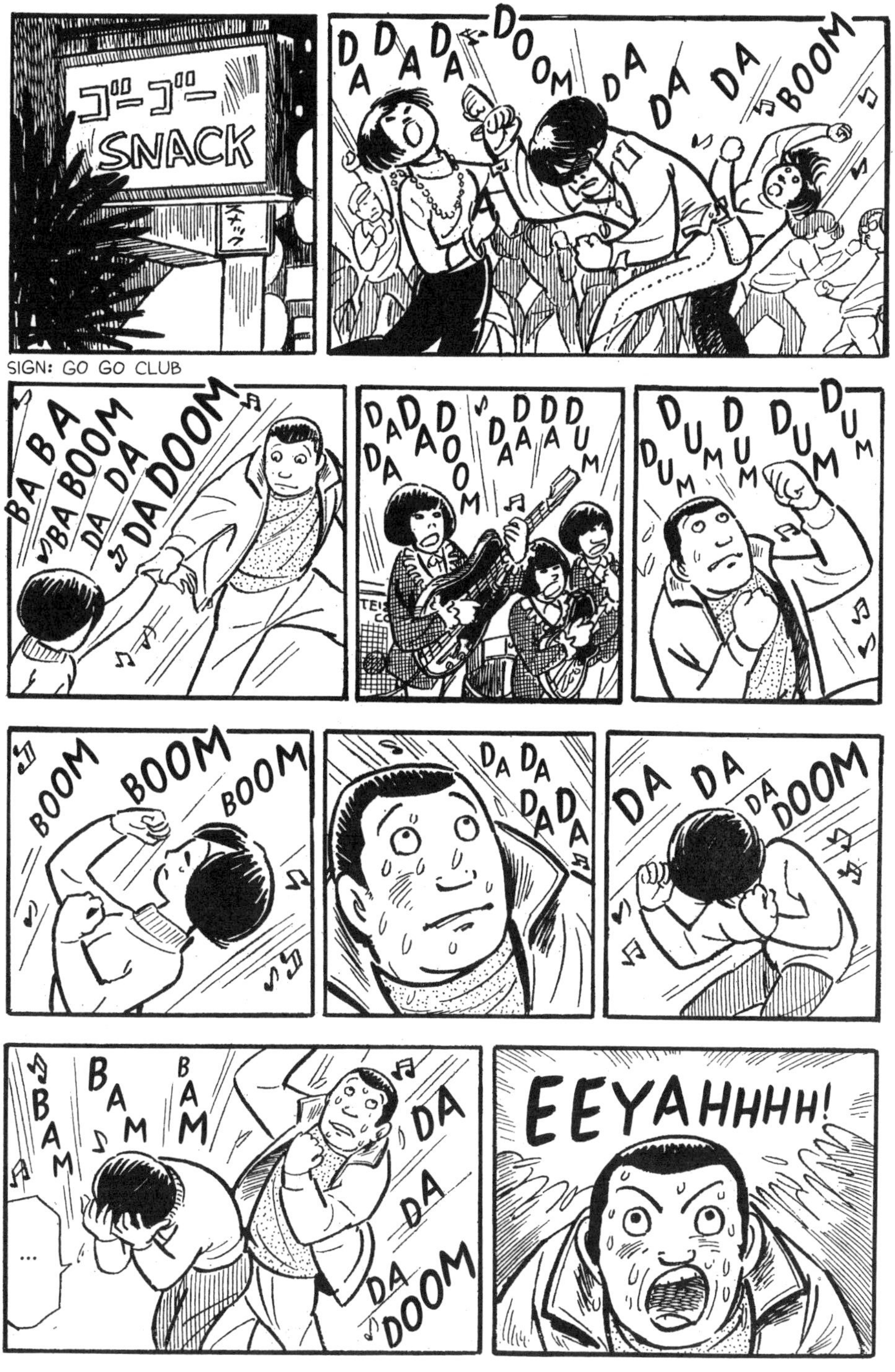
ゴーゴー
SNACK
スナック
DA DA DA DA DOOM DA DA DA BOOM
SIGN: GO GO CLUB
BA BA BA BOOM DA DA DA DOOM
DA DA DA DOOM DA DA DA DUM
DUM DUM DUM DUM DUM
BOOM BOOM BOOM
DA DA DA DA DA
DA DA DA DOOM
BAM BAM BAM DA DA DA DOOM
...
EEYAHHHH!

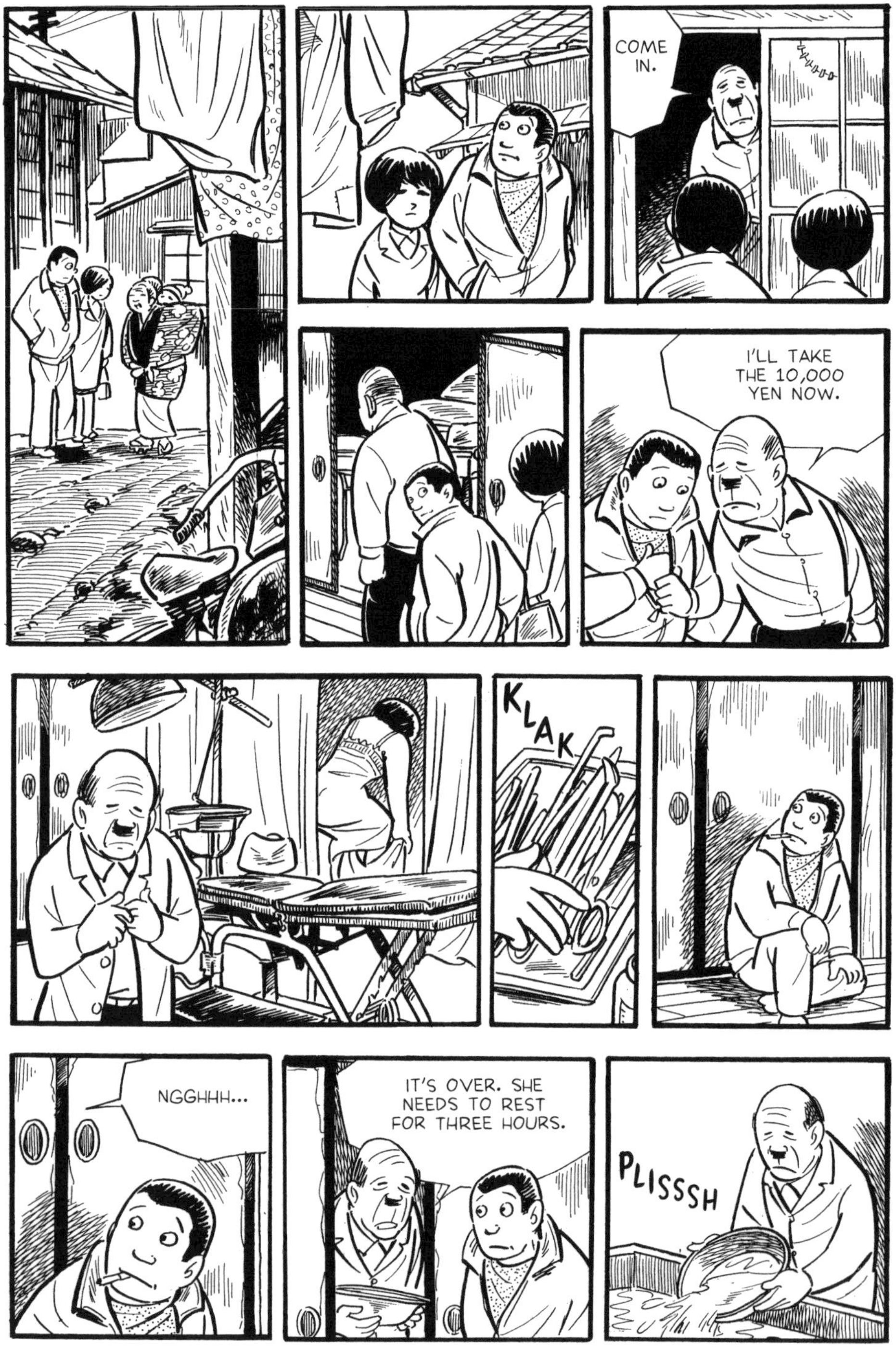
COME IN.
I'LL TAKE THE 10,000 YEN NOW.
KLAK
NGGHHH...
IT'S OVER. SHE NEEDS TO REST FOR THREE HOURS.
PLISSSH

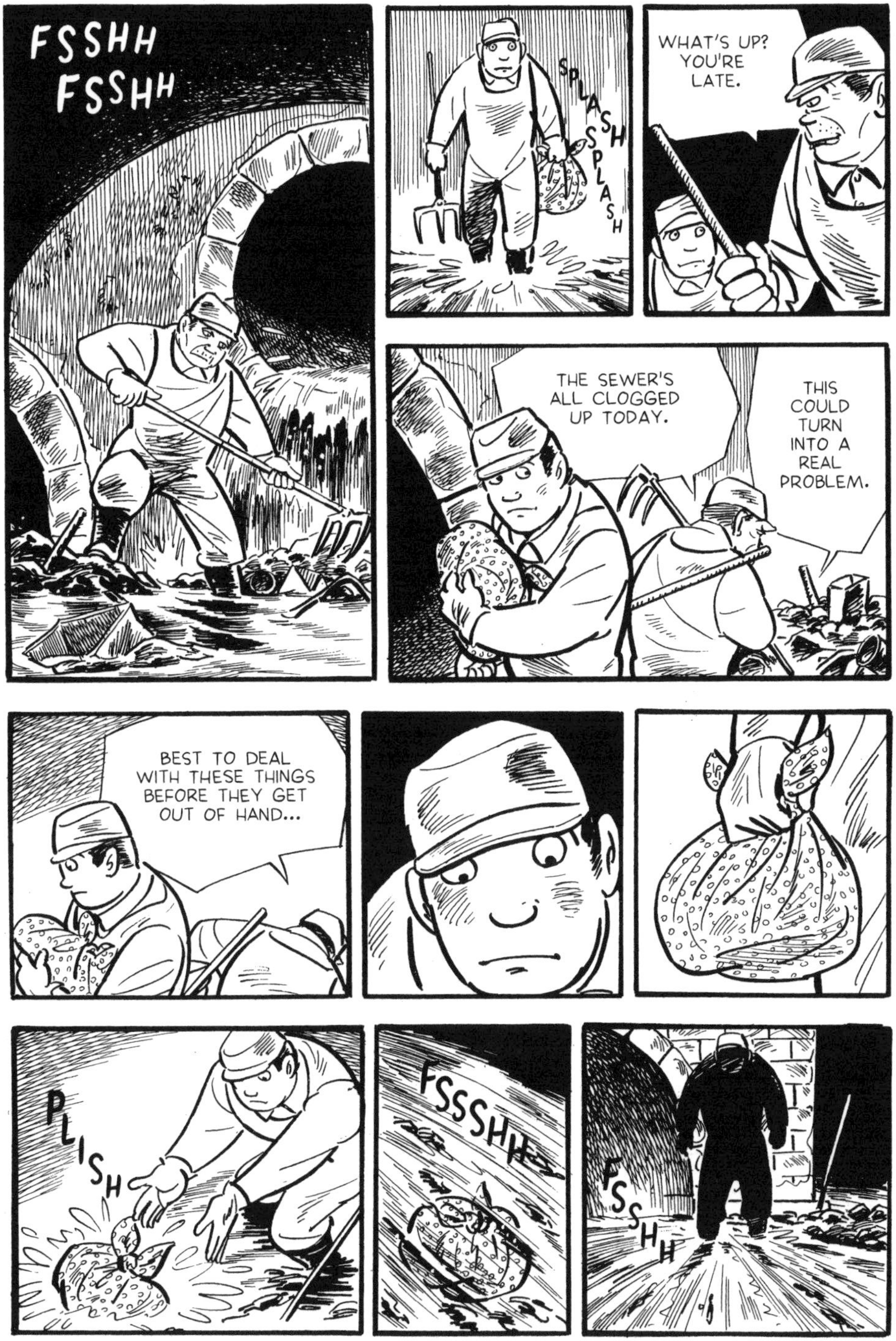
FSSHH FSSHH
SPLASH SPLASH
WHAT'S UP? YOU'RE LATE.
THE SEWER'S ALL CLOGGED UP TODAY.
THIS COULD TURN INTO A REAL PROBLEM.
BEST TO DEAL WITH THESE THINGS BEFORE THEY GET OUT OF HAND...
PLISH
FSSSHH
FSSHH

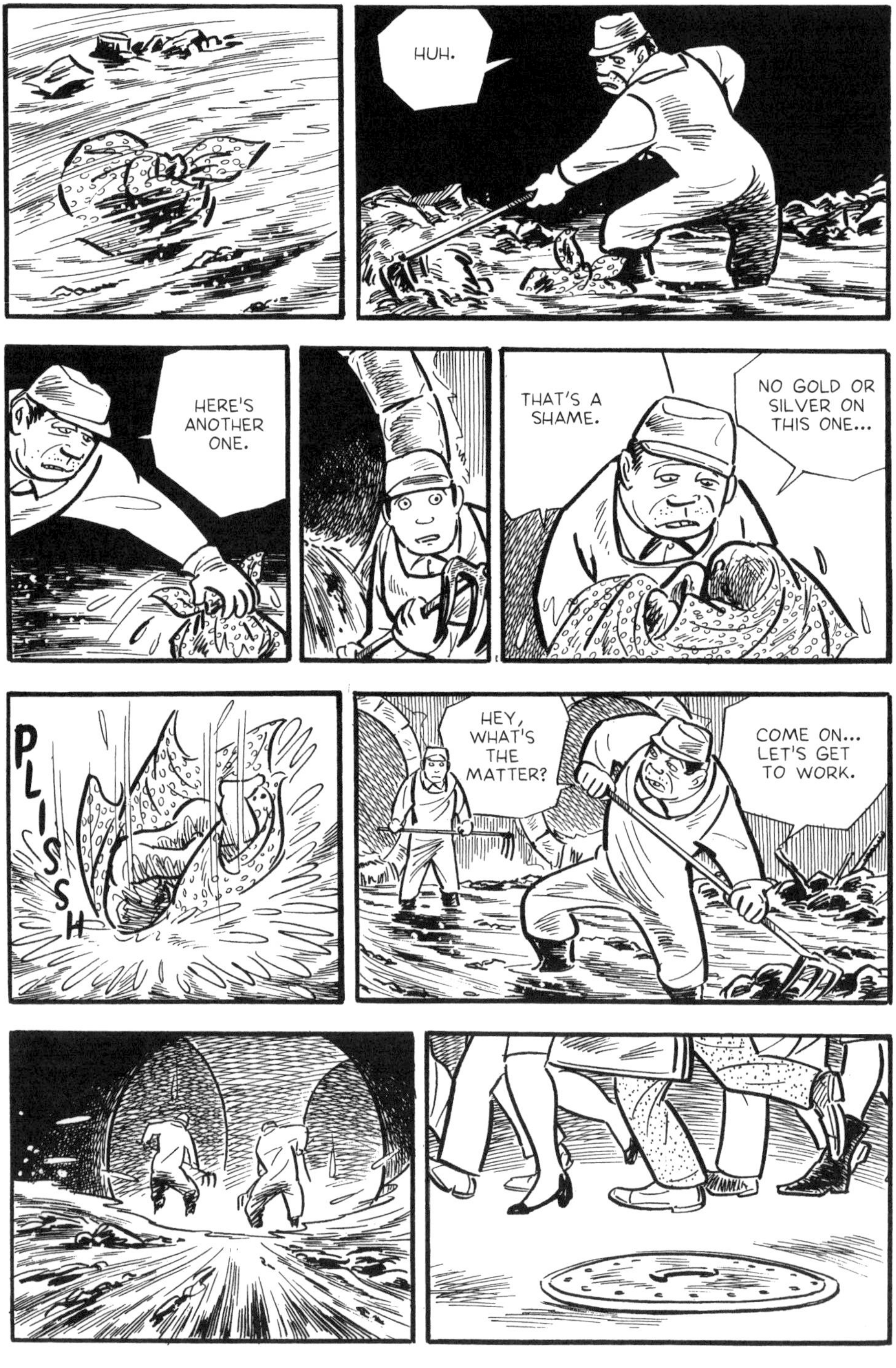
HUH.
HERE'S ANOTHER ONE.
THAT'S A SHAME.
NO GOLD OR SILVER ON THIS ONE...
PLISSH
HEY, WHAT'S THE MATTER?
COME ON... LET'S GET TO WORK.

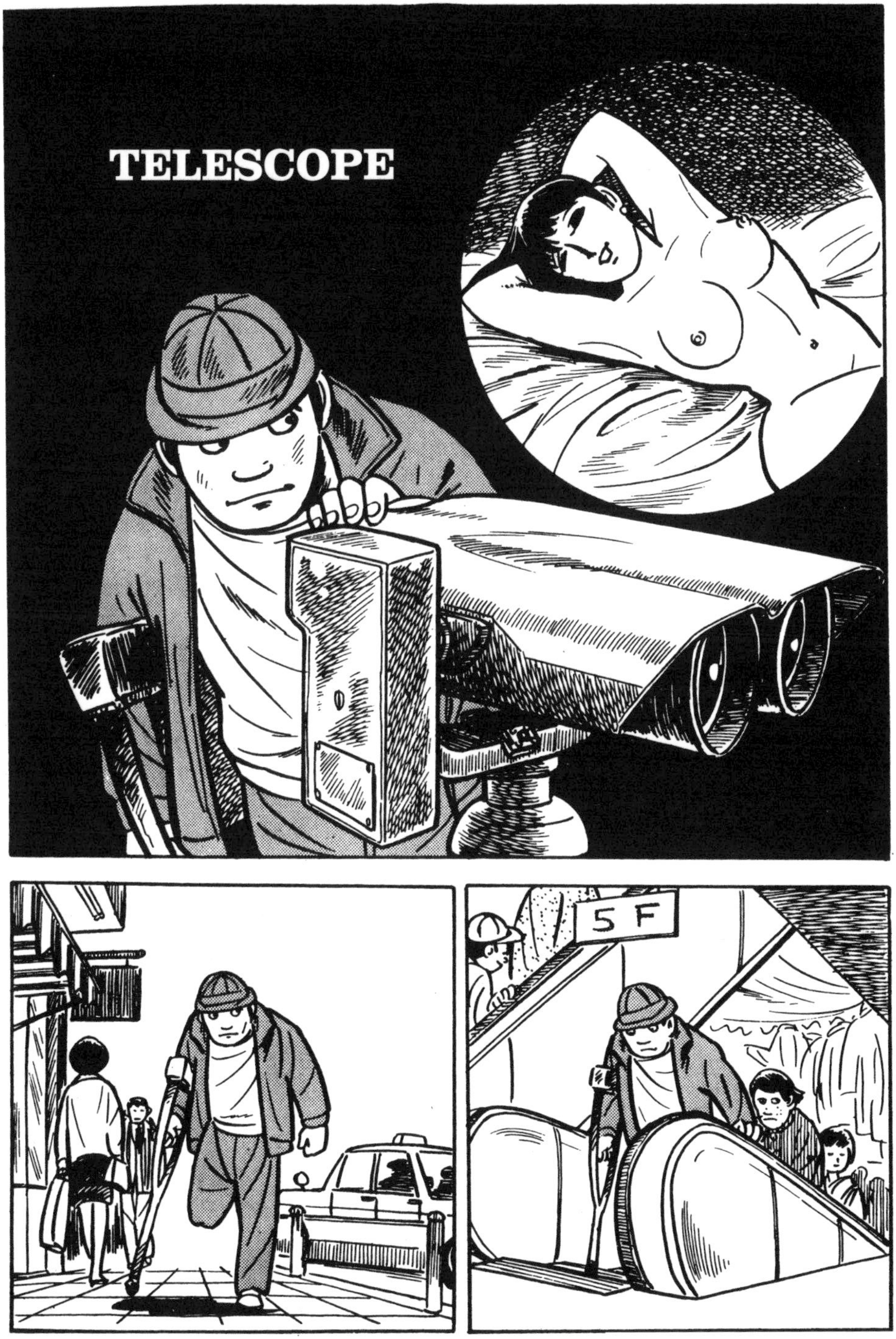
TELESCOPE
5 F

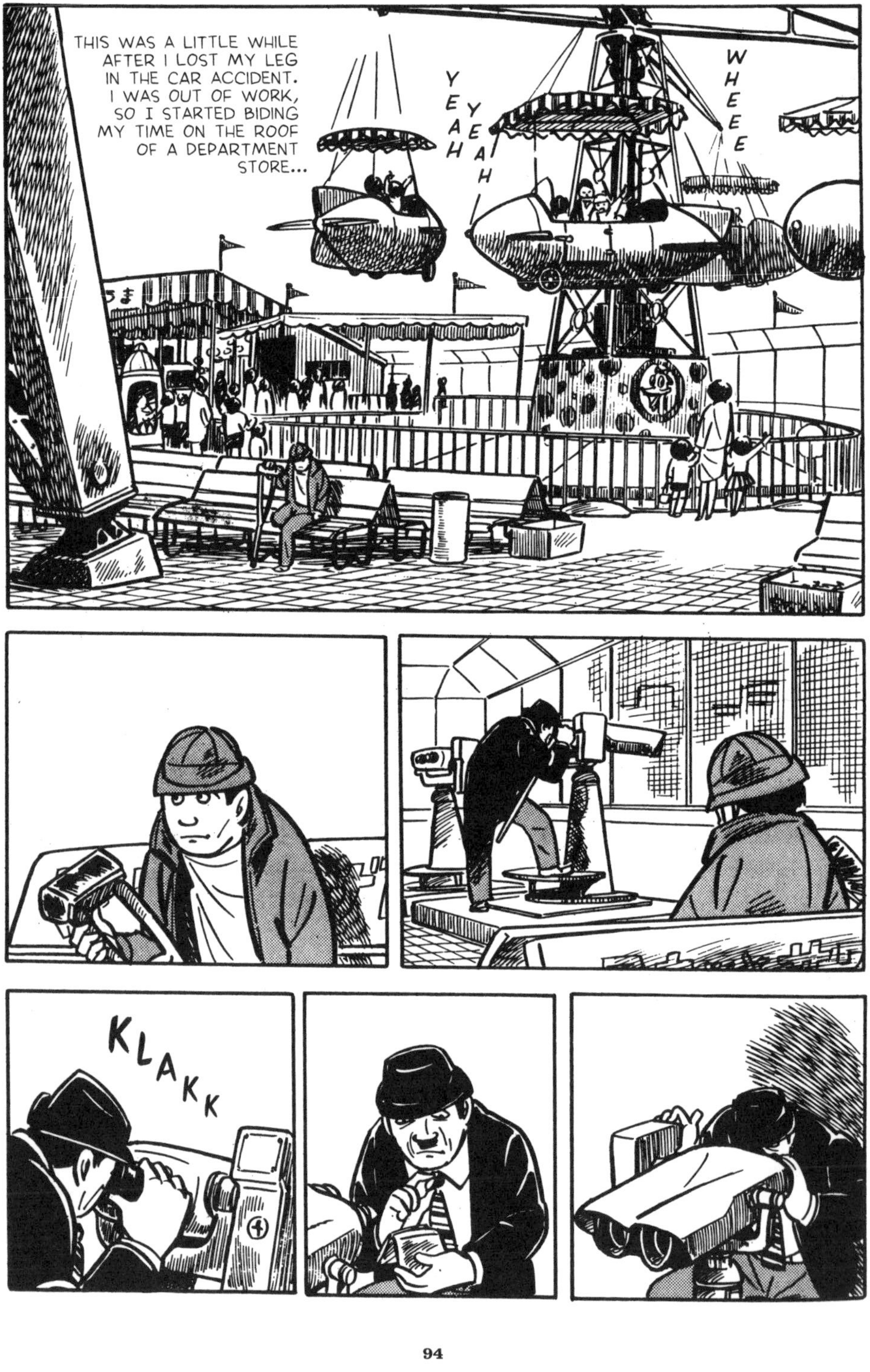
THIS WAS A LITTLE WHILE AFTER I LOST MY LEG IN THE CAR ACCIDENT. I WAS OUT OF WORK, SO I STARTED BIDING MY TIME ON THE ROOF OF A DEPARTMENT STORE...
YEAH
YEAH
WHEEE
KLAKK

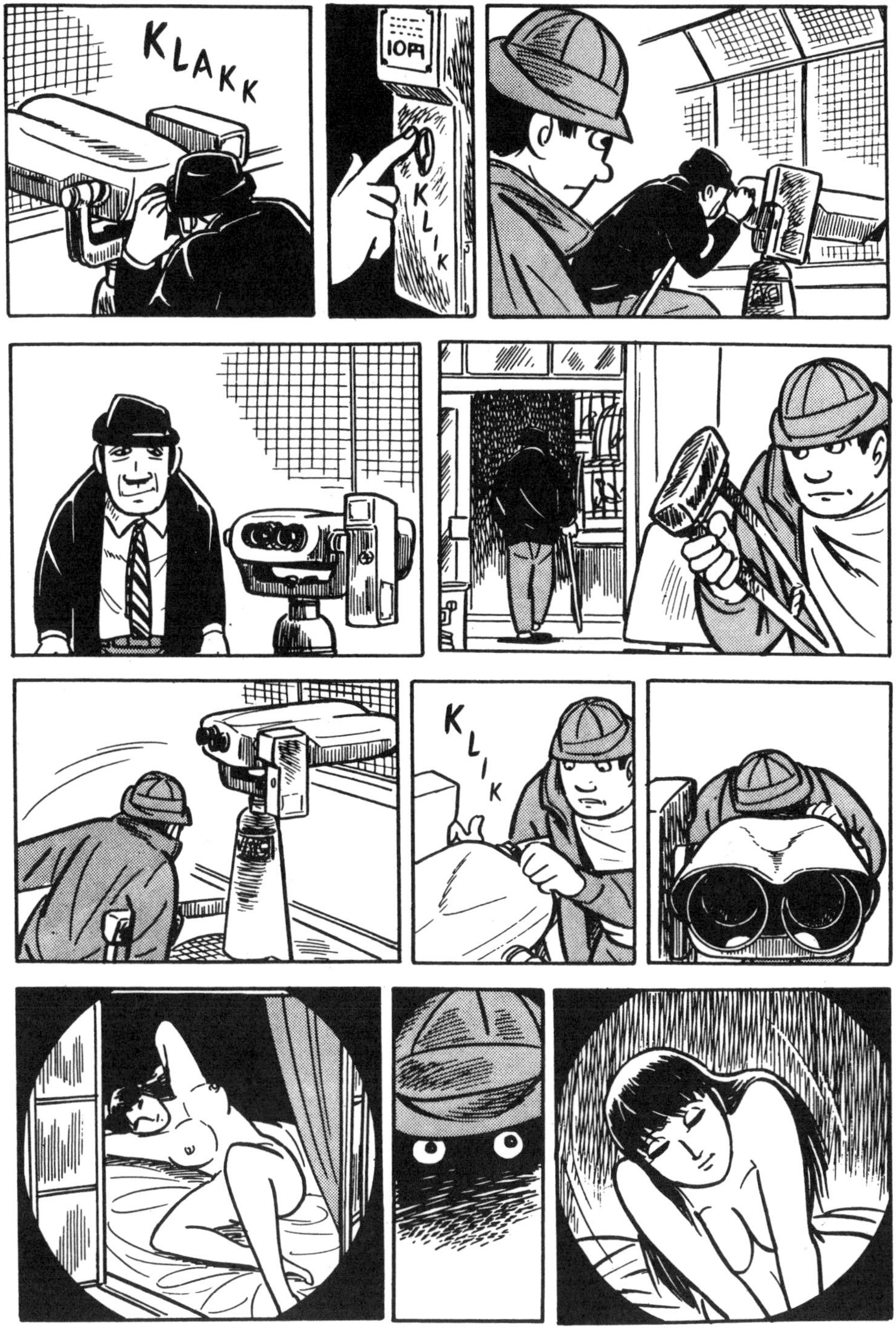
KLAKK
10円
KLIK
KLIK

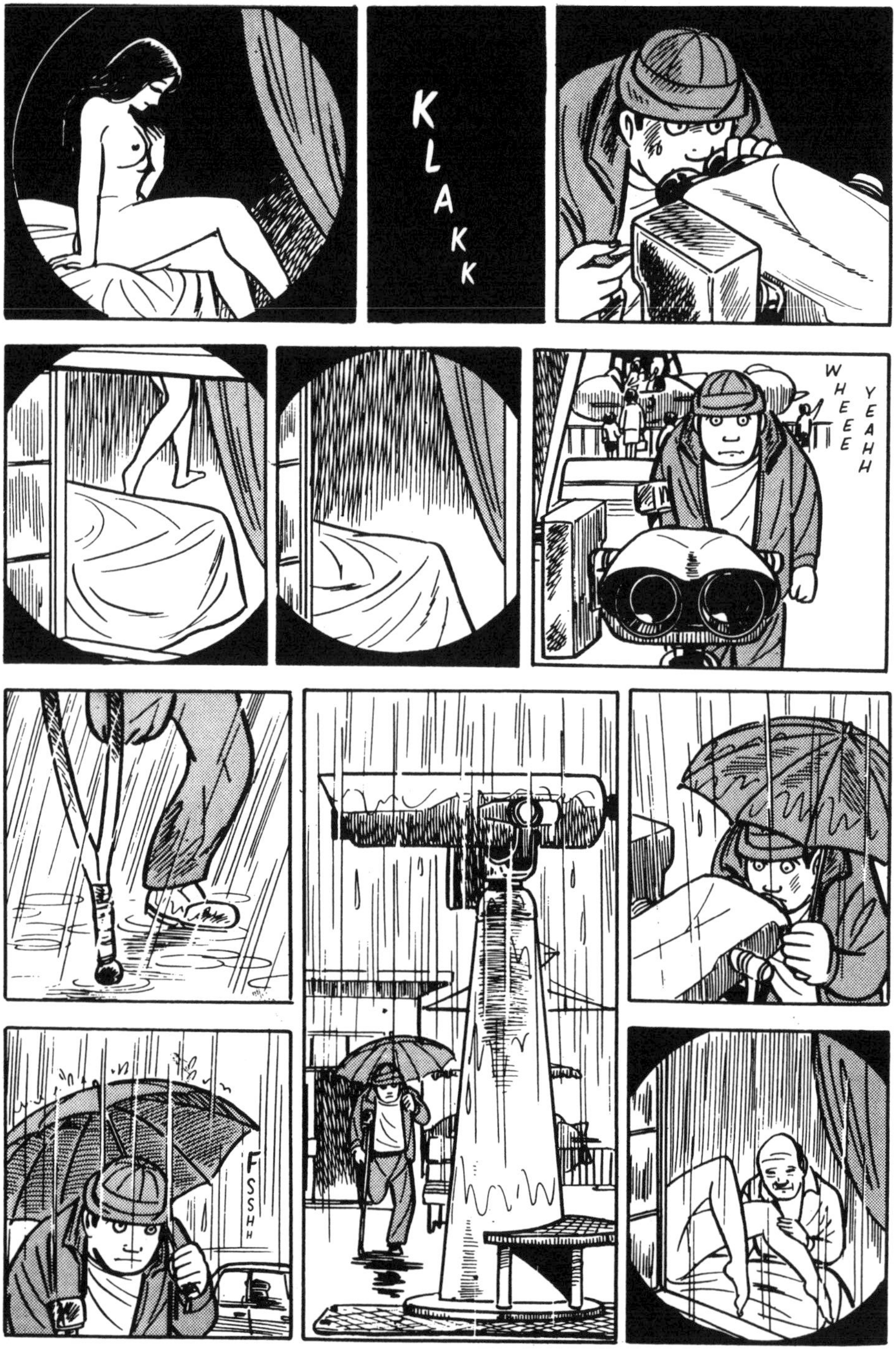
KLAKK
WHEEE
YEAHH
FSSHH

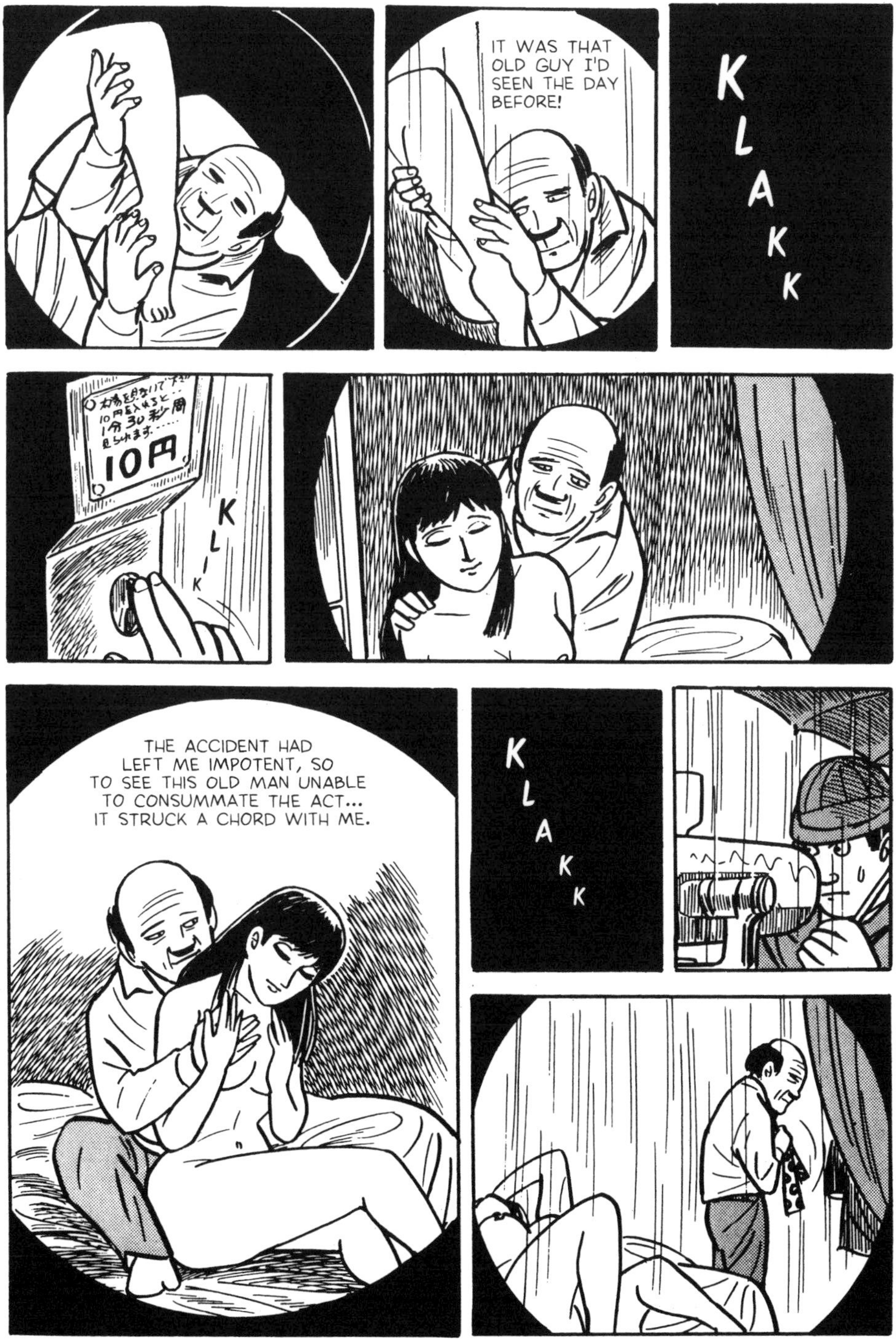
IT WAS THAT OLD GUY I'D SEEN THE DAY BEFORE!
KLAKK
10円を入れると
1分30秒間
見られます
10円
KLIK
THE ACCIDENT HAD LEFT ME IMPOTENT, SO TO SEE THIS OLD MAN UNABLE TO CONSUMMATE THE ACT... IT STRUCK A CHORD WITH ME.
KLAKK

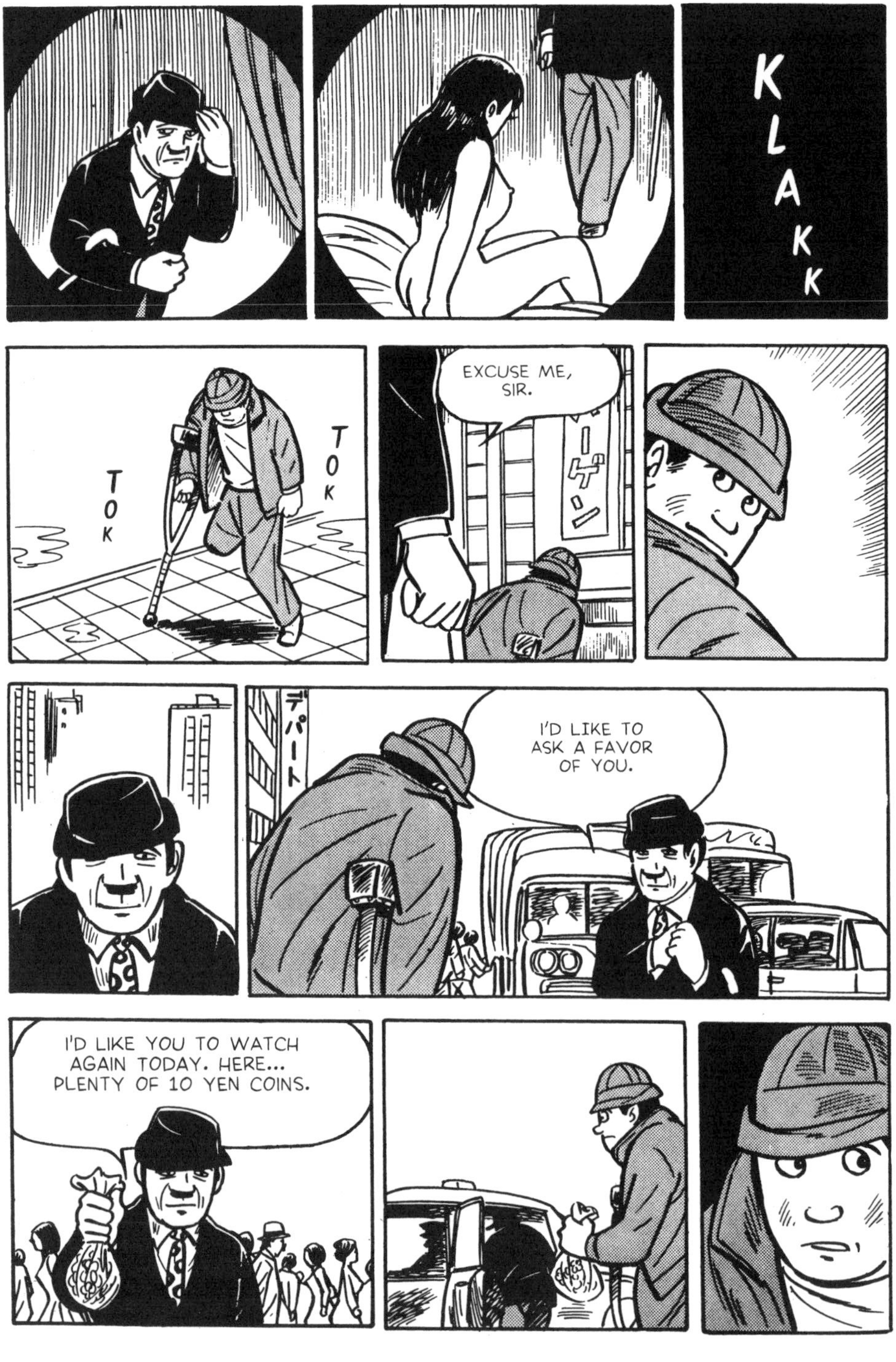
KLAKK
TOK
TOK
EXCUSE ME, SIR.
I'D LIKE TO ASK A FAVOR OF YOU.
I'D LIKE YOU TO WATCH AGAIN TODAY. HERE... PLENTY OF 10 YEN COINS.

YOU SEEM TO BE IN A GOOD MOOD TODAY.

COME HERE...

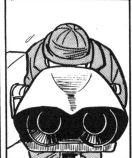

AAAA...

IT FELT SO DIFFERENT. YOU'RE A NEW MAN...

I KNOW.

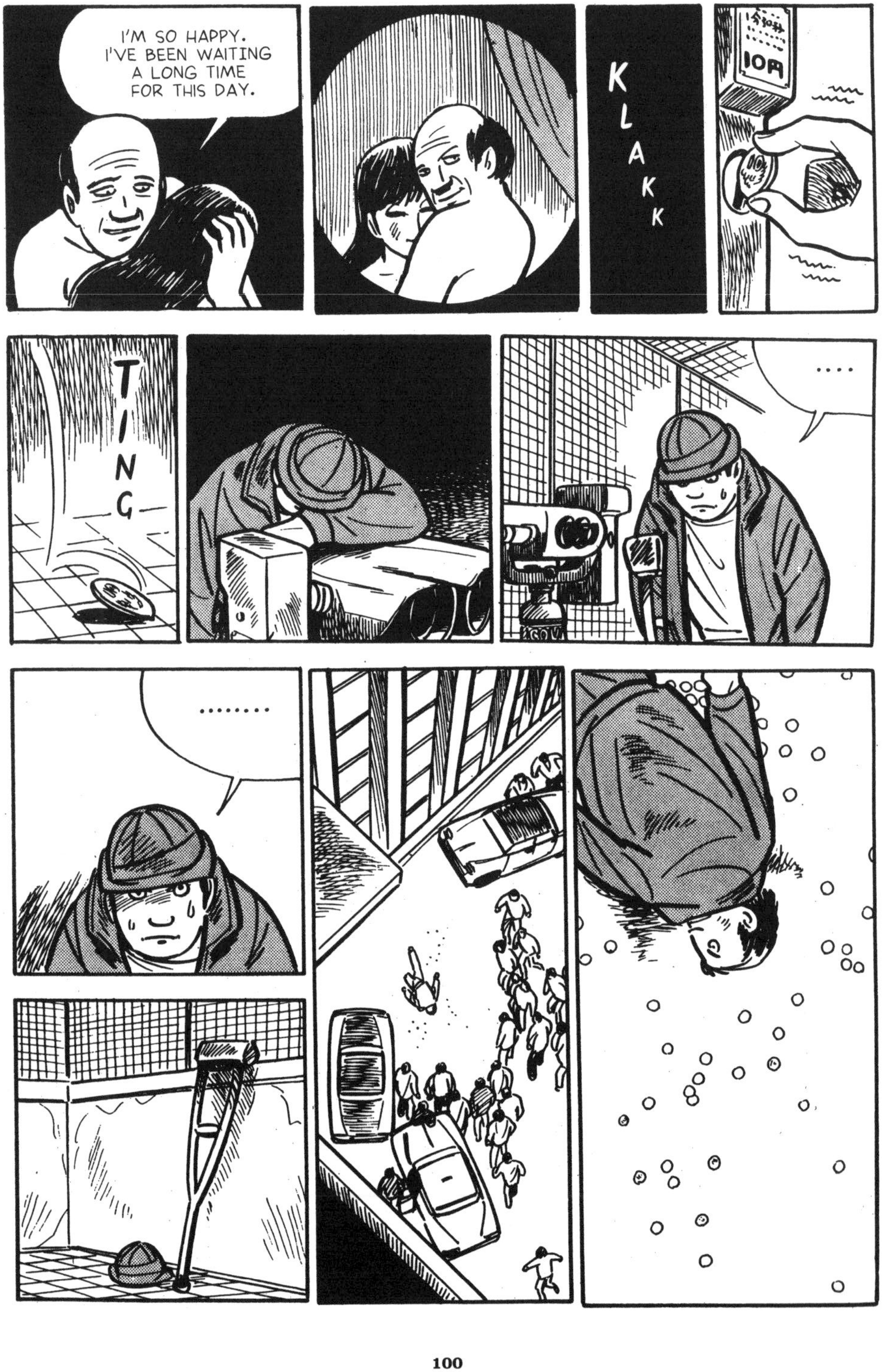
I'M SO HAPPY. I'VE BEEN WAITING A LONG TIME FOR THIS DAY.
KLAKK
10円
TING
....
....

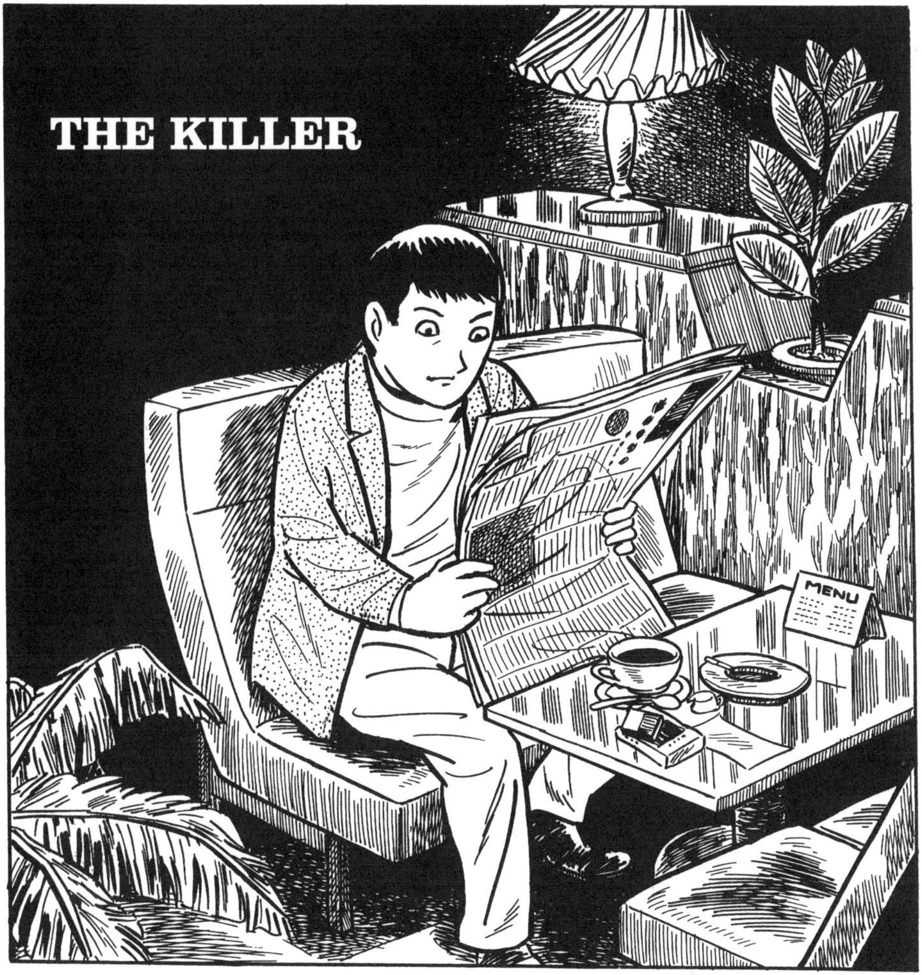
THE KILLER
MENU

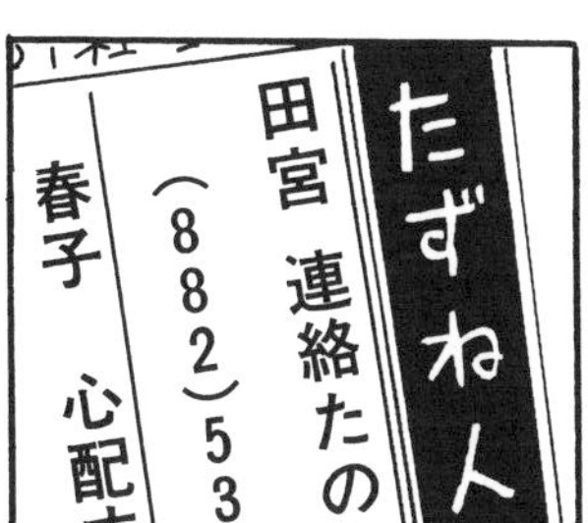
たずね人
田宮 連絡たのむ
(882)5394
春子 心配するな

PERSONALS TAMIYA: CONTACT ME

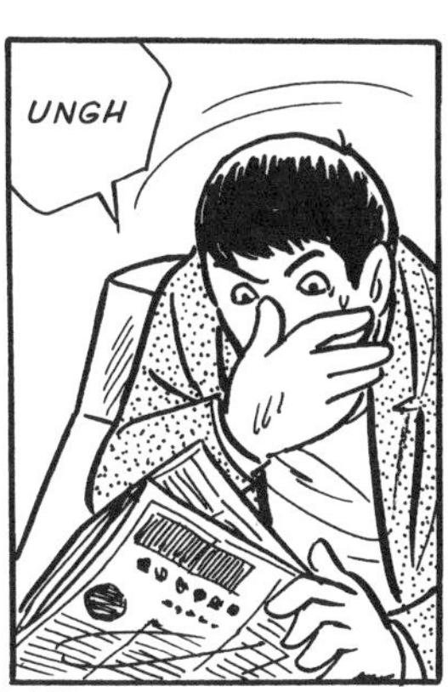
UNGH

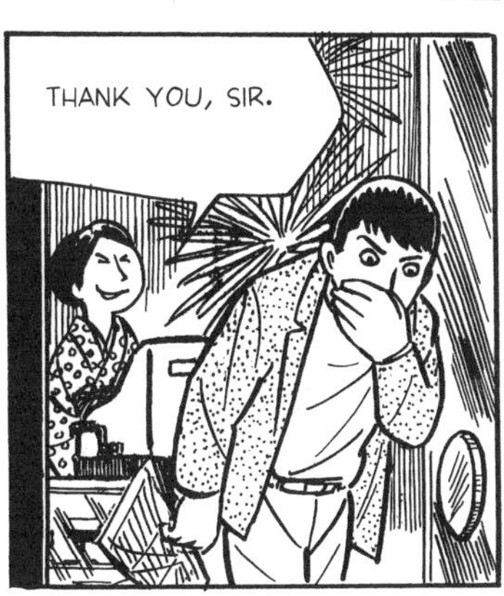
THANK YOU, SIR.

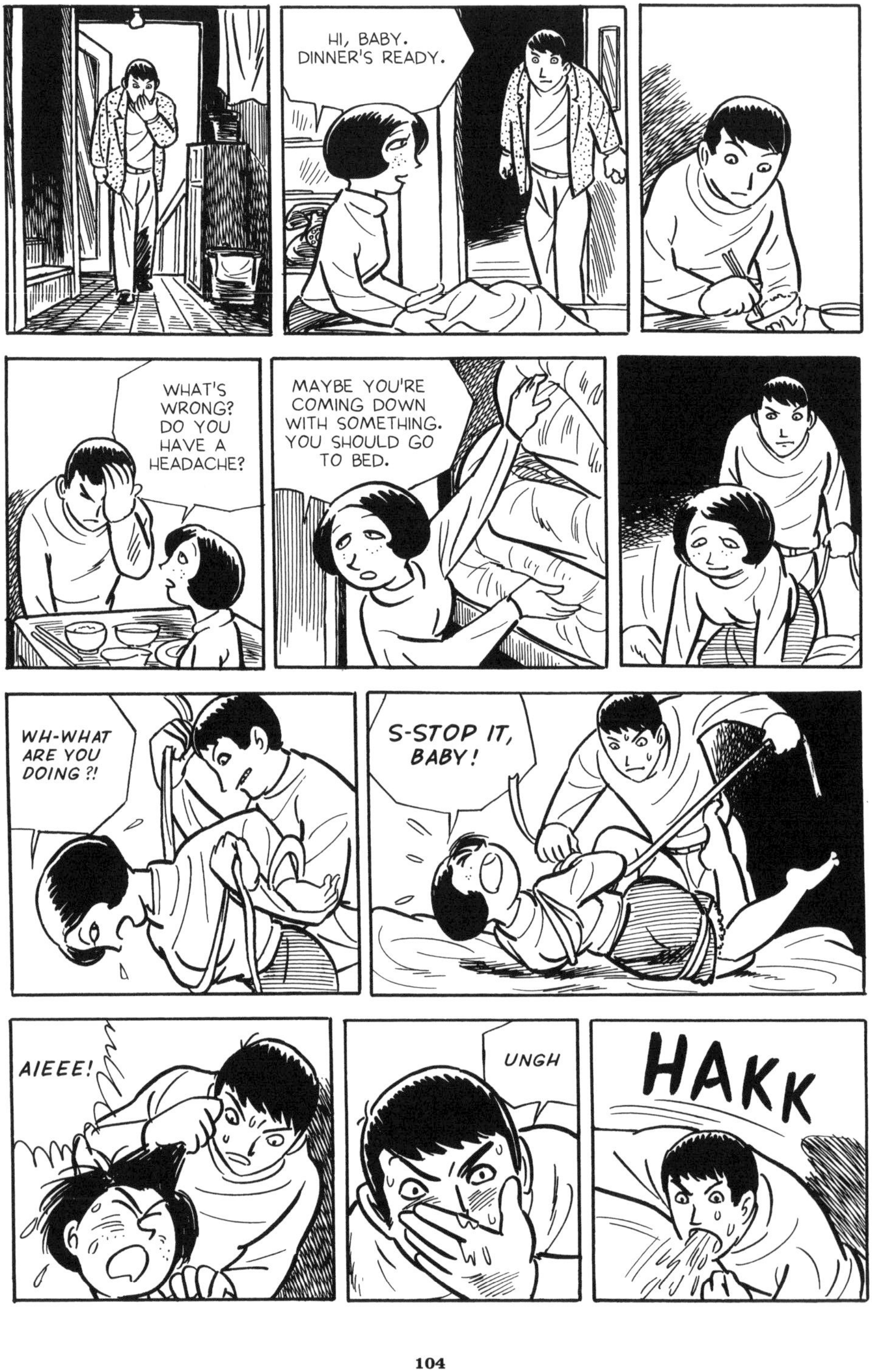
HI, BABY. DINNER'S READY.
WHAT'S WRONG? DO YOU HAVE A HEADACHE?
MAYBE YOU'RE COMING DOWN WITH SOMETHING. YOU SHOULD GO TO BED.
WH-WHAT ARE YOU DOING?!
S-STOP IT, BABY!
AIEEE!
UNGH
HAKK

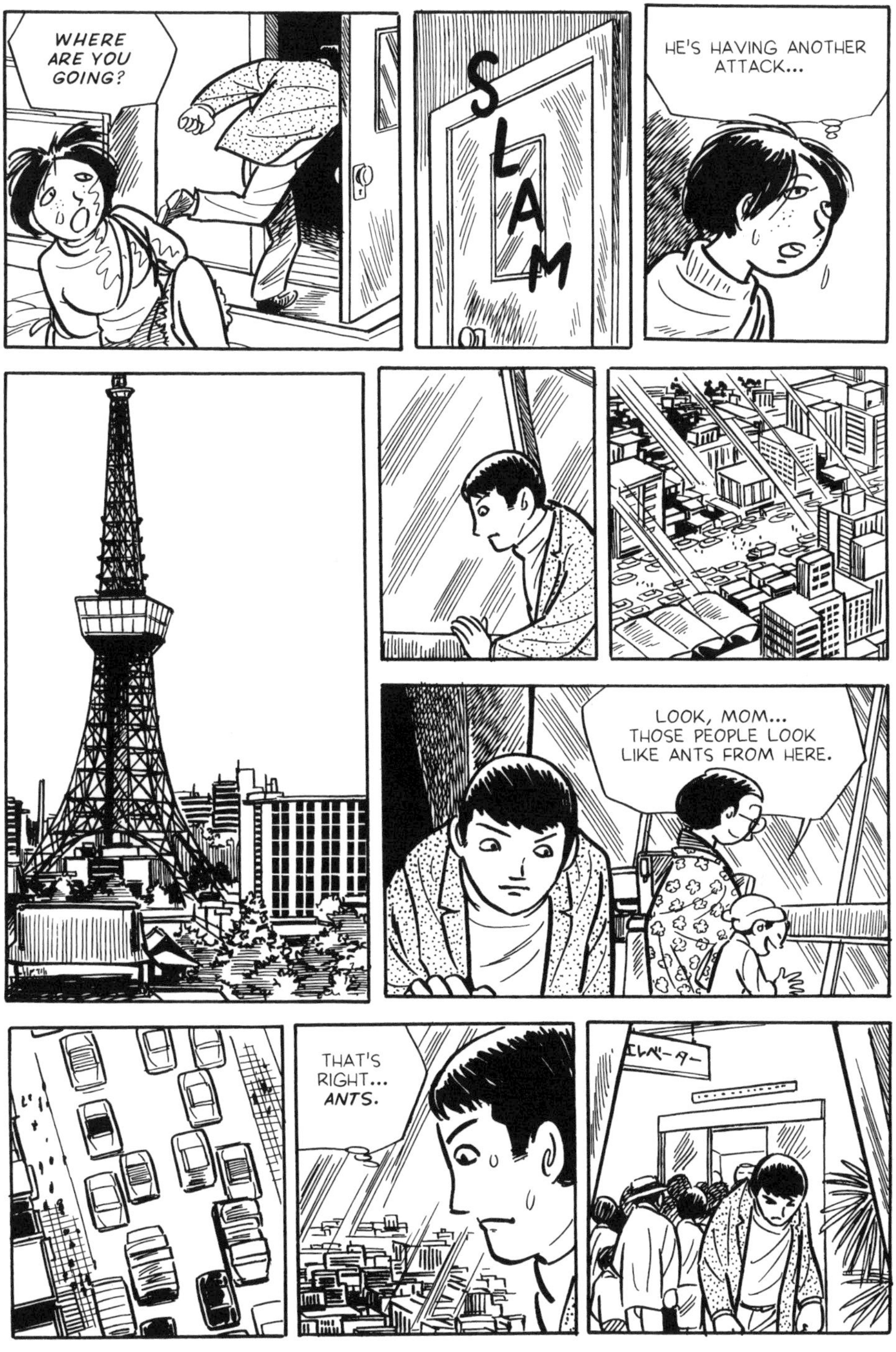
WHERE ARE YOU GOING?
SLAM
HE'S HAVING ANOTHER ATTACK...
LOOK, MOM... THOSE PEOPLE LOOK LIKE ANTS FROM HERE.
THAT'S RIGHT... ANTS.
エレベーター

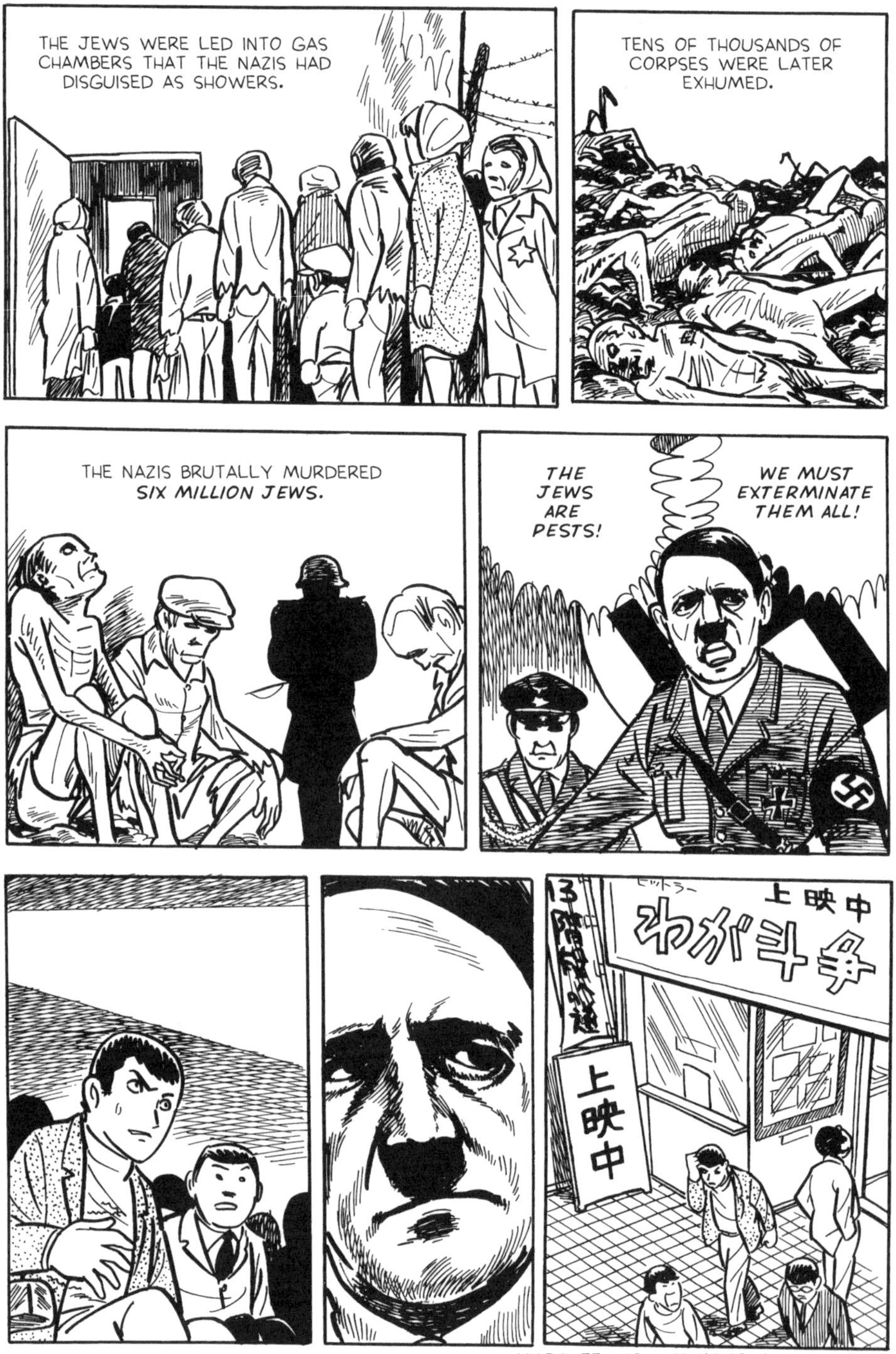
THE JEWS WERE LED INTO GAS CHAMBERS THAT THE NAZIS HAD DISGUISED AS SHOWERS.
TENS OF THOUSANDS OF CORPSES WERE LATER EXHUMED.
THE NAZIS BRUTALLY MURDERED *SIX MILLION JEWS.*
THE JEWS ARE PESTS!
WE MUST EXTERMINATE THEM ALL!
上映中
わが斗争
上映中

MARQUEE: NOW PLAYING ***MEIN KAMPF***

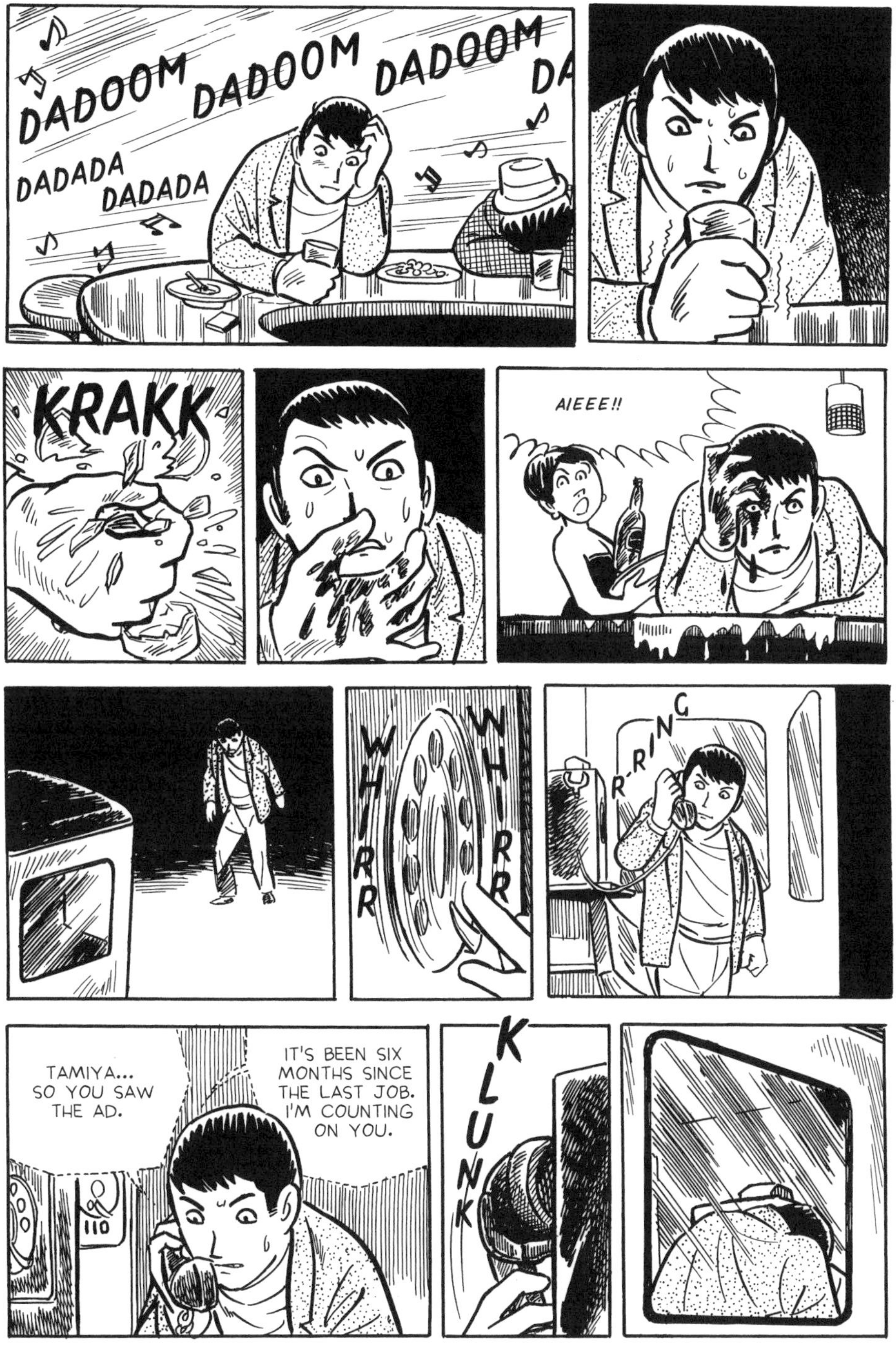
DADOOM
DADOOM
DADOOM
DA
DADADA
DADADA
KRAKK
AIEEE!!
WHIRR
WHIRR
R-RING
110
TAMIYA... SO YOU SAW THE AD.
IT'S BEEN SIX MONTHS SINCE THE LAST JOB. I'M COUNTING ON YOU.
KLUNK

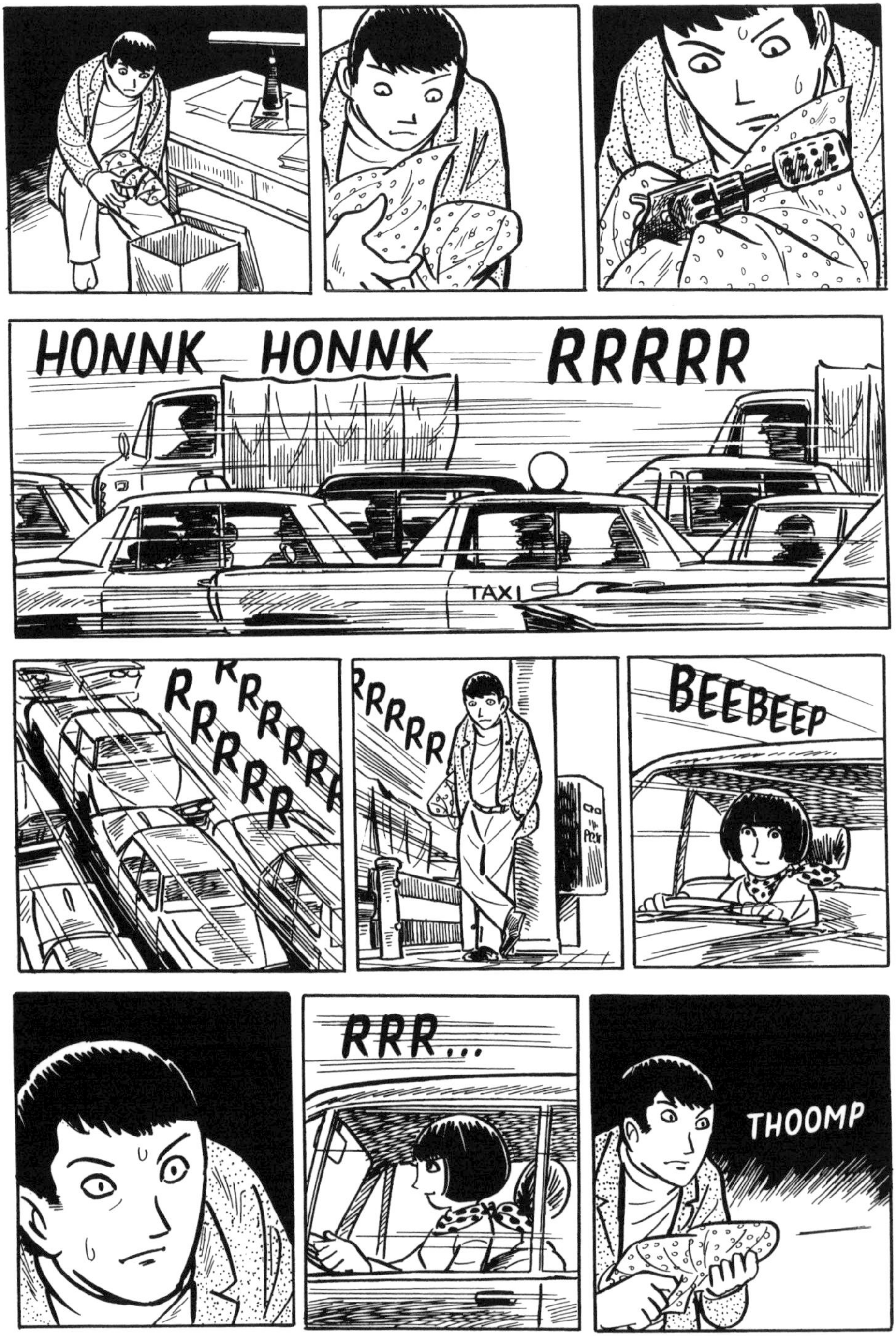
HONNK HONNK
RRRRR
TAXI
RRRRRRRRRR
RRRRRR
BEEBEEP
RRR...
THOOMP

SKREEEECH
BAMM
KRRRRRRRR
WEEYOO WEEYOO
YAWN
WEEYOO WEEYOO
POLICE
純喫茶
ゴンドラ
THIS IS FOR YOU, MR.TAMIYA.
東京駅ロッカー
35

SIGN: CAFÉ GONDOLA

NOTE: TOKYO STATION COIN LOCKER

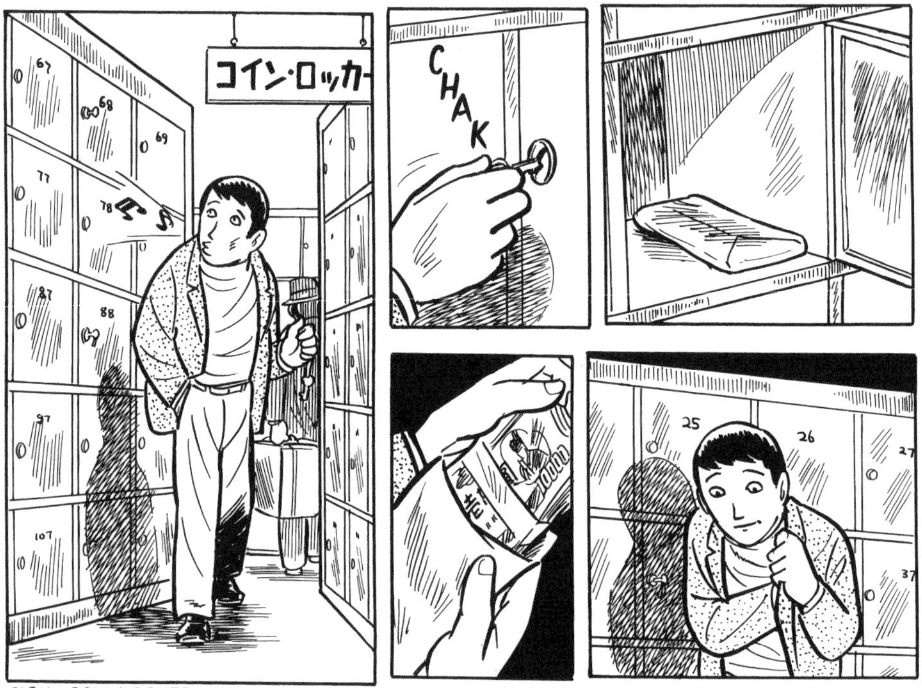
コイン・ロッカー
CHAK

SIGN: COIN LOCKER

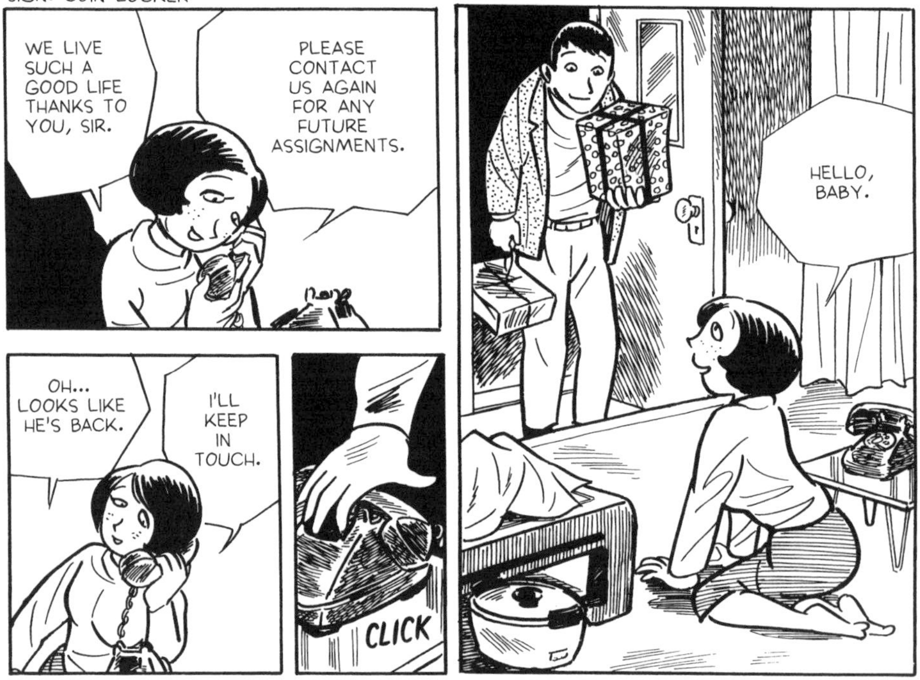
WE LIVE SUCH A GOOD LIFE THANKS TO YOU, SIR.
PLEASE CONTACT US AGAIN FOR ANY FUTURE ASSIGNMENTS.
OH... LOOKS LIKE HE'S BACK.
I'LL KEEP IN TOUCH.
CLICK
HELLO, BABY.

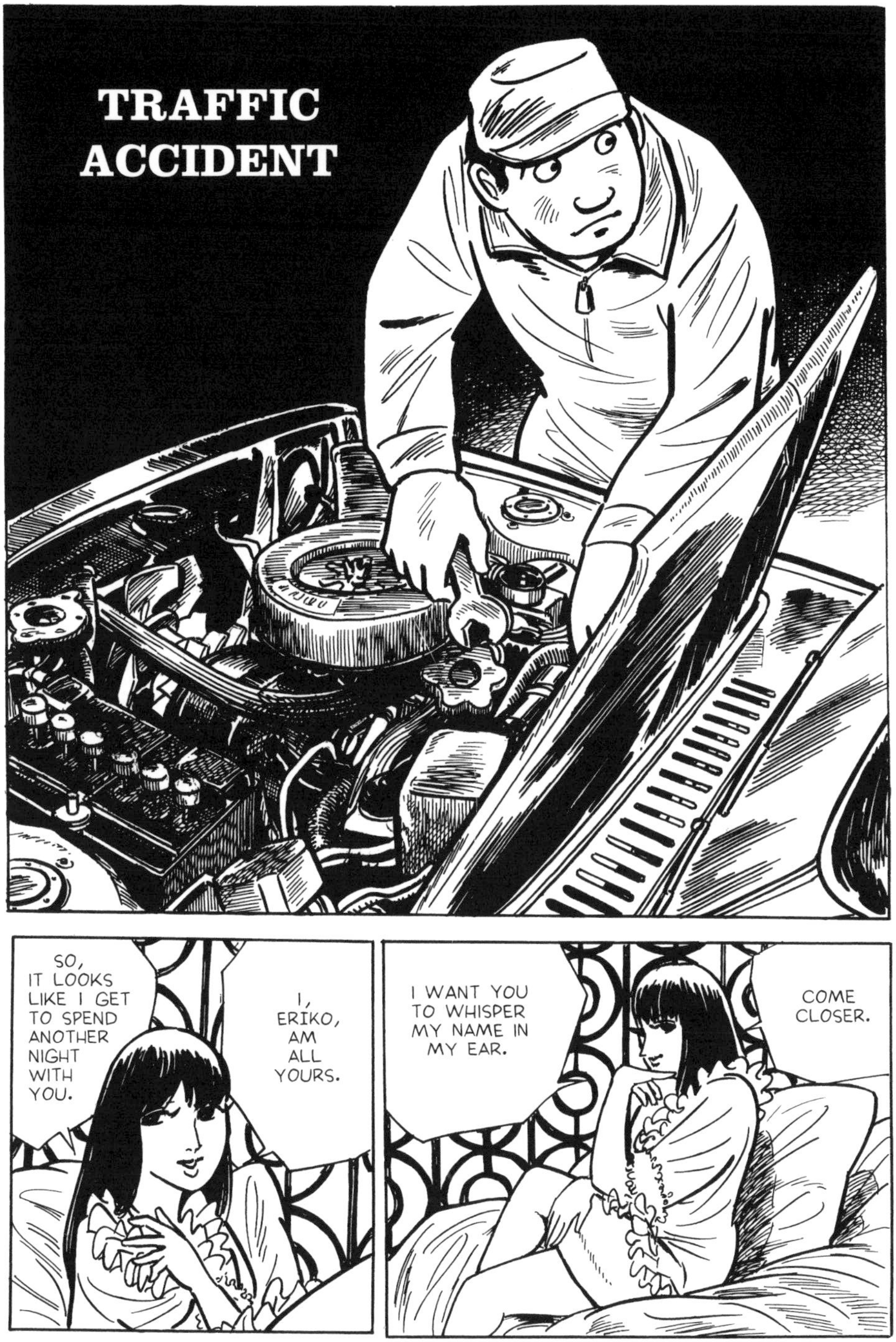
TRAFFIC ACCIDENT
SO, IT LOOKS LIKE I GET TO SPEND ANOTHER NIGHT WITH YOU.
I, ERIKO, AM ALL YOURS.
I WANT YOU TO WHISPER MY NAME IN MY EAR.
COME CLOSER.

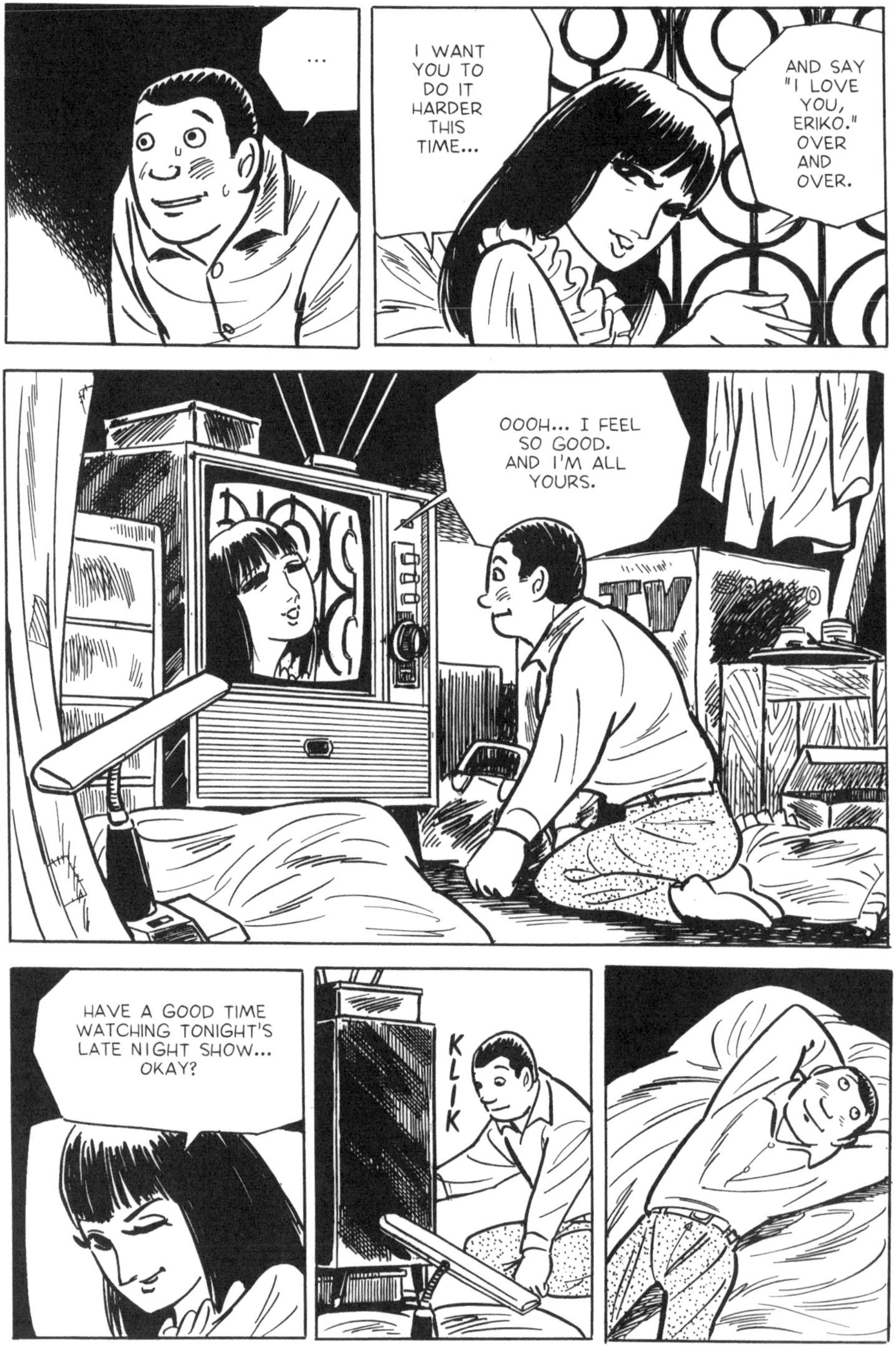
...
I WANT YOU TO DO IT HARDER THIS TIME...
AND SAY "I LOVE YOU, ERIKO." OVER AND OVER.
OOOH... I FEEL SO GOOD. AND I'M ALL YOURS.
TV
HAVE A GOOD TIME WATCHING TONIGHT'S LATE NIGHT SHOW... OKAY?
KLIK

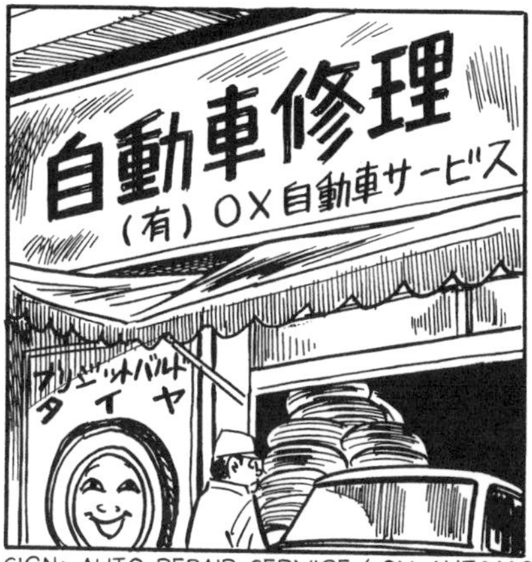
自動車修理
(有) OX自動車サービス
タイヤ

SIGN: AUTO REPAIR SERVICE/ OX AUTOMOBILE SERVICES INC.

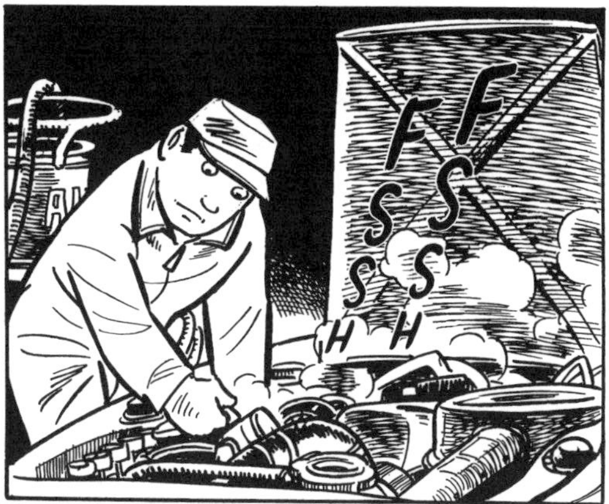
FSSH
FSSH

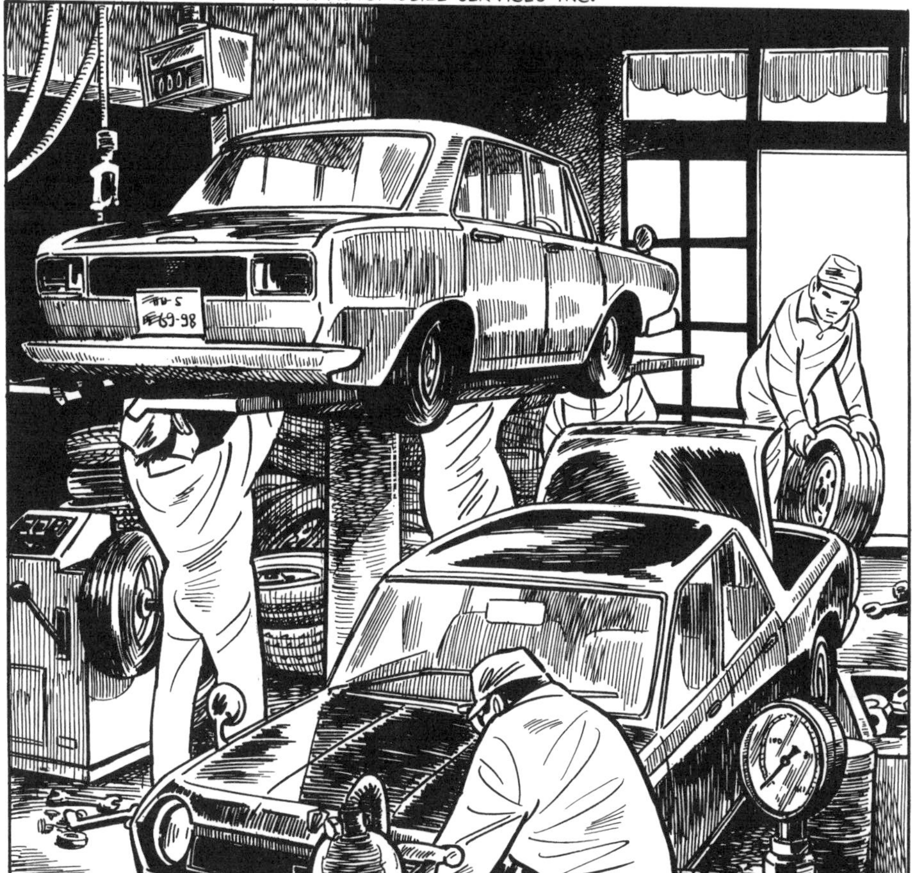

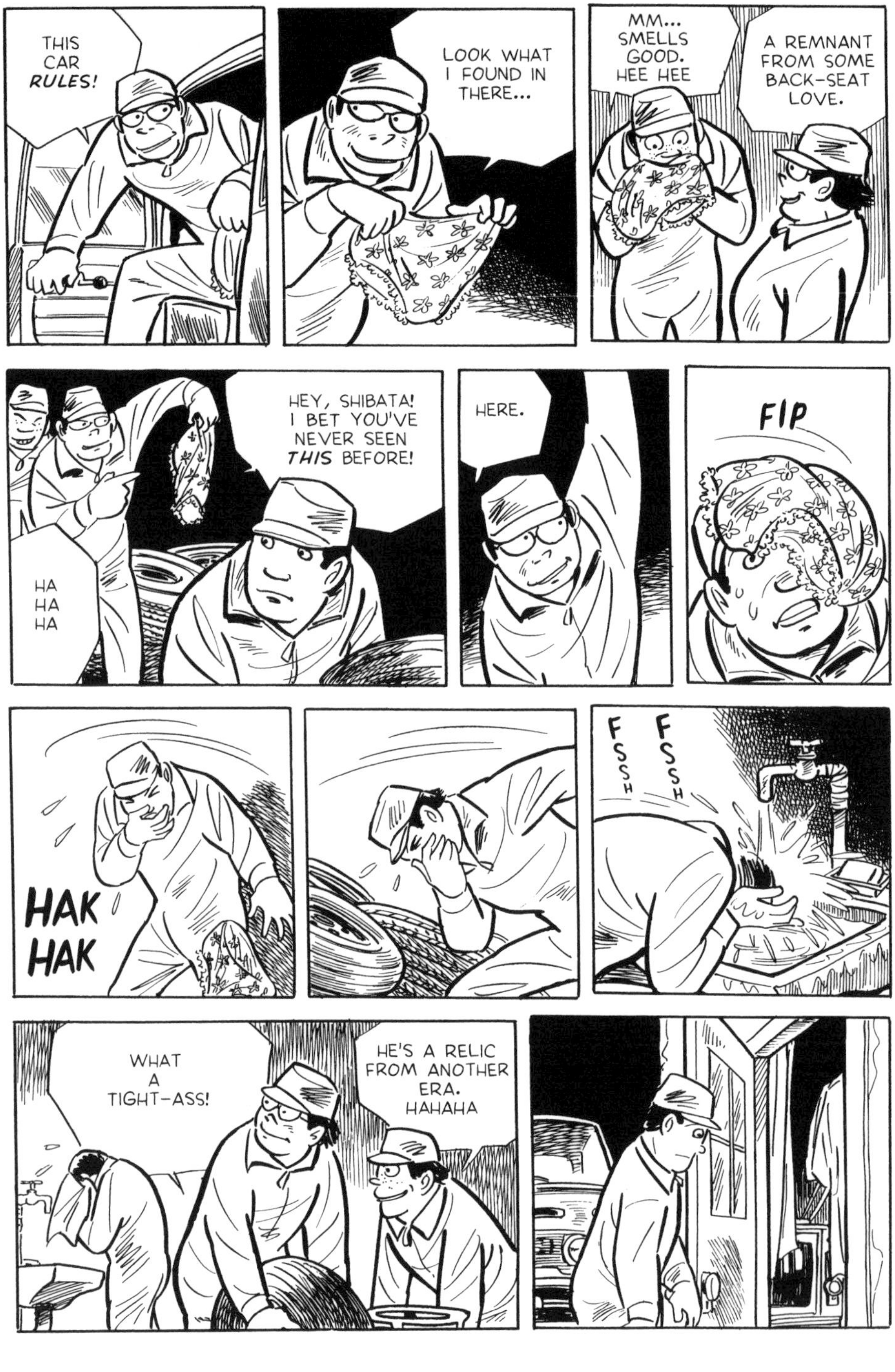
THIS CAR *RULES!*
LOOK WHAT I FOUND IN THERE...
MM... SMELLS GOOD. HEE HEE
A REMNANT FROM SOME BACK-SEAT LOVE.
HEY, SHIBATA! I BET YOU'VE NEVER SEEN *THIS* BEFORE!
HA HA HA
HERE.
FIP
HAK HAK
FSSH FSSH
WHAT A TIGHT-ASS!
HE'S A RELIC FROM ANOTHER ERA. HAHAHA

BRRRING

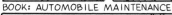
BOOK: AUTOMOBILE MAINTENANCE

KLIK

SO YOU STAYED AWAKE FOR ME AGAIN, HM?

I'M ALL YOURS TONIGHT. WILL YOU TREAT ME NICE AGAIN?

I WANT YOU TO WHISPER IN MY EAR AGAIN...

...AND SAY "MY SWEET ERIKO."

HOLD ME TIGHT AND DON'T LET GO.

117

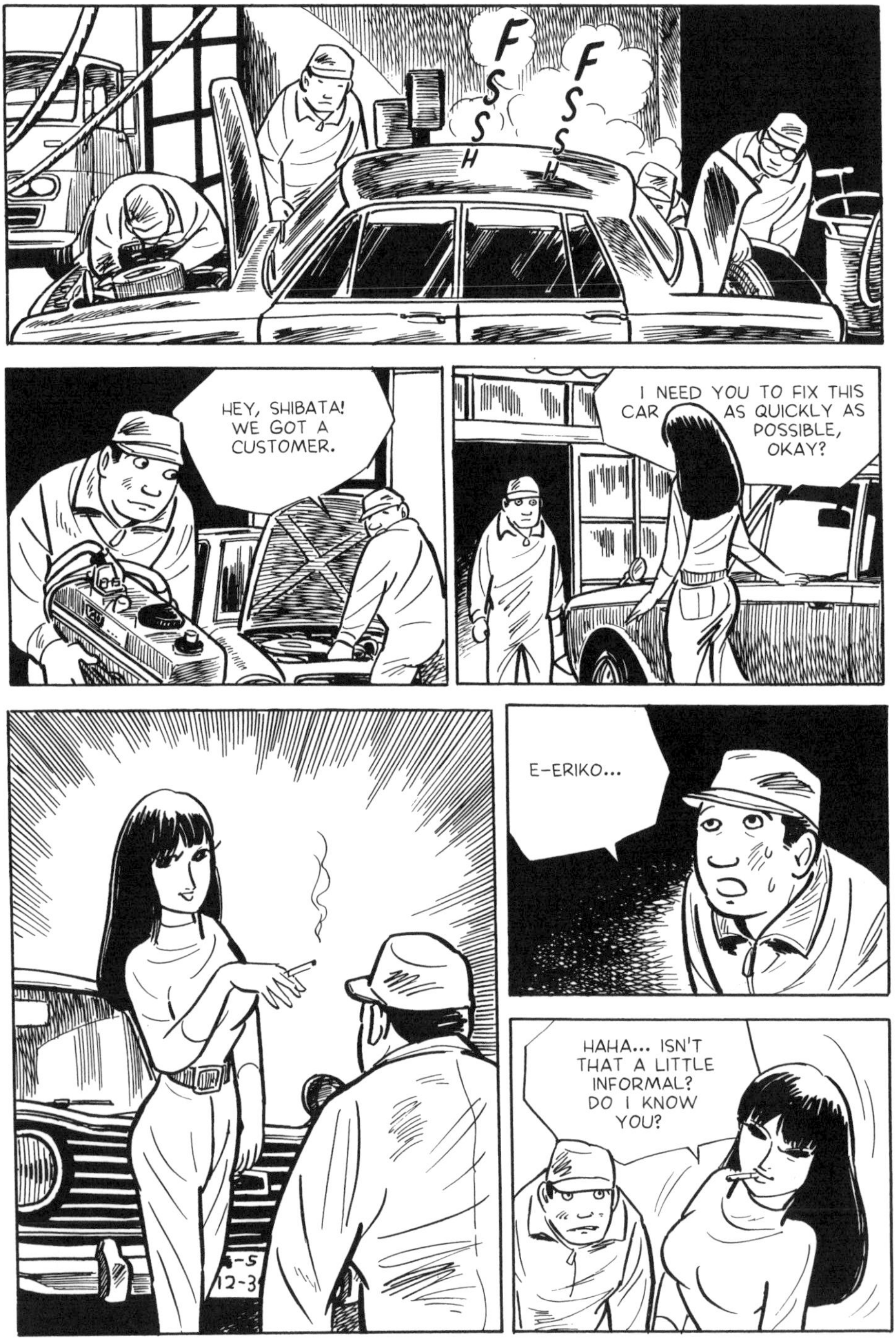
F S S H
F S S H
HEY, SHIBATA! WE GOT A CUSTOMER.
I NEED YOU TO FIX THIS CAR AS QUICKLY AS POSSIBLE, OKAY?
E-ERIKO...
HAHA... ISN'T THAT A LITTLE INFORMAL? DO I KNOW YOU?

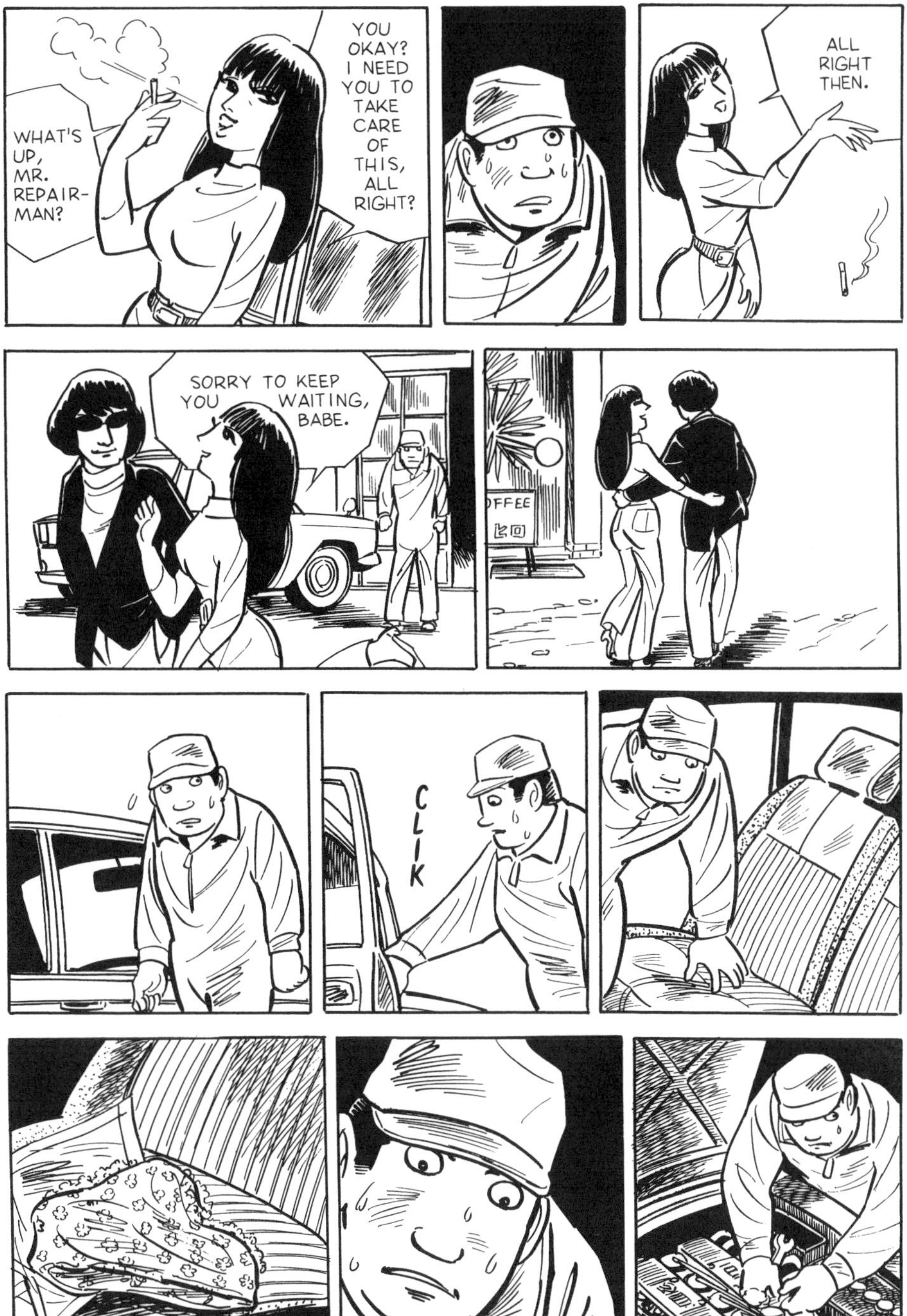
WHAT'S UP, MR. REPAIR-MAN?
YOU OKAY? I NEED YOU TO TAKE CARE OF THIS, ALL RIGHT?
ALL RIGHT THEN.
SORRY TO KEEP YOU WAITING, BABE.
OFFEE
ヒロ
CLIK

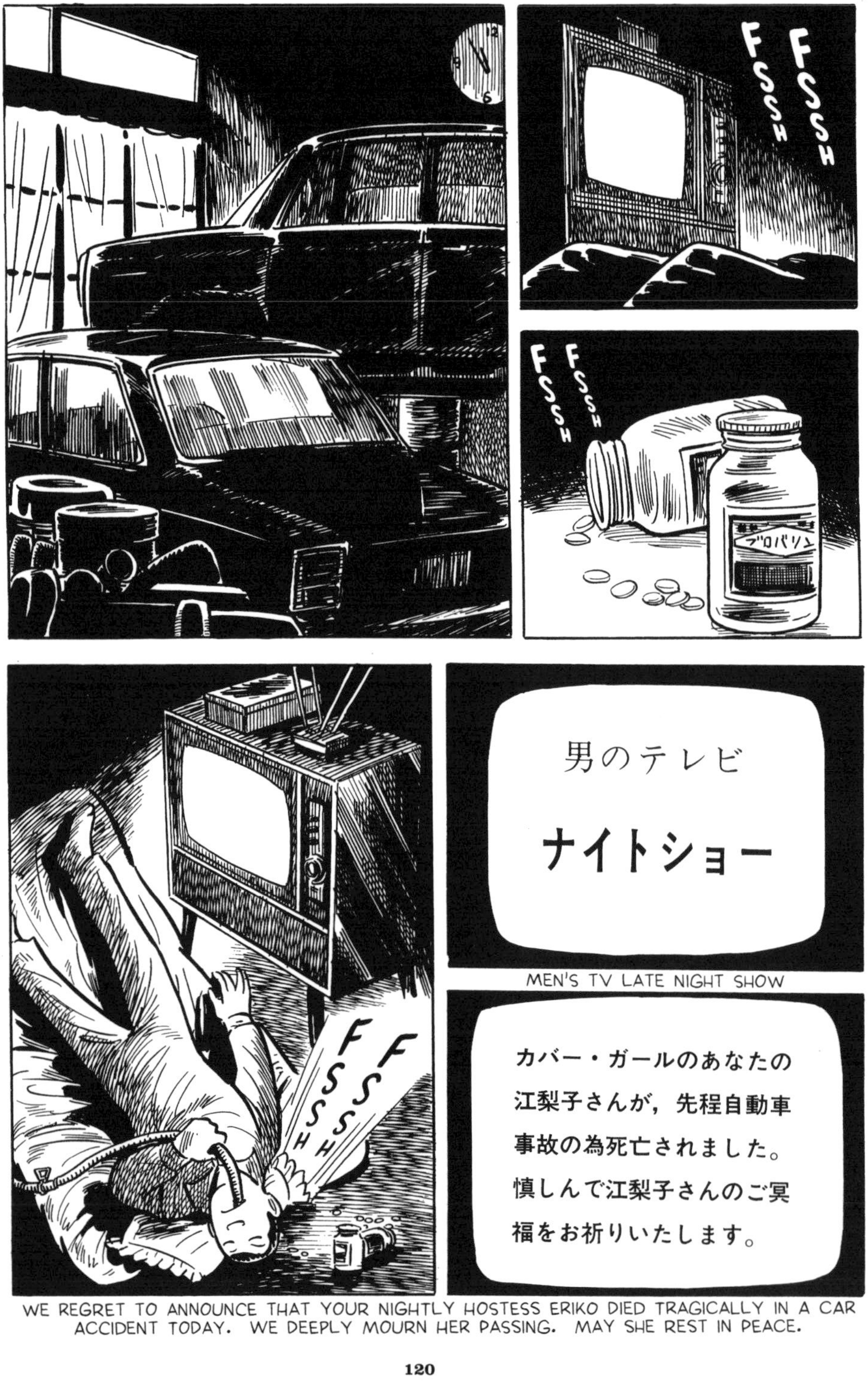
FSSSH
FSSSH
FSSSH
FSSSH
ブロバリン
FSSSH
FSSSH
男のテレビ
ナイトショー
MEN'S TV LATE NIGHT SHOW
カバー・ガールのあなたの
江梨子さんが，先程自動車
事故の為死亡されました。
慎しんで江梨子さんのご冥
福をお祈りいたします。

WE REGRET TO ANNOUNCE THAT YOUR NIGHTLY HOSTESS ERIKO DIED TRAGICALLY IN A CAR ACCIDENT TODAY. WE DEEPLY MOURN HER PASSING. MAY SHE REST IN PEACE.

MAKE-UP

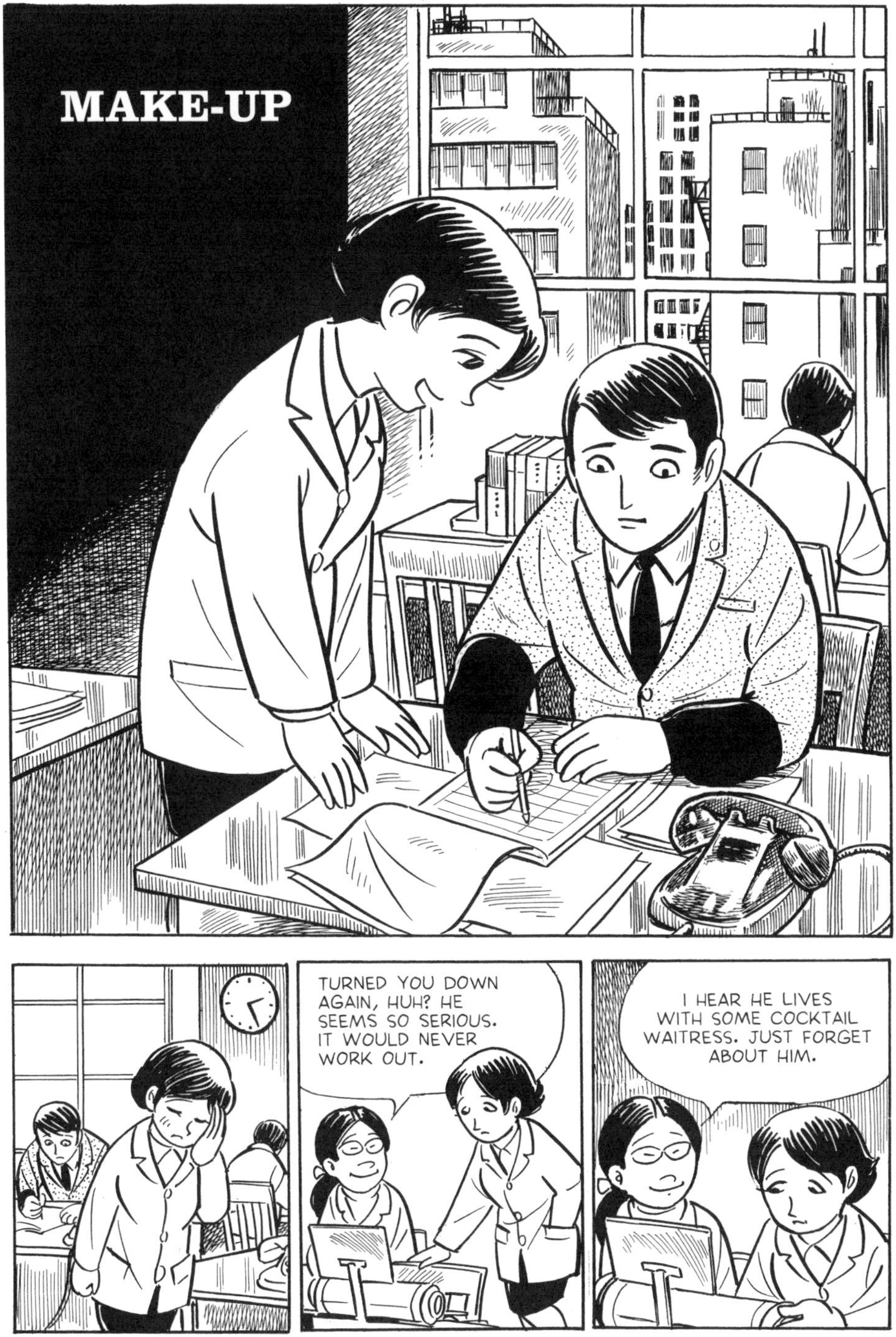
TURNED YOU DOWN AGAIN, HUH? HE SEEMS SO SERIOUS. IT WOULD NEVER WORK OUT.
I HEAR HE LIVES WITH SOME COCKTAIL WAITRESS. JUST FORGET ABOUT HIM.

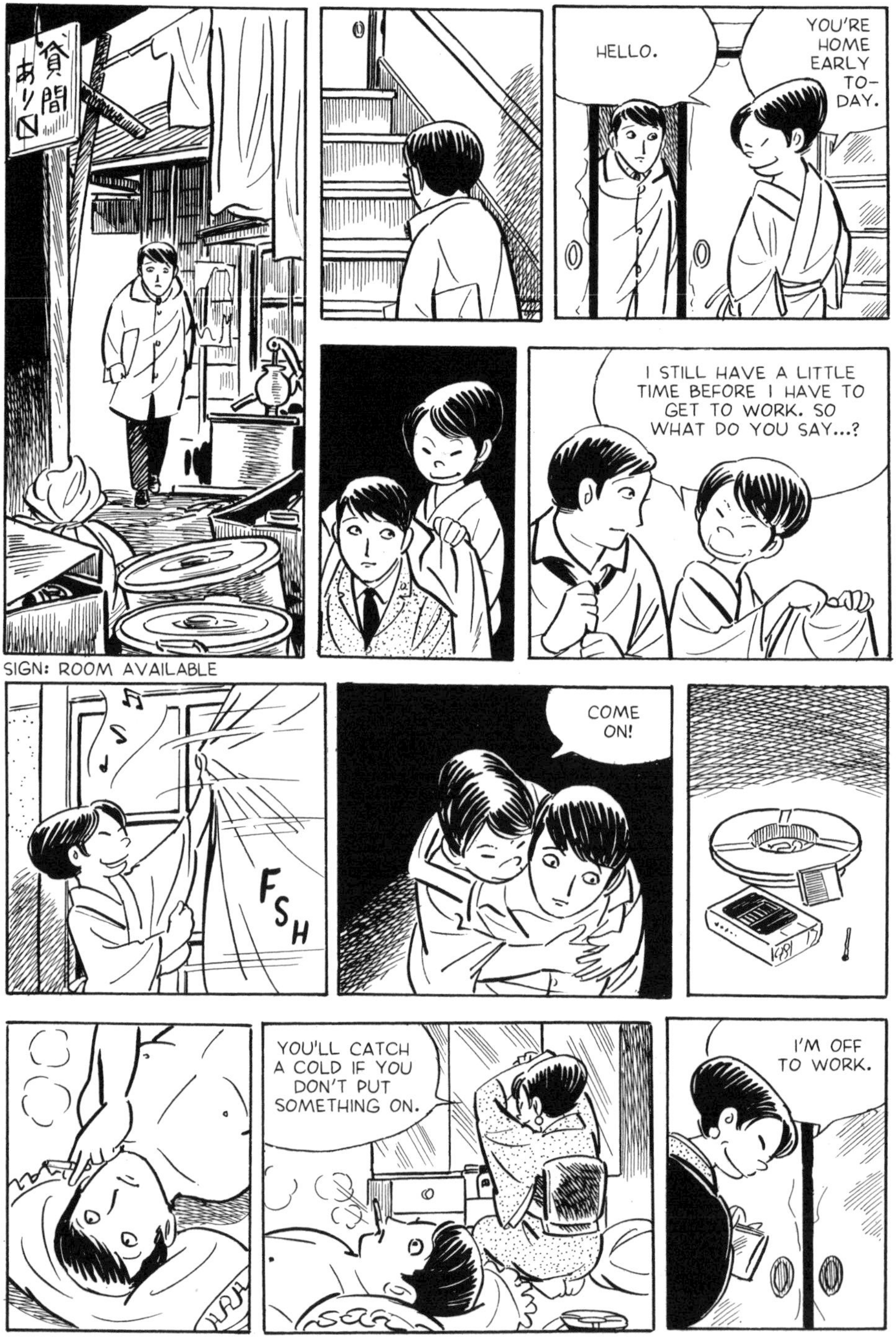

貸間あり〼
SIGN: ROOM AVAILABLE
HELLO.
YOU'RE HOME EARLY TO-DAY.
I STILL HAVE A LITTLE TIME BEFORE I HAVE TO GET TO WORK. SO WHAT DO YOU SAY...?
FSH
COME ON!
YOU'LL CATCH A COLD IF YOU DON'T PUT SOMETHING ON.
I'M OFF TO WORK.

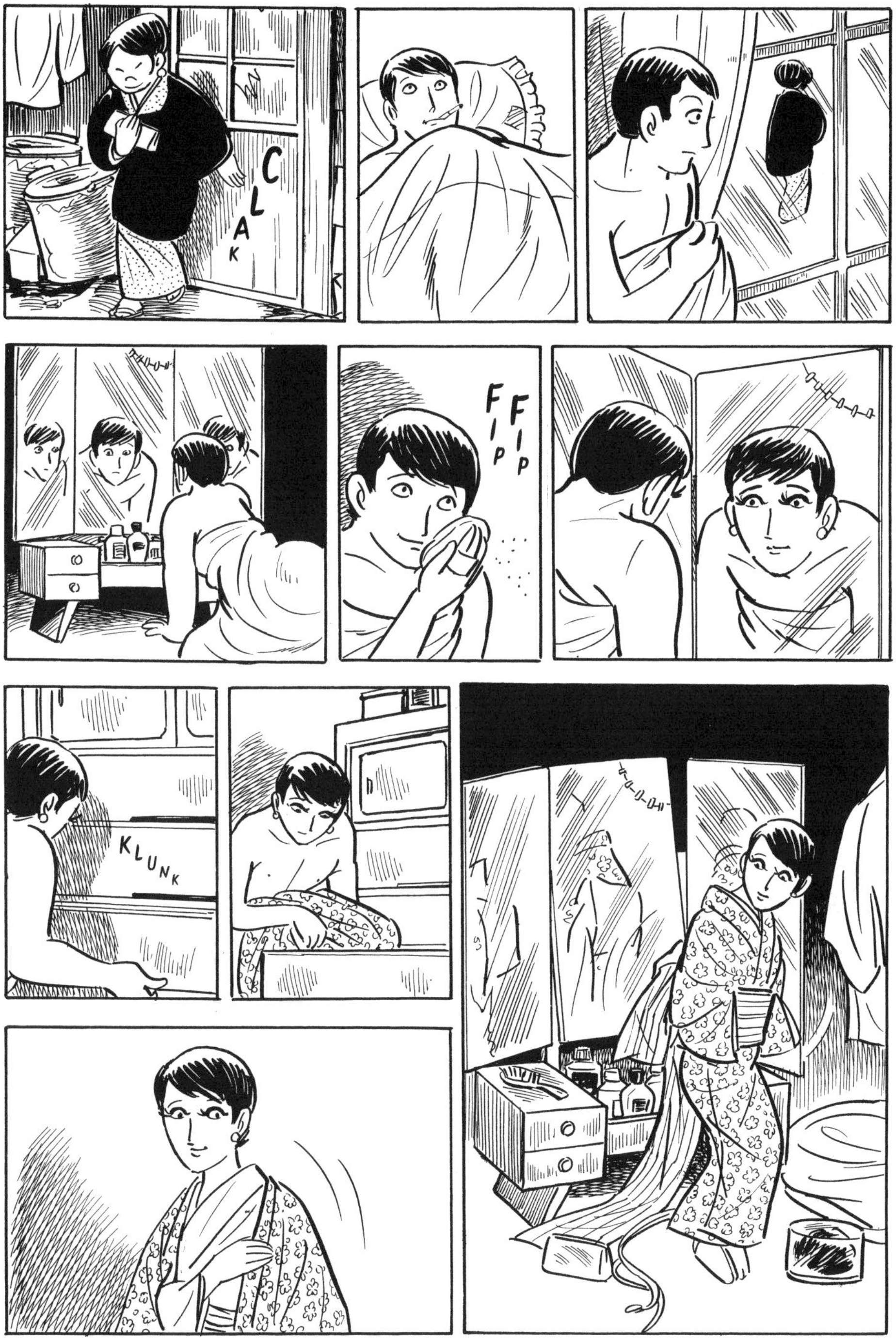
CLAK
FLIP FLIP
KLUNK

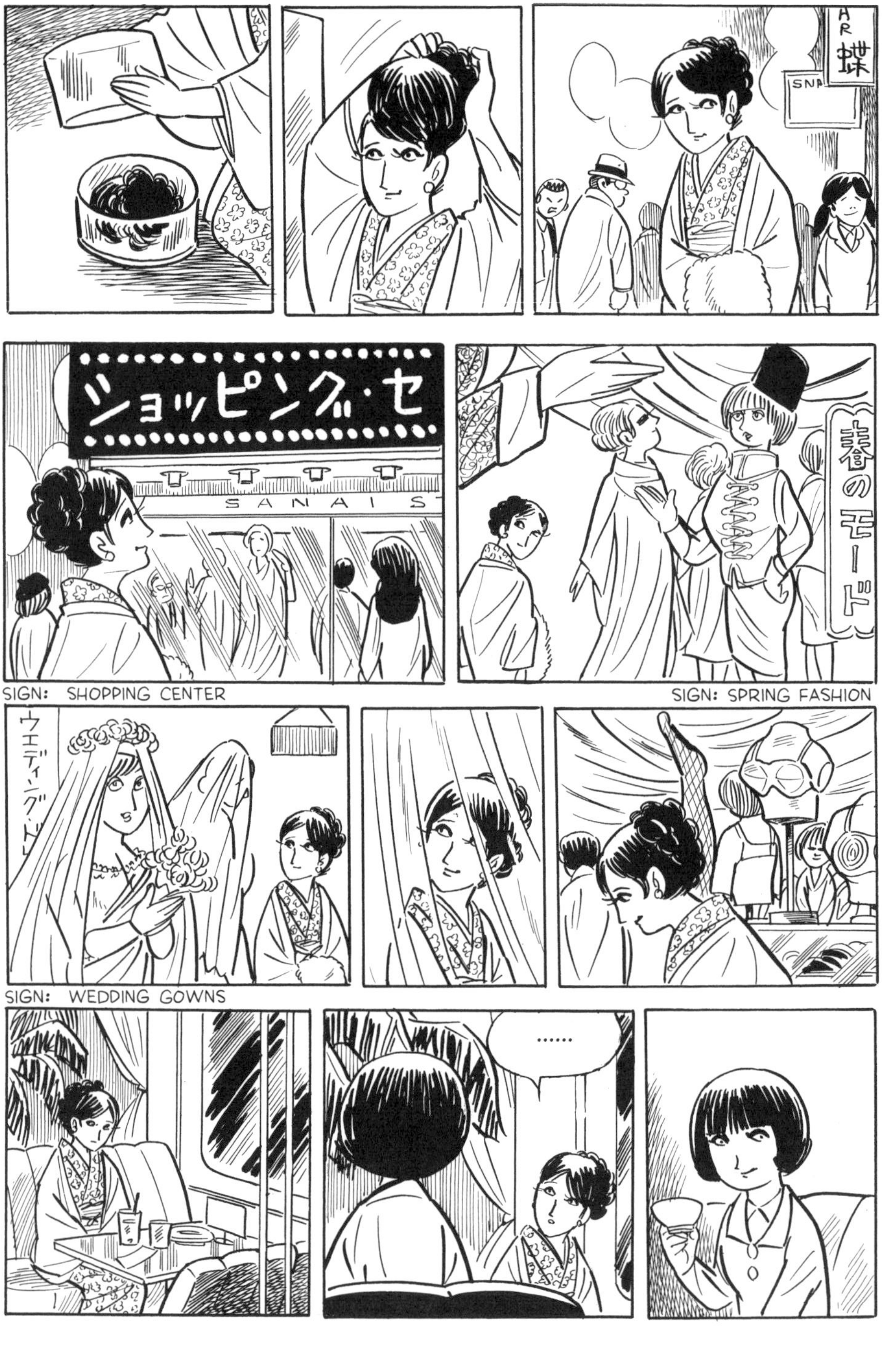
AR 蝶
SNA
ショッピング・セ
SANAI S
SIGN: SHOPPING CENTER
春のモード
SIGN: SPRING FASHION
ウエディング・
SIGN: WEDDING GOWNS
......

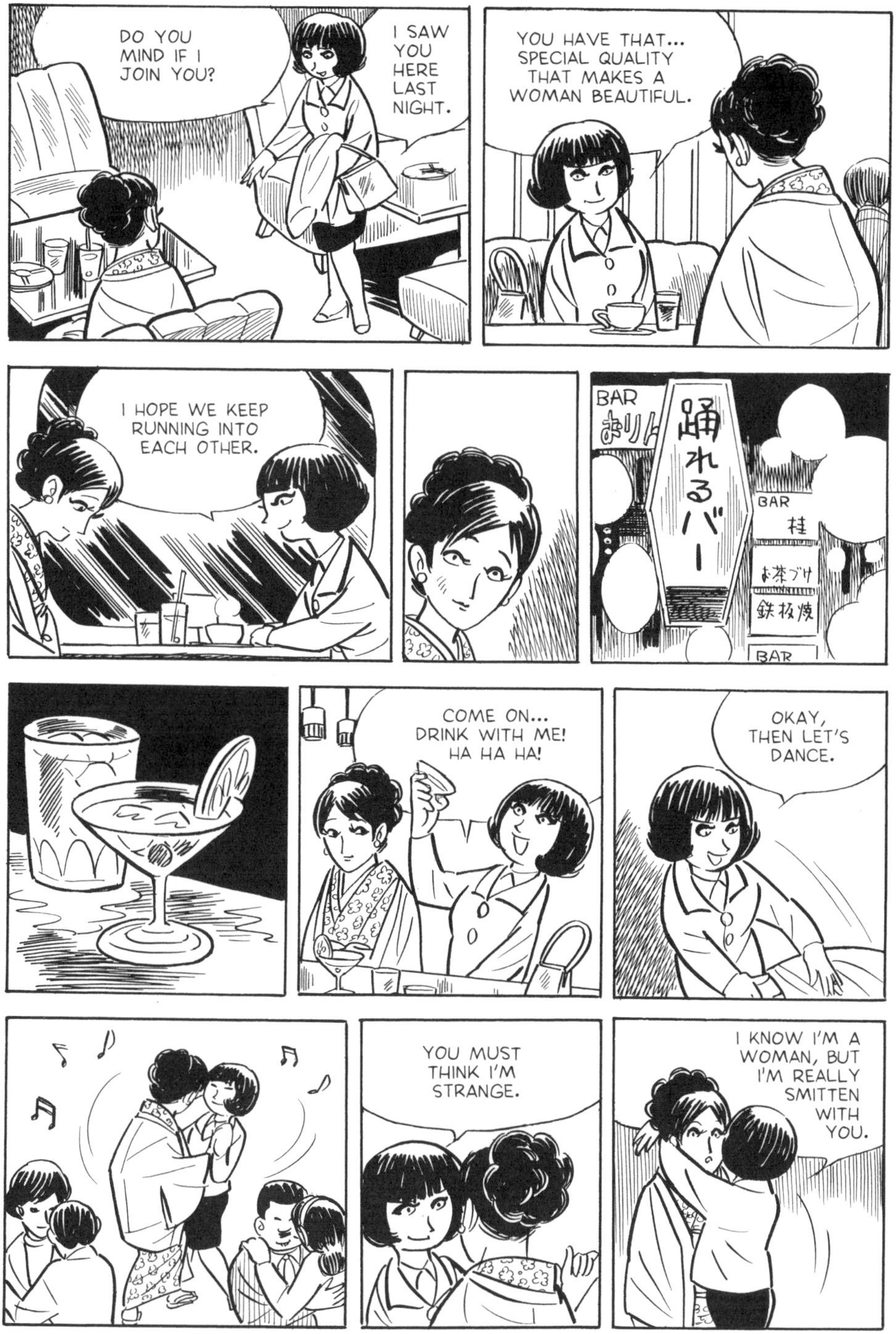
DO YOU MIND IF I JOIN YOU?
I SAW YOU HERE LAST NIGHT.
YOU HAVE THAT... SPECIAL QUALITY THAT MAKES A WOMAN BEAUTIFUL.
I HOPE WE KEEP RUNNING INTO EACH OTHER.
BAR
踊れるバー
BAR
桂
お茶づけ
鉄板焼
BAR
COME ON... DRINK WITH ME! HA HA HA!
OKAY, THEN LET'S DANCE.
YOU MUST THINK I'M STRANGE.
I KNOW I'M A WOMAN, BUT I'M REALLY SMITTEN WITH YOU.

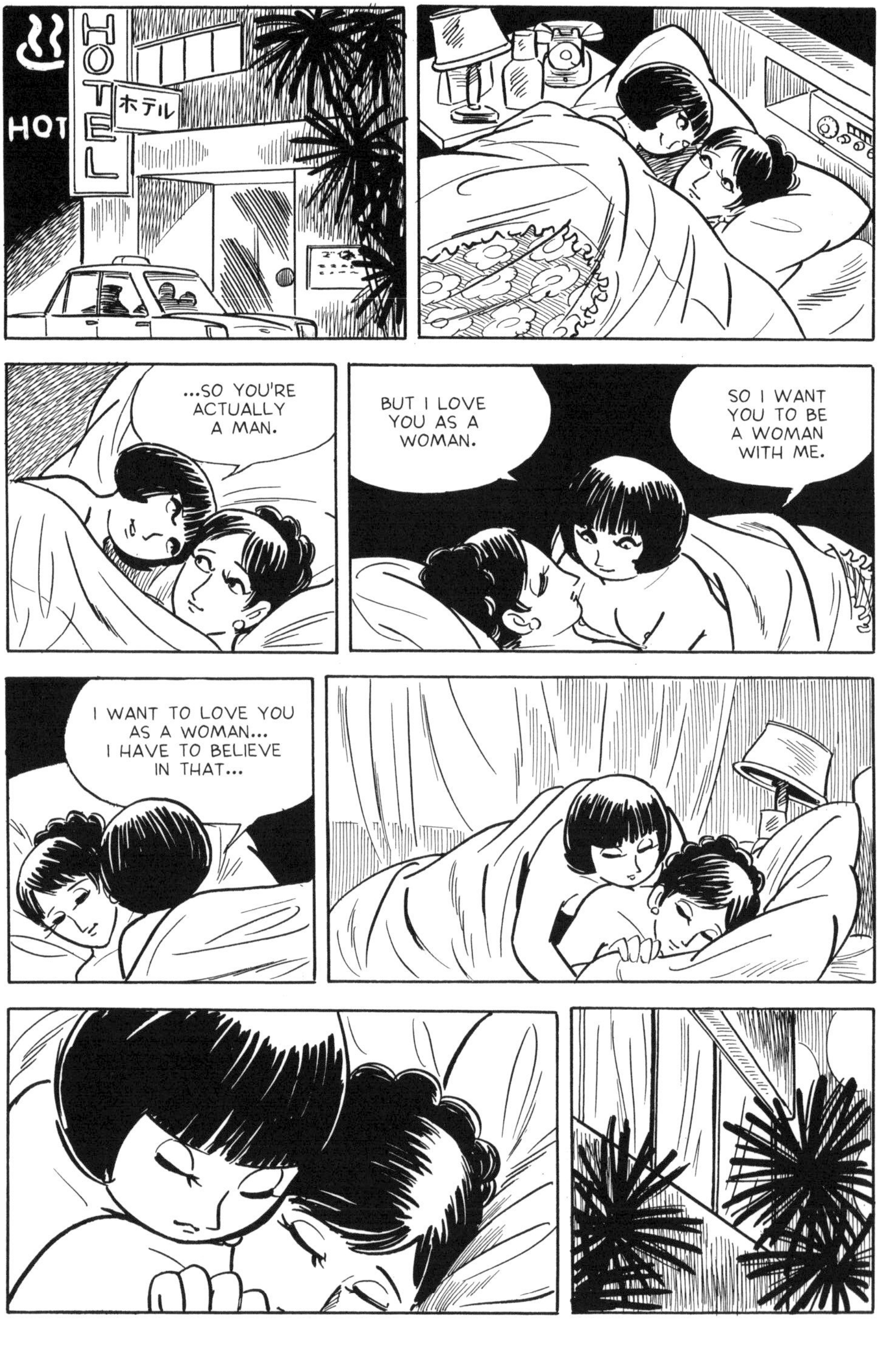
HOTEL
ホテル
HOT
...SO YOU'RE ACTUALLY A MAN.
BUT I LOVE YOU AS A WOMAN.
SO I WANT YOU TO BE A WOMAN WITH ME.
I WANT TO LOVE YOU AS A WOMAN... I HAVE TO BELIEVE IN THAT...

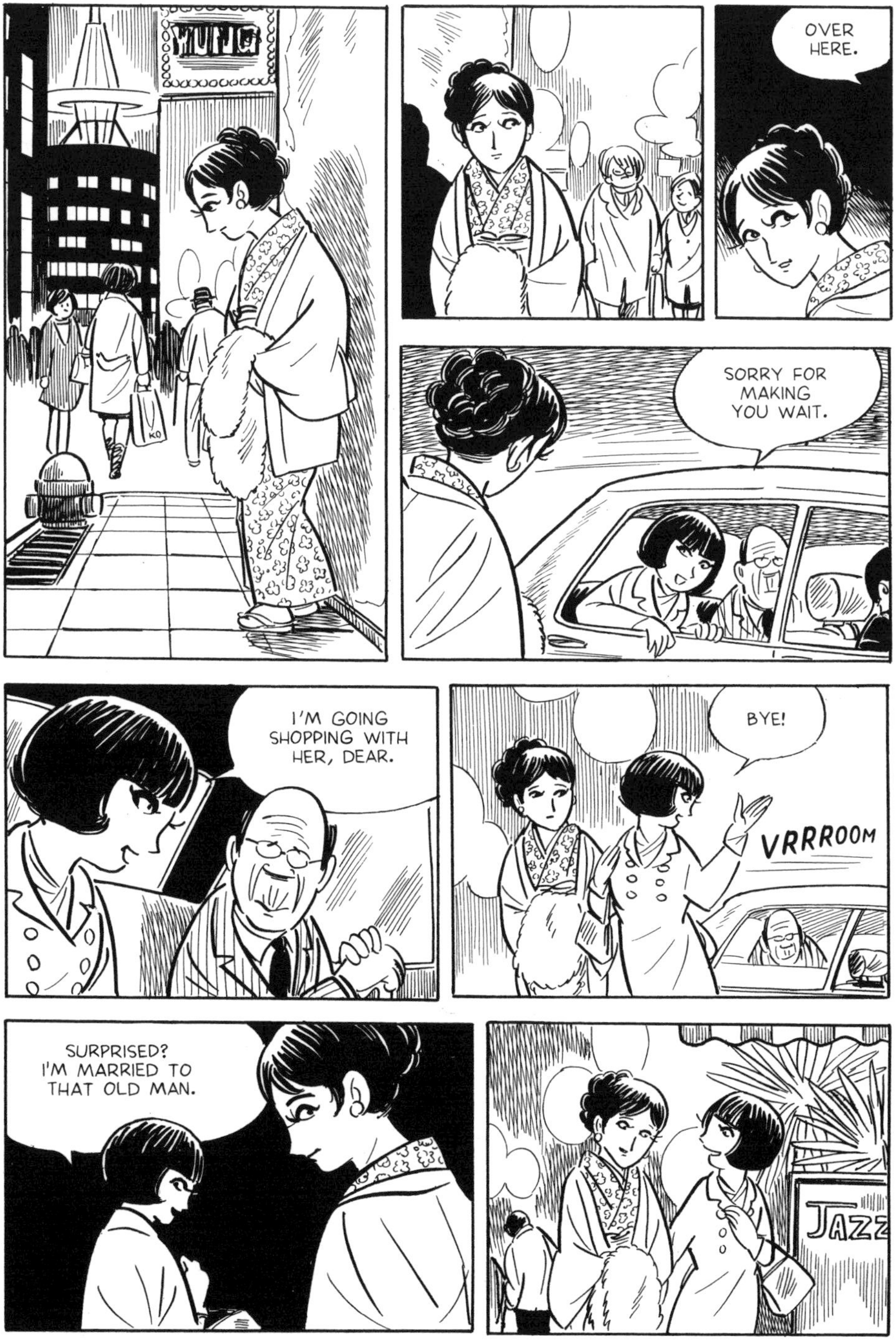
KO
OVER HERE.
SORRY FOR MAKING YOU WAIT.
I'M GOING SHOPPING WITH HER, DEAR.
BYE!
VRRROOM
SURPRISED? I'M MARRIED TO THAT OLD MAN.

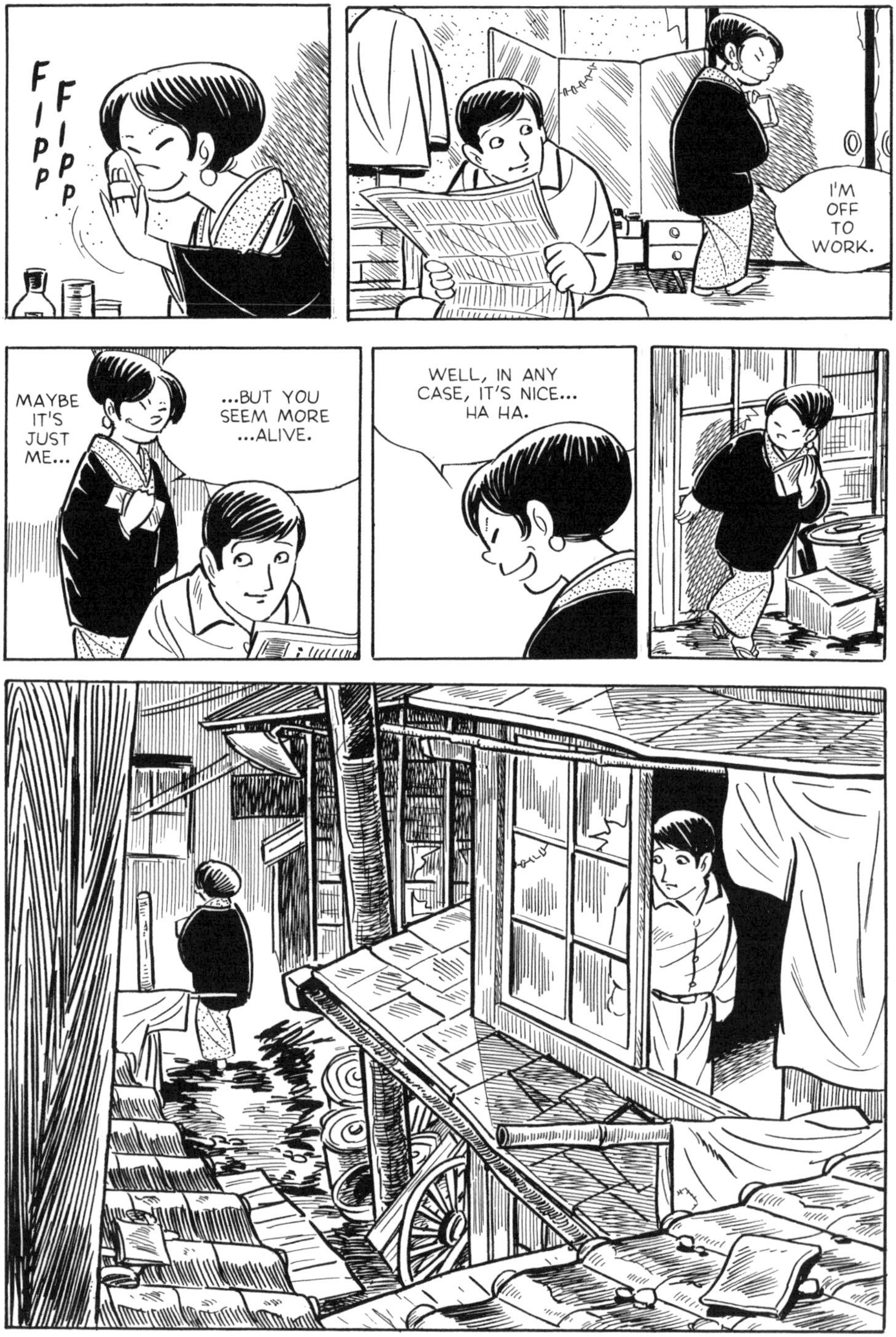
FIPP FIPP
I'M OFF TO WORK.
MAYBE IT'S JUST ME...
...BUT YOU SEEM MORE ...ALIVE.
WELL, IN ANY CASE, IT'S NICE... HA HA.

DISINFECTION

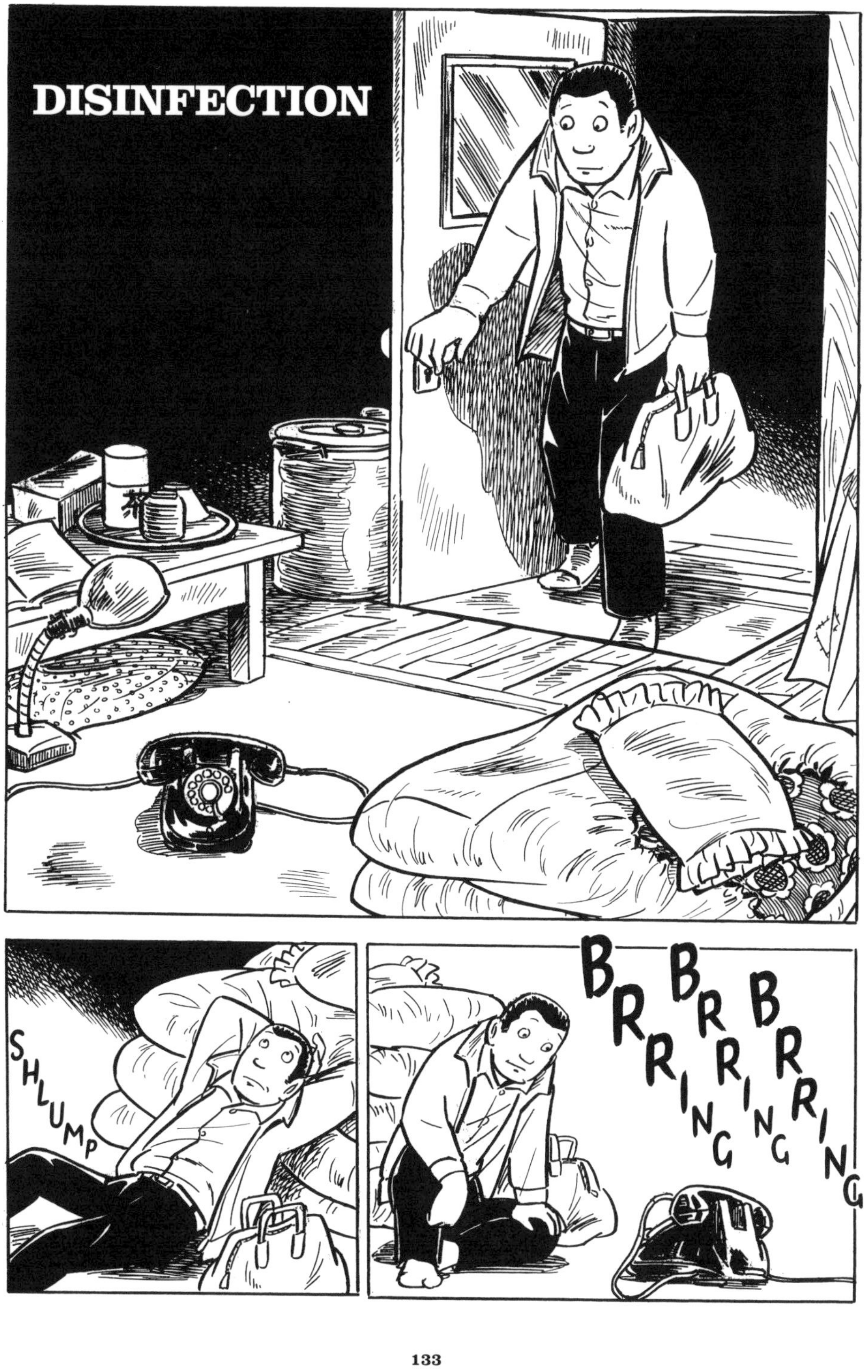
SHLUMP
BRRING
BRRING
BRRING

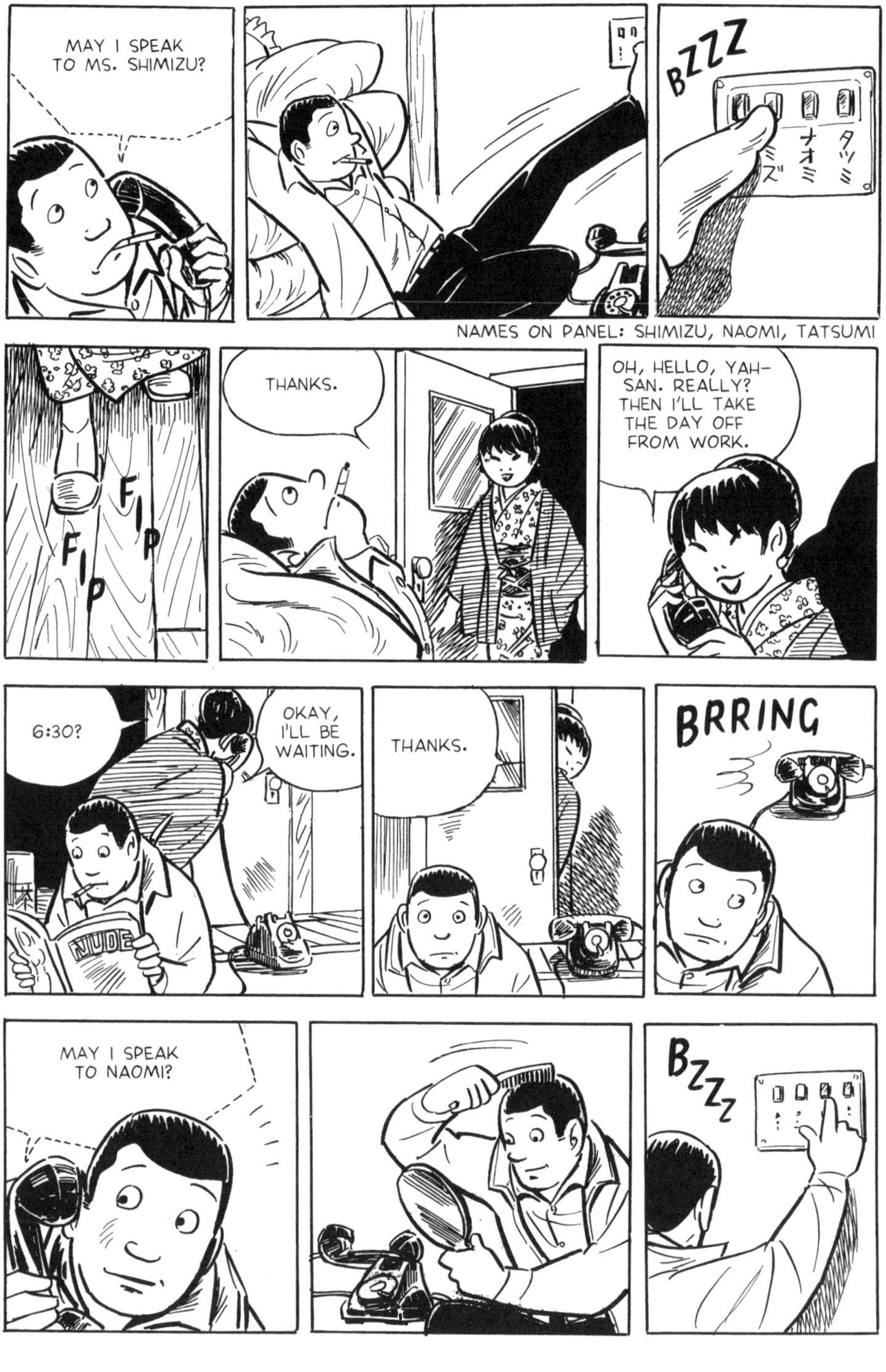
MAY I SPEAK TO MS. SHIMIZU?
BZZZ
タツミ
ナオミ
シミズ
NAMES ON PANEL: SHIMIZU, NAOMI, TATSUMI
FIP
FIP
FIP
THANKS.
OH, HELLO, YAH-SAN. REALLY? THEN I'LL TAKE THE DAY OFF FROM WORK.
6:30?
OKAY, I'LL BE WAITING.
NUDE
THANKS.
BRRING
MAY I SPEAK TO NAOMI?
BZZZ

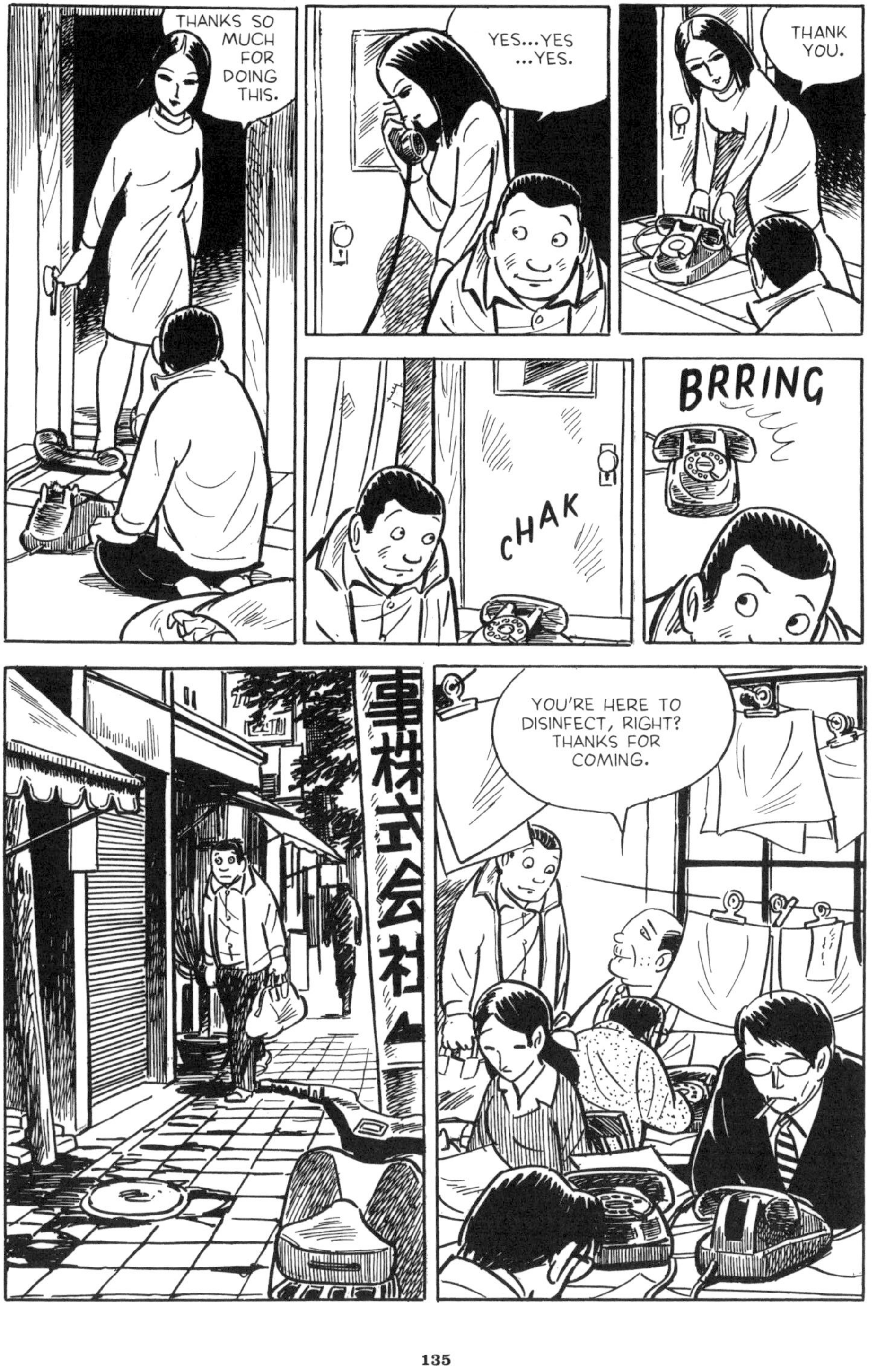
THANKS SO MUCH FOR DOING THIS.
YES...YES ...YES.
THANK YOU.
CHAK
BRRING
事株式会社
YOU'RE HERE TO DISINFECT, RIGHT? THANKS FOR COMING.

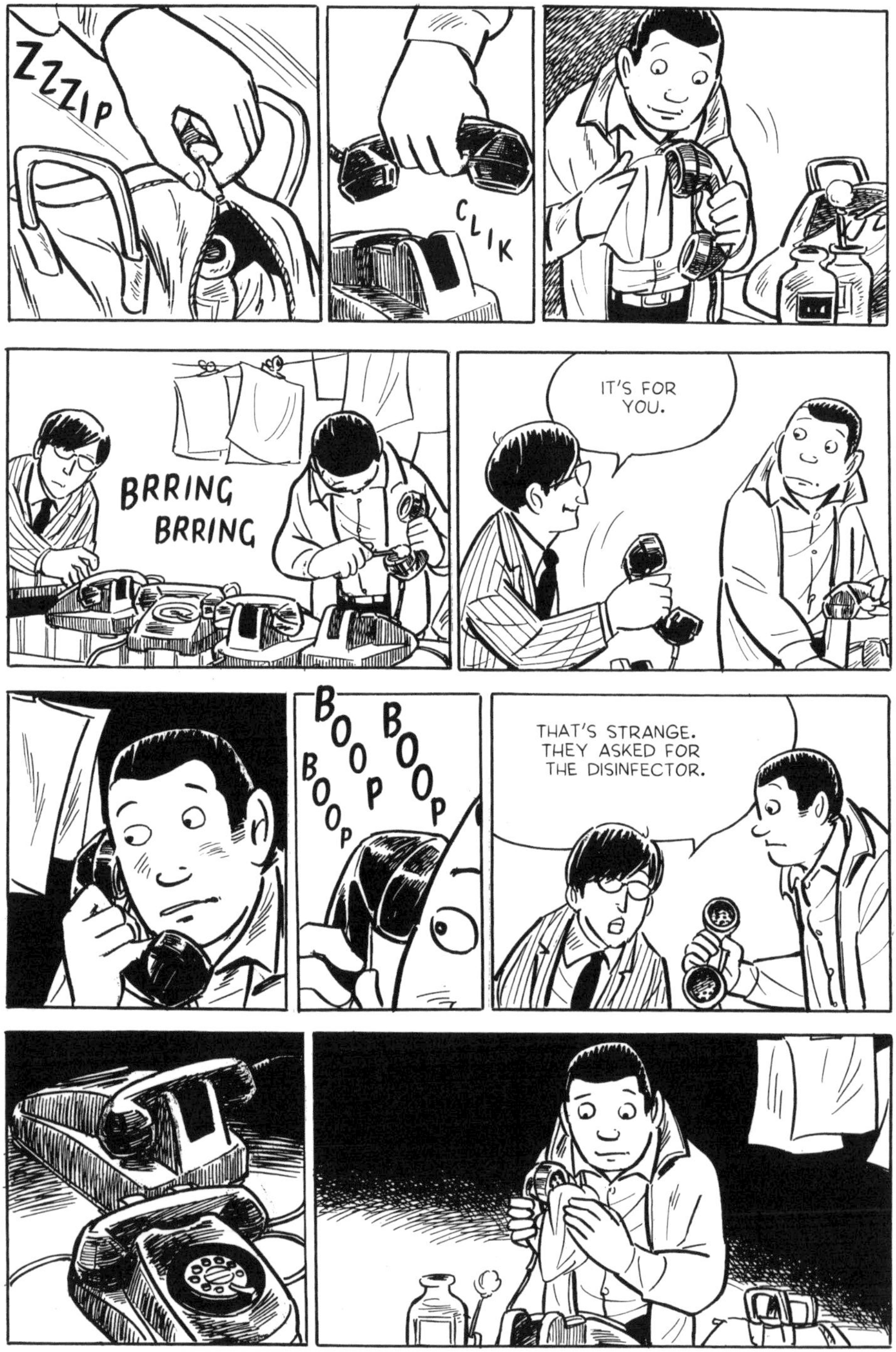
ZZZIP
CLIK
BRRING BRRING
IT'S FOR YOU.
BOOP BOOP BOOP
THAT'S STRANGE. THEY ASKED FOR THE DISINFECTOR.

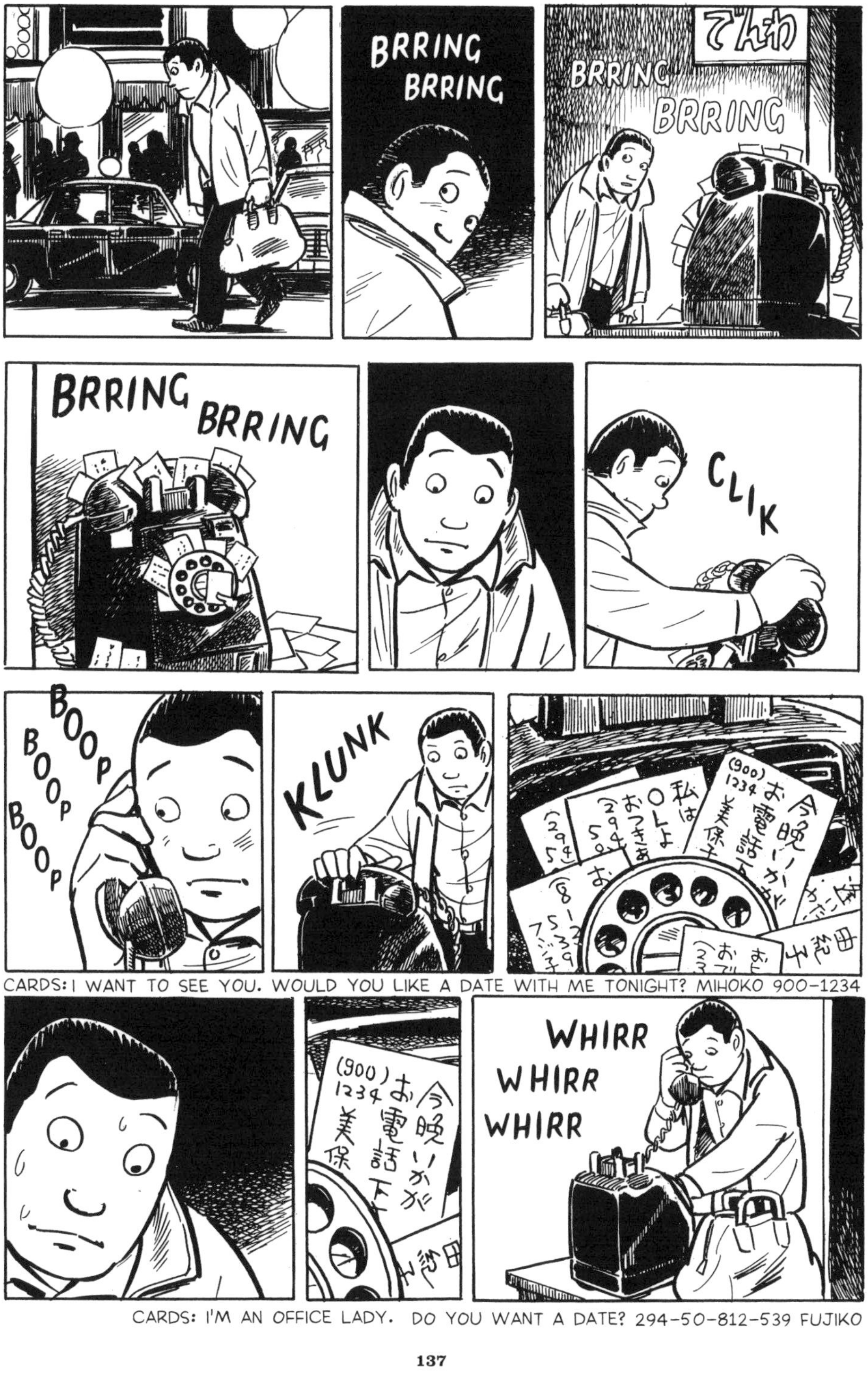

BRRING
BRRING
でんわ
BRRING
BRRING
BRRING
BRRING
CLIK
BOOP
BOOP
BOOP
BOOP
KLUNK
CARDS: I WANT TO SEE YOU. WOULD YOU LIKE A DATE WITH ME TONIGHT? MIHOKO 900-1234
WHIRR
WHIRR
WHIRR
CARDS: I'M AN OFFICE LADY. DO YOU WANT A DATE? 294-50-812-539 FUJIKO

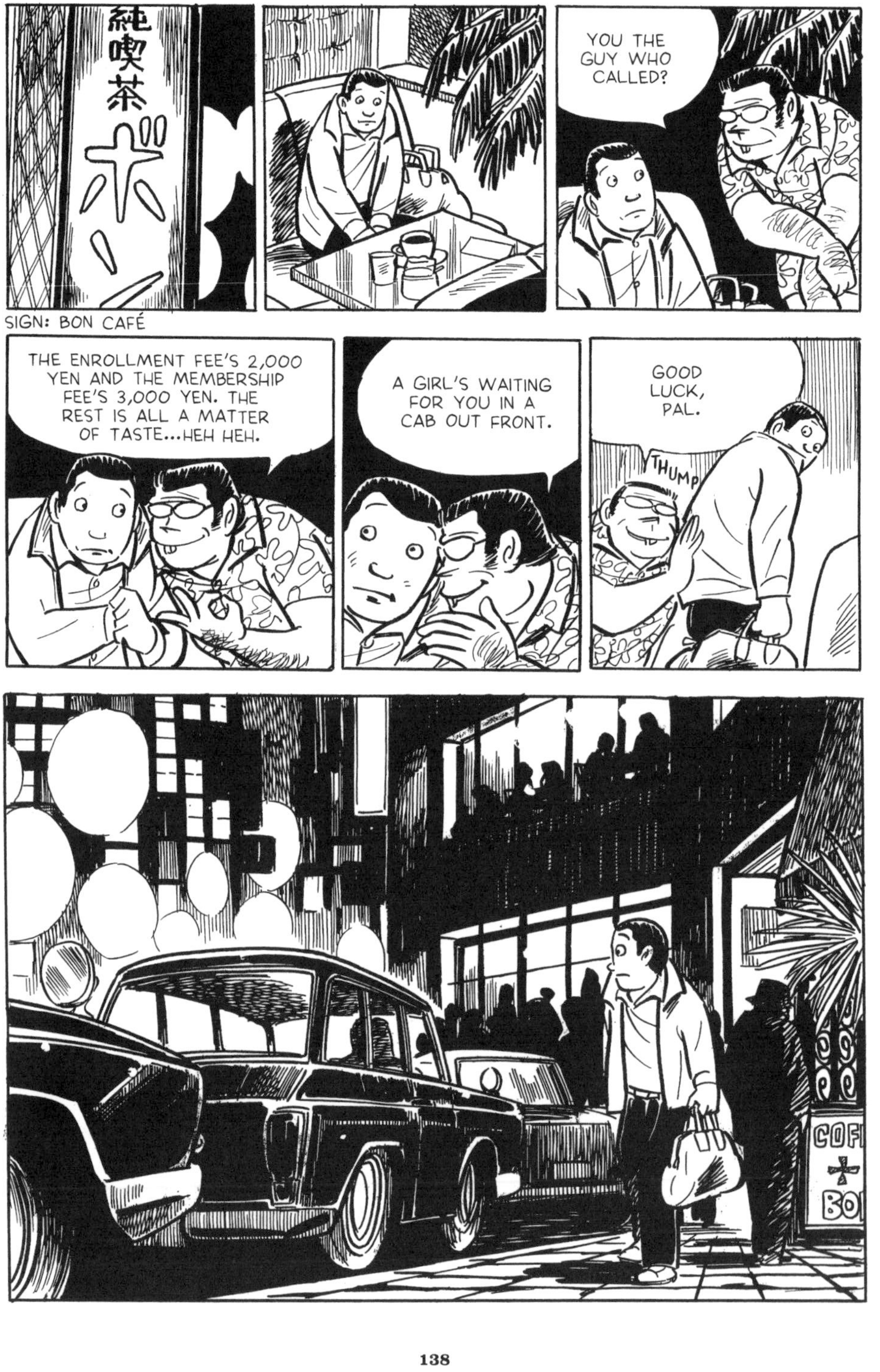
純喫茶
SIGN: BON CAFÉ
YOU THE GUY WHO CALLED?
THE ENROLLMENT FEE'S 2,000 YEN AND THE MEMBERSHIP FEE'S 3,000 YEN. THE REST IS ALL A MATTER OF TASTE...HEH HEH.
A GIRL'S WAITING FOR YOU IN A CAB OUT FRONT.
GOOD LUCK, PAL.
THUMP

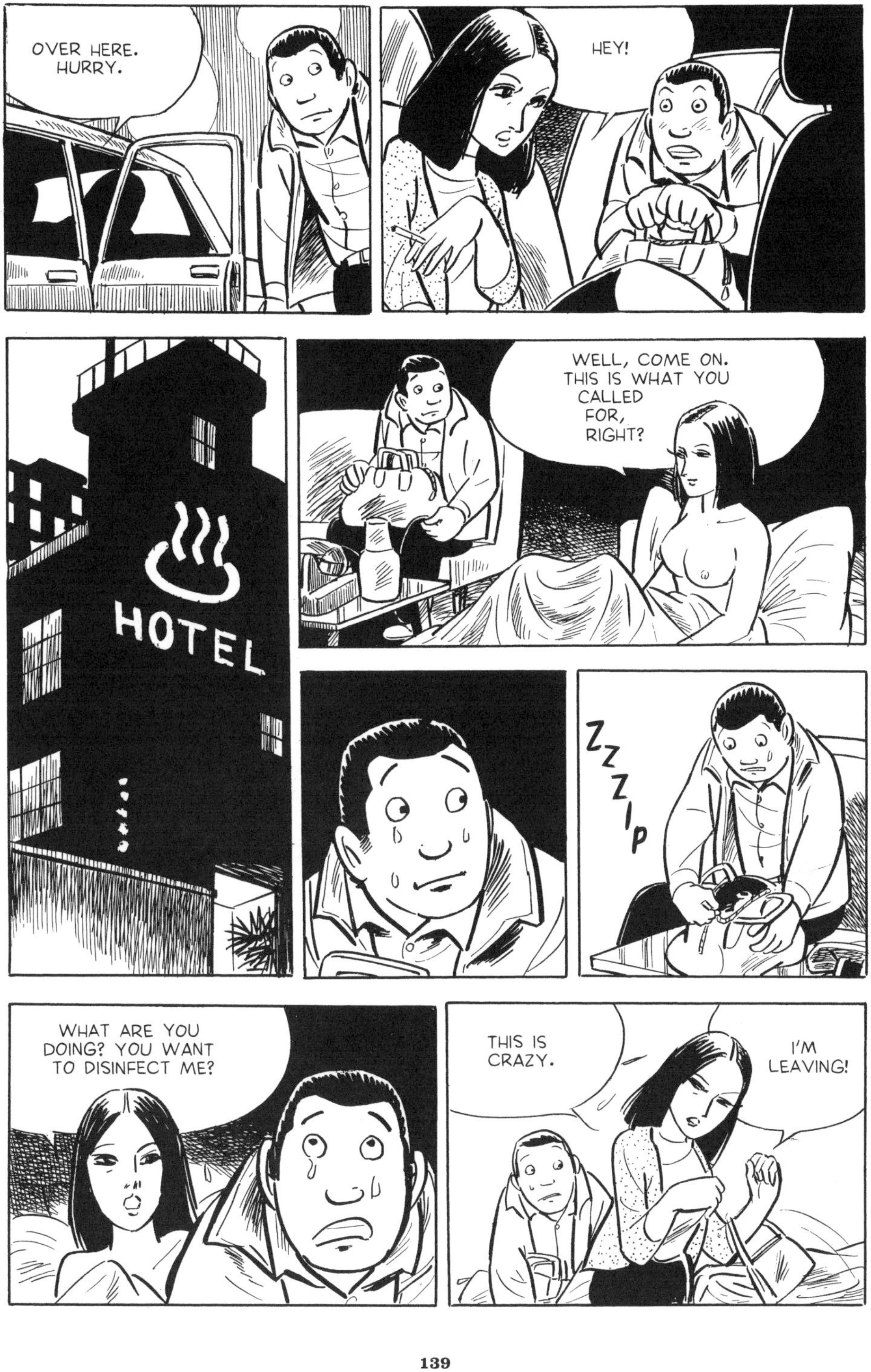
OVER HERE. HURRY.
HEY!
HOTEL
WELL, COME ON. THIS IS WHAT YOU CALLED FOR, RIGHT?
ZZZIP
WHAT ARE YOU DOING? YOU WANT TO DISINFECT ME?
THIS IS CRAZY.
I'M LEAVING!

BRRING
BRRING

BRRING
BRRING

CLIK

HELLO
?

NAOMI...
I'VE GOT
ANOTHER
JOB FOR
YOU.
HELLO?

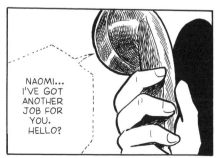

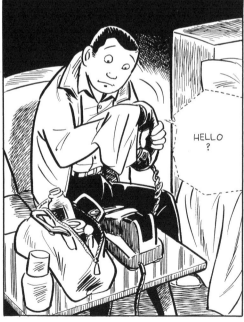

HELLO
?

WHO ARE YOU?

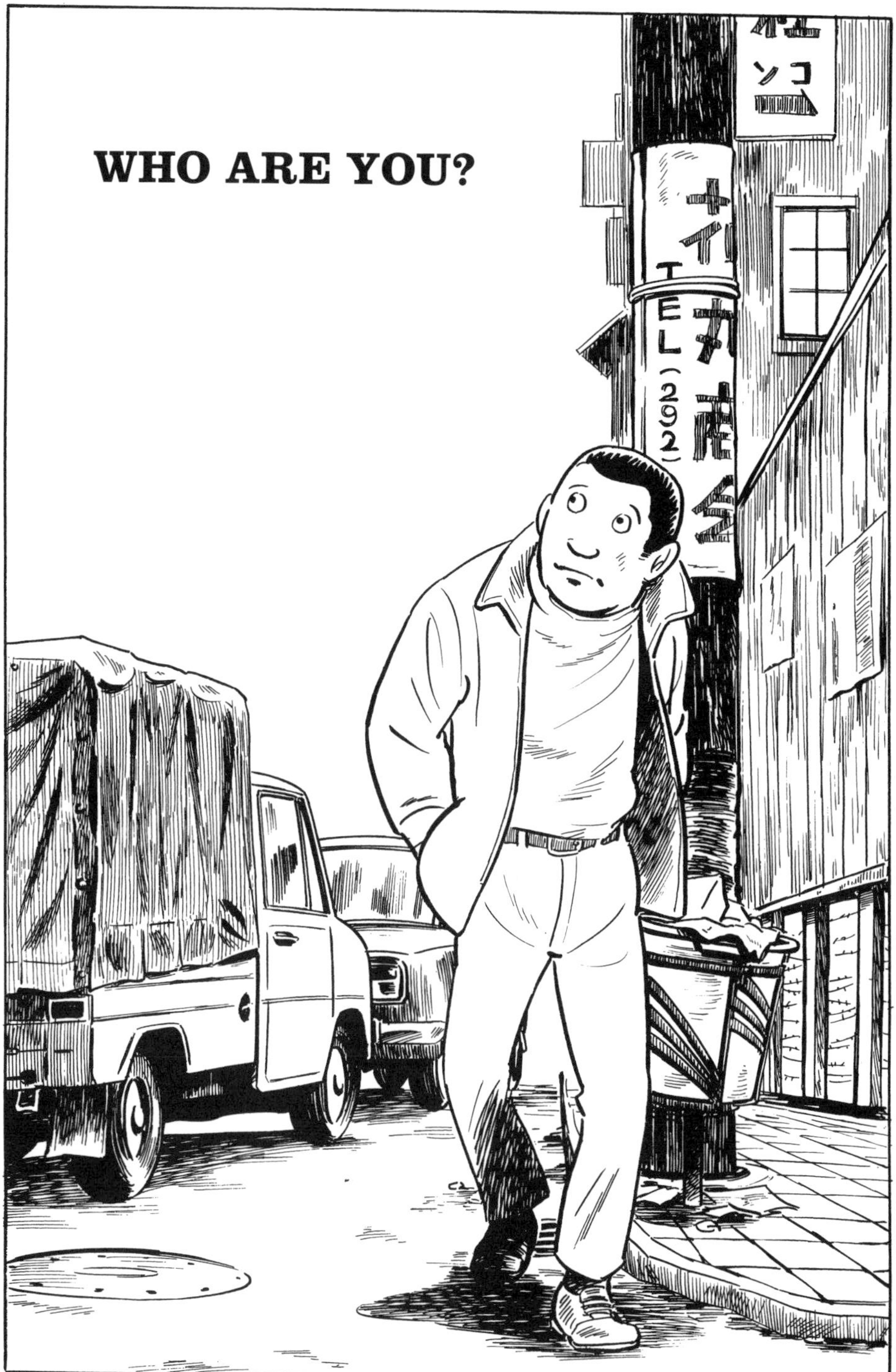
TEL (292)

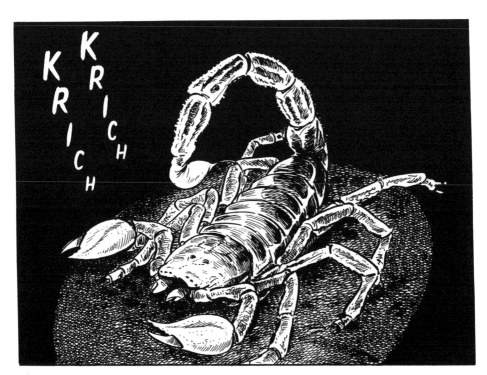

< WHO ARE YOU? >

< WHO ARE YOU? WHAT ARE YOU DOING HERE? >

< ENGLISH >

< WHAT ARE YOU DOING HERE? >

KRICH KRICH

144

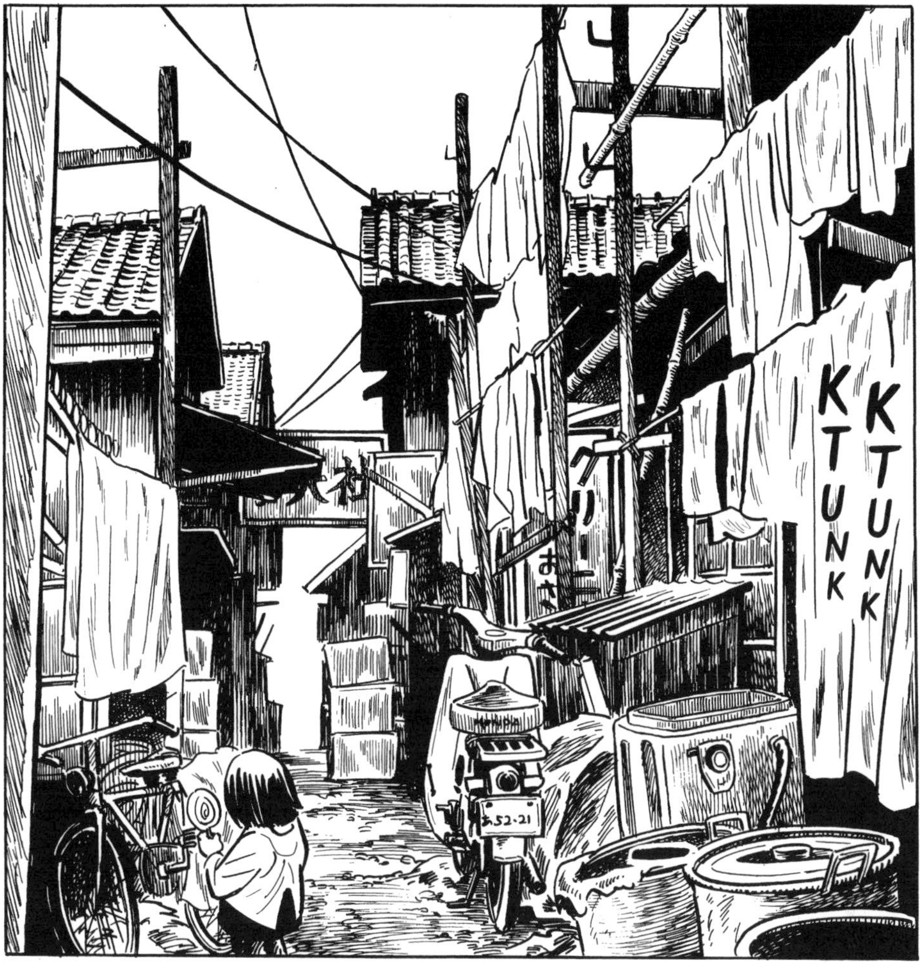
KTUNK
KTUNK

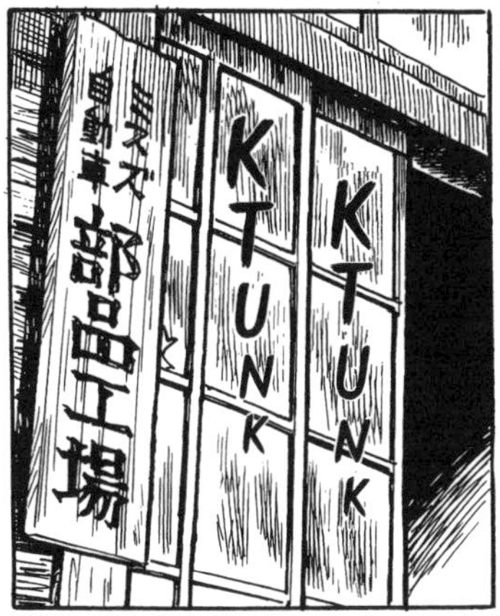
ミスズ自動車部品工場
KTUNK
KTUNK

SIGN: MISUZU AUTOMOBILE PARTS PLANT

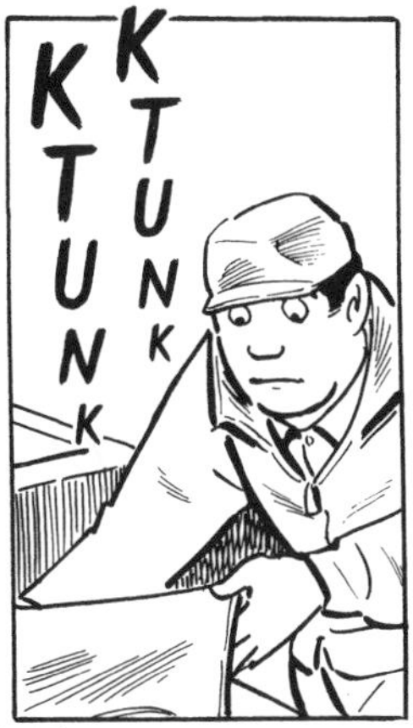
KTUNK
KTUNK

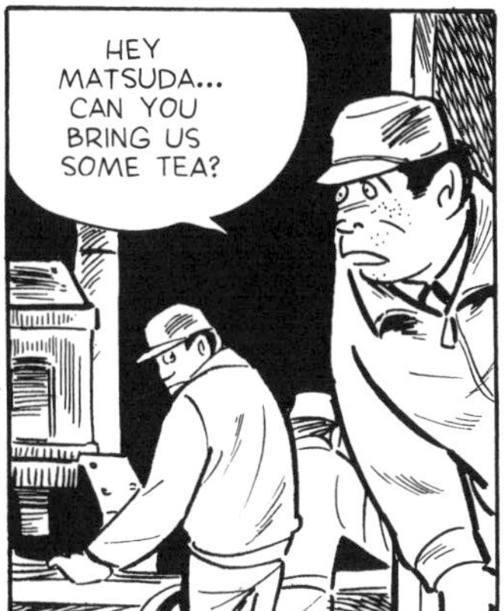
HEY MATSUDA... CAN YOU BRING US SOME TEA?

WINDOW: OFFICE   DOOR: STAFF ONLY

KLUNK

YOU DID IT AGAIN, YOU DUMB HICK!

HOW MANY TIMES DO I HAVE TO WARN YOU?

I WAS THE ONE WHO TOOK IN THIS EX-CON.

PLEASE, SIR! WE'RE SHORT ON STAFF. IF YOU COULD JUST CUT HIM SOME SLACK...

WHAT?

HE'S GOT NOWHERE ELSE TO GO.

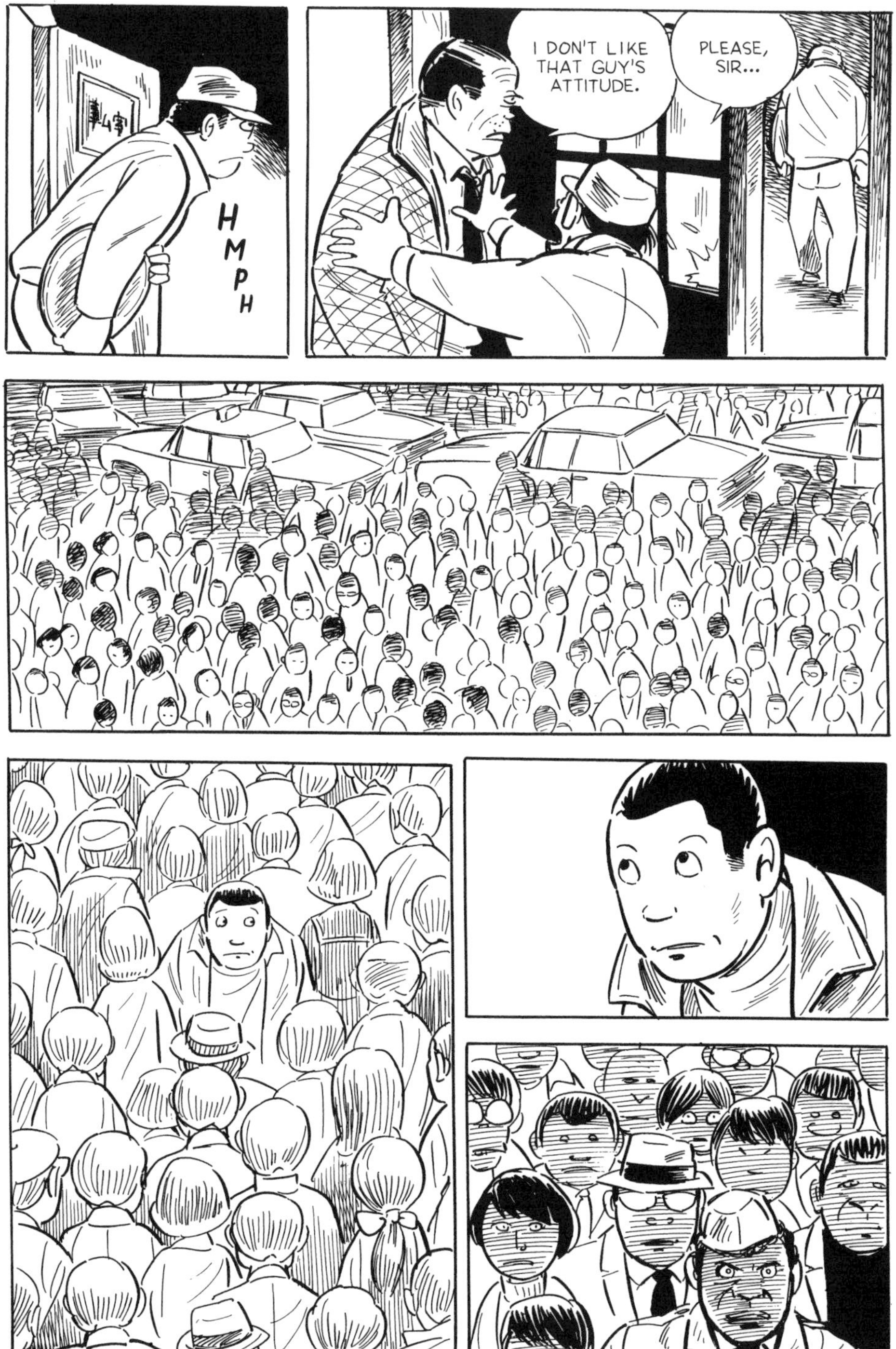
HMPH
I DON'T LIKE THAT GUY'S ATTITUDE.
PLEASE, SIR...

<WHO ARE YOU? >
<WHO ARE YOU? WHAT ARE YOU DOING HERE? >
珈琲店
ソコ
双葉荘
廊下は静かに
KRICH KRICH

DOOR: FUTABA APARTMENTS

SIGN: WALK QUIETLY IN HALLWAY

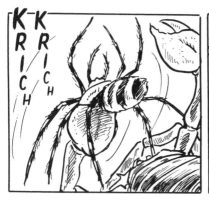

OH...YOU'RE HOME.
IS IT THAT LATE?

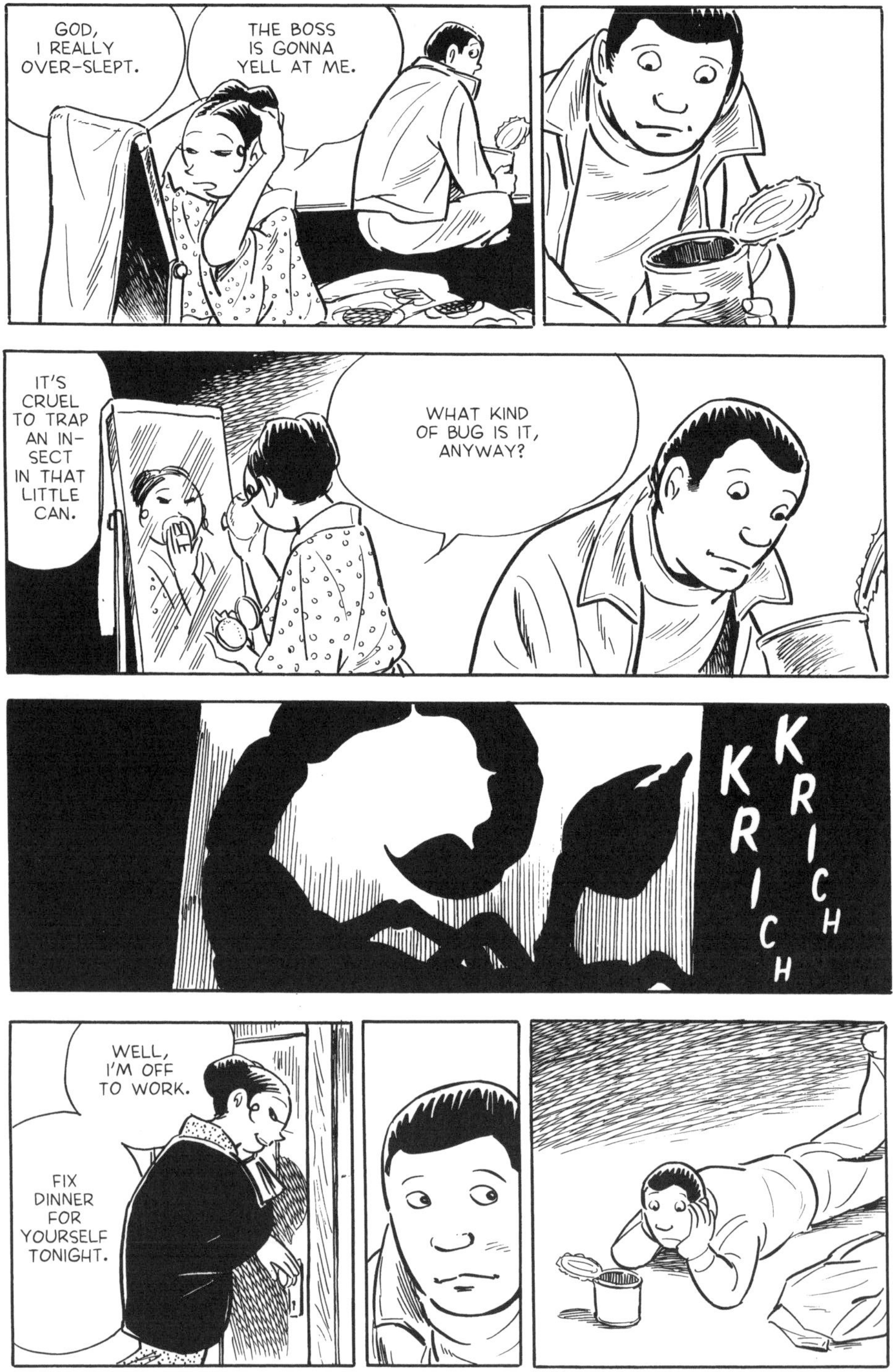
GOD, I REALLY OVER-SLEPT.
THE BOSS IS GONNA YELL AT ME.
IT'S CRUEL TO TRAP AN IN-SECT IN THAT LITTLE CAN.
WHAT KIND OF BUG IS IT, ANYWAY?
KRICH
KRICH
WELL, I'M OFF TO WORK.
FIX DINNER FOR YOURSELF TONIGHT.

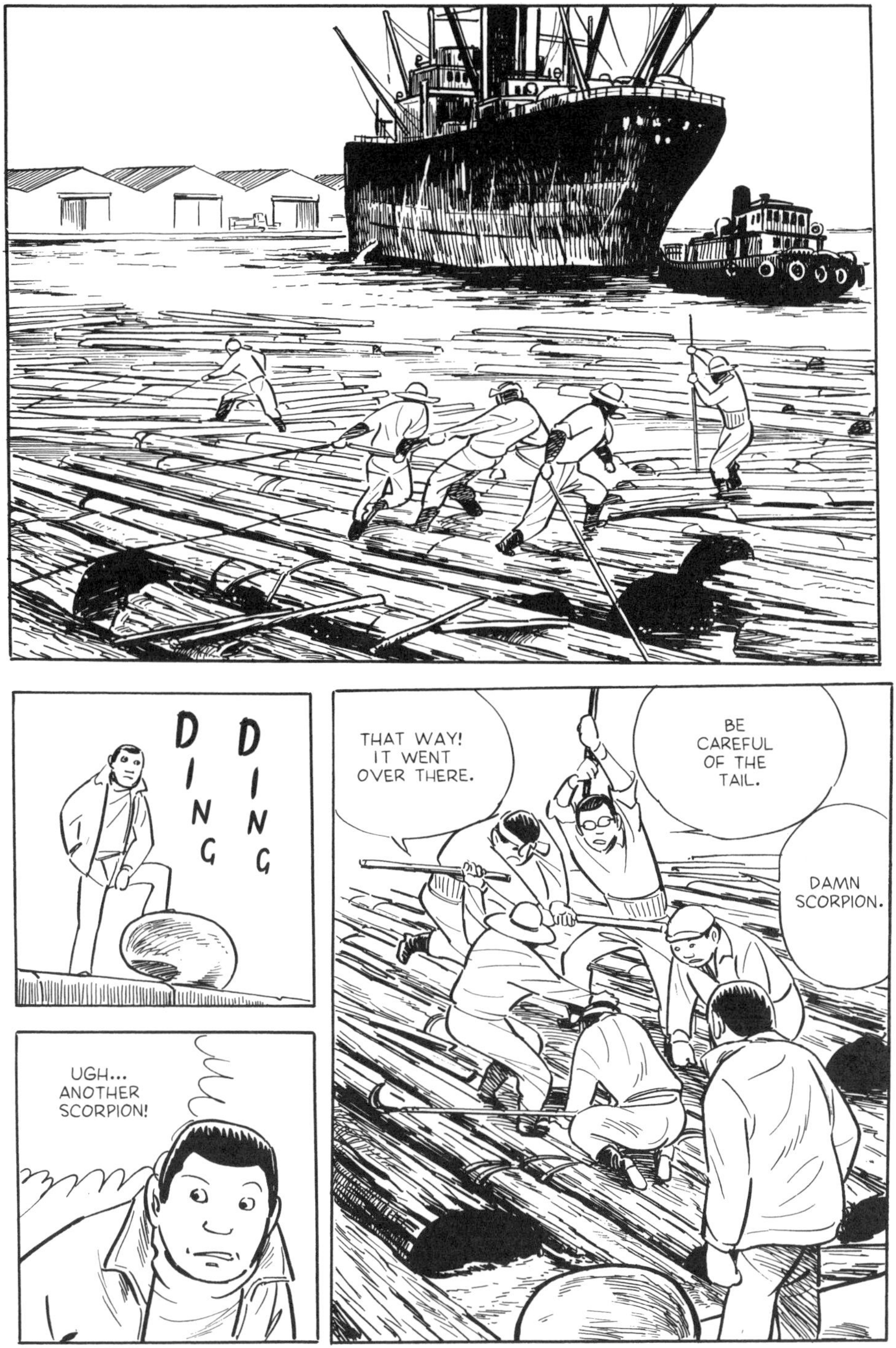
DING DING
UGH... ANOTHER SCORPION!
THAT WAY! IT WENT OVER THERE.
BE CAREFUL OF THE TAIL.
DAMN SCORPION.

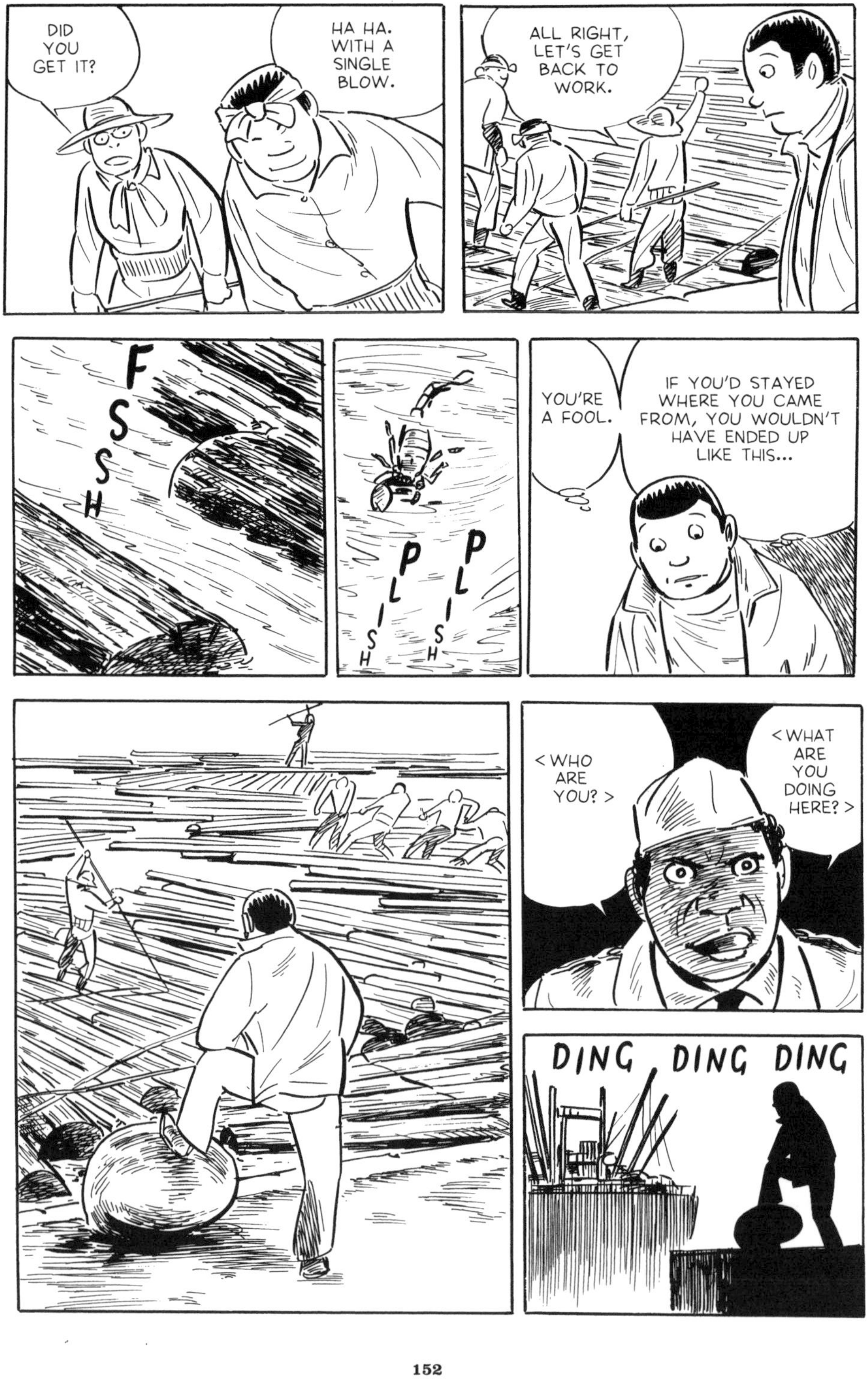
DID YOU GET IT?
HA HA. WITH A SINGLE BLOW.
ALL RIGHT, LET'S GET BACK TO WORK.
FSSH
PLISH
PLISH
YOU'RE A FOOL.
IF YOU'D STAYED WHERE YOU CAME FROM, YOU WOULDN'T HAVE ENDED UP LIKE THIS...
< WHO ARE YOU? >
<WHAT ARE YOU DOING HERE? >
DING DING DING

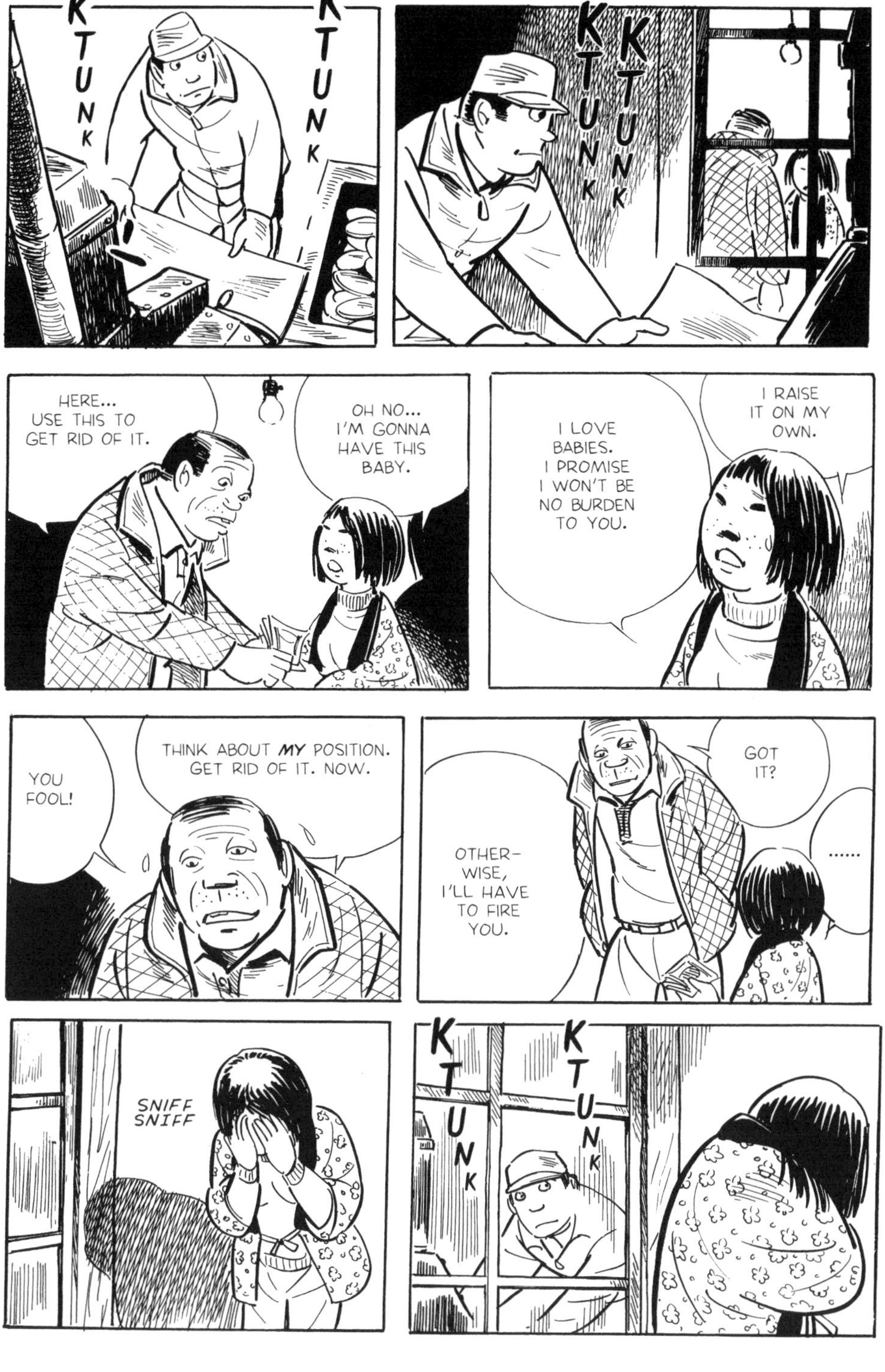
KTUNK
KTUNK
KTUNK
KTUNK
HERE... USE THIS TO GET RID OF IT.
OH NO... I'M GONNA HAVE THIS BABY.
I LOVE BABIES. I PROMISE I WON'T BE NO BURDEN TO YOU.
I RAISE IT ON MY OWN.
YOU FOOL!
THINK ABOUT *MY* POSITION. GET RID OF IT. NOW.
OTHER-WISE, I'LL HAVE TO FIRE YOU.
GOT IT?
......
SNIFF SNIFF
KTUNK
KTUNK

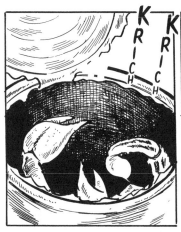

KRICH KRICH

OH, YOU'RE HOME.

SORRY, BUT I'M GONNA TAKE OFF FOR A FEW DAYS.

I GOT THIS URGE TO GO VISIT MY OLD HOME IN THE COUNTRY.

YOU DON'T BELIEVE ME, DO YOU? I'M VISITING HOME... REALLY.

LOOK AFTER OUR PLACE, ALL RIGHT?

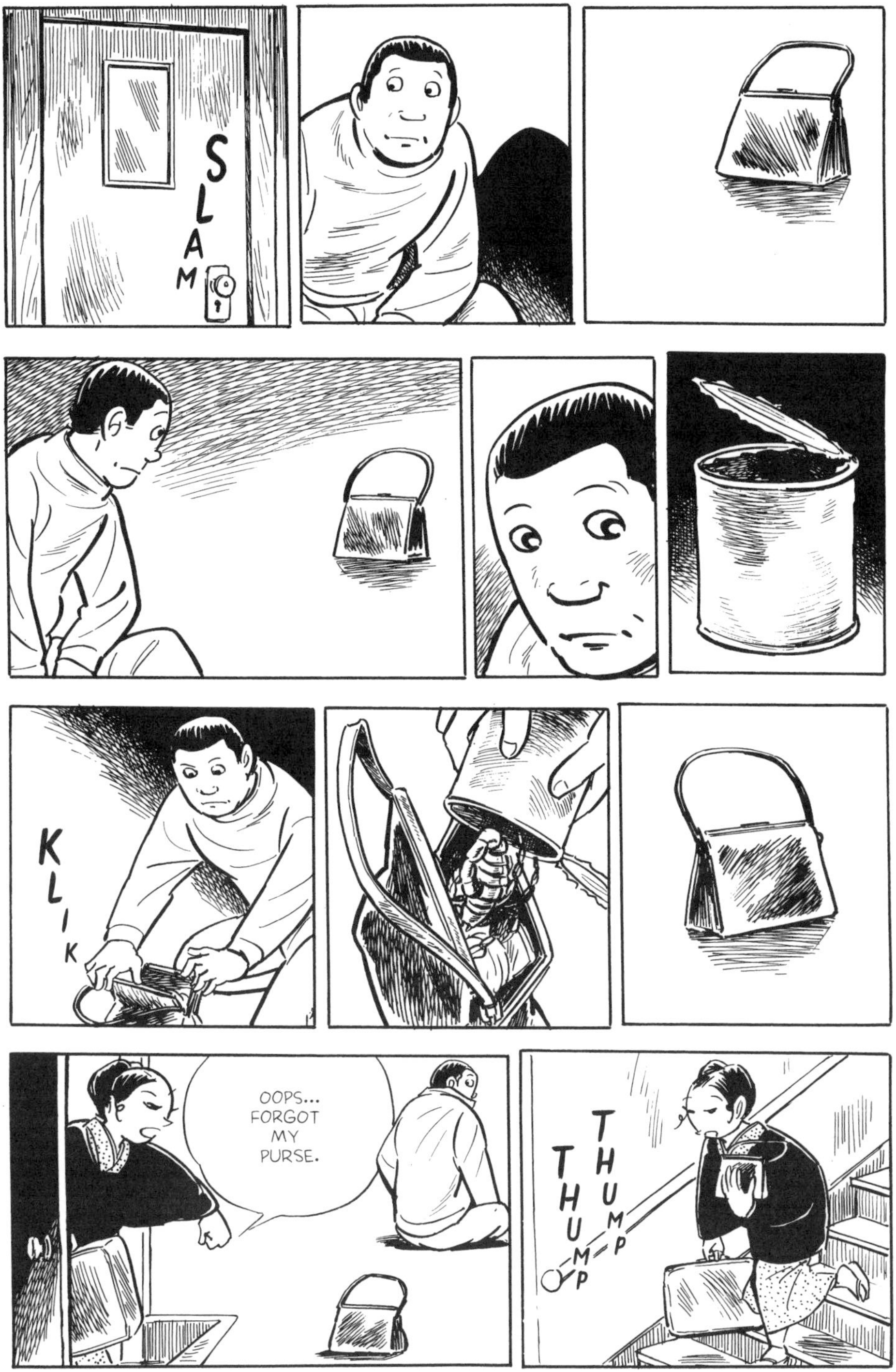
SLAM
KLIK
OOPS... FORGOT MY PURSE.
THUMP
THUMP

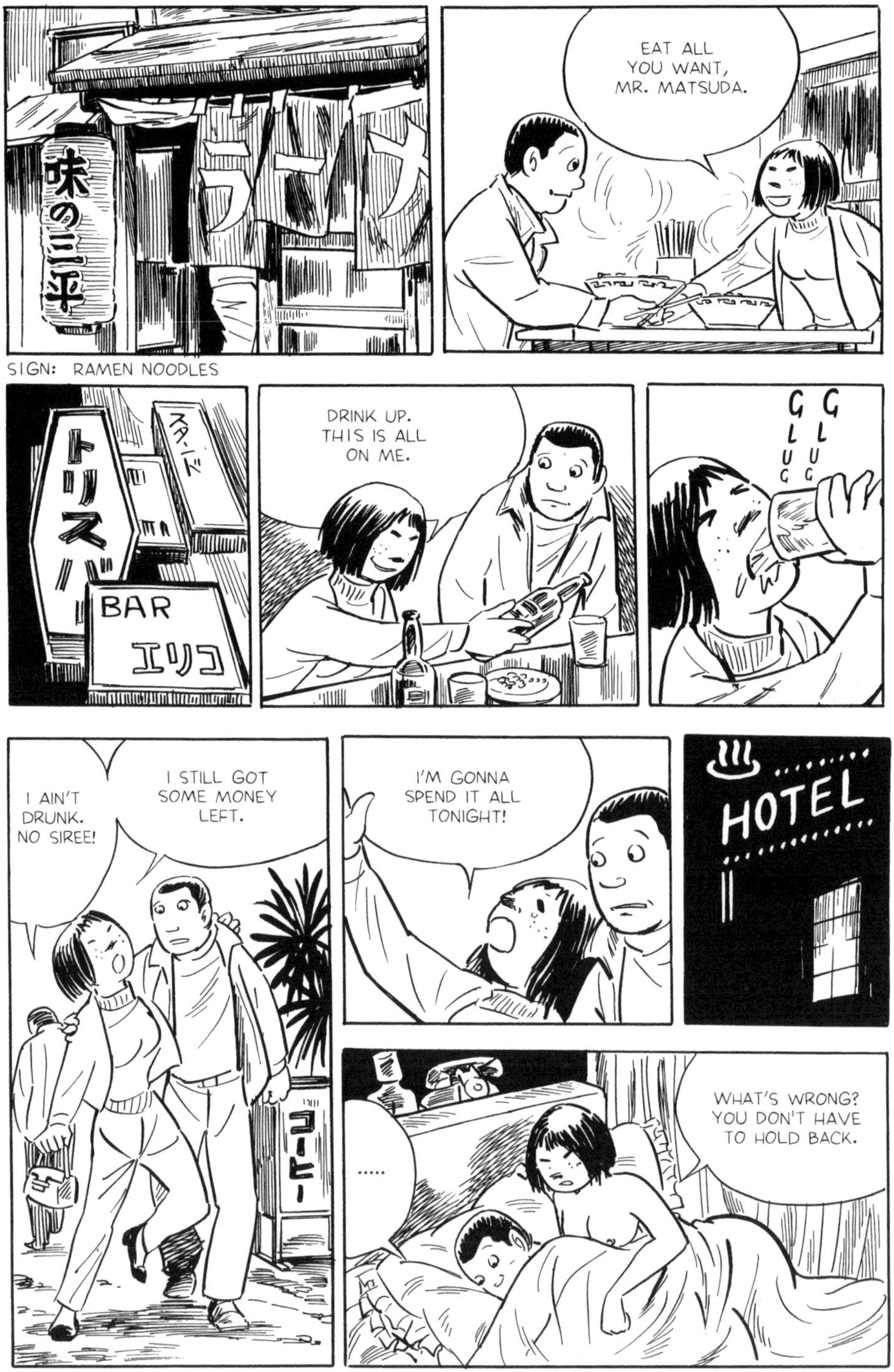
味の三平
EAT ALL YOU WANT, MR. MATSUDA.
SIGN: RAMEN NOODLES
スタンド
トリスバー
BAR
エリコ
DRINK UP. THIS IS ALL ON ME.
GLUG GLUG
I AIN'T DRUNK. NO SIREE!
I STILL GOT SOME MONEY LEFT.
コーヒー
I'M GONNA SPEND IT ALL TONIGHT!
HOTEL
.....
WHAT'S WRONG? YOU DON'T HAVE TO HOLD BACK.

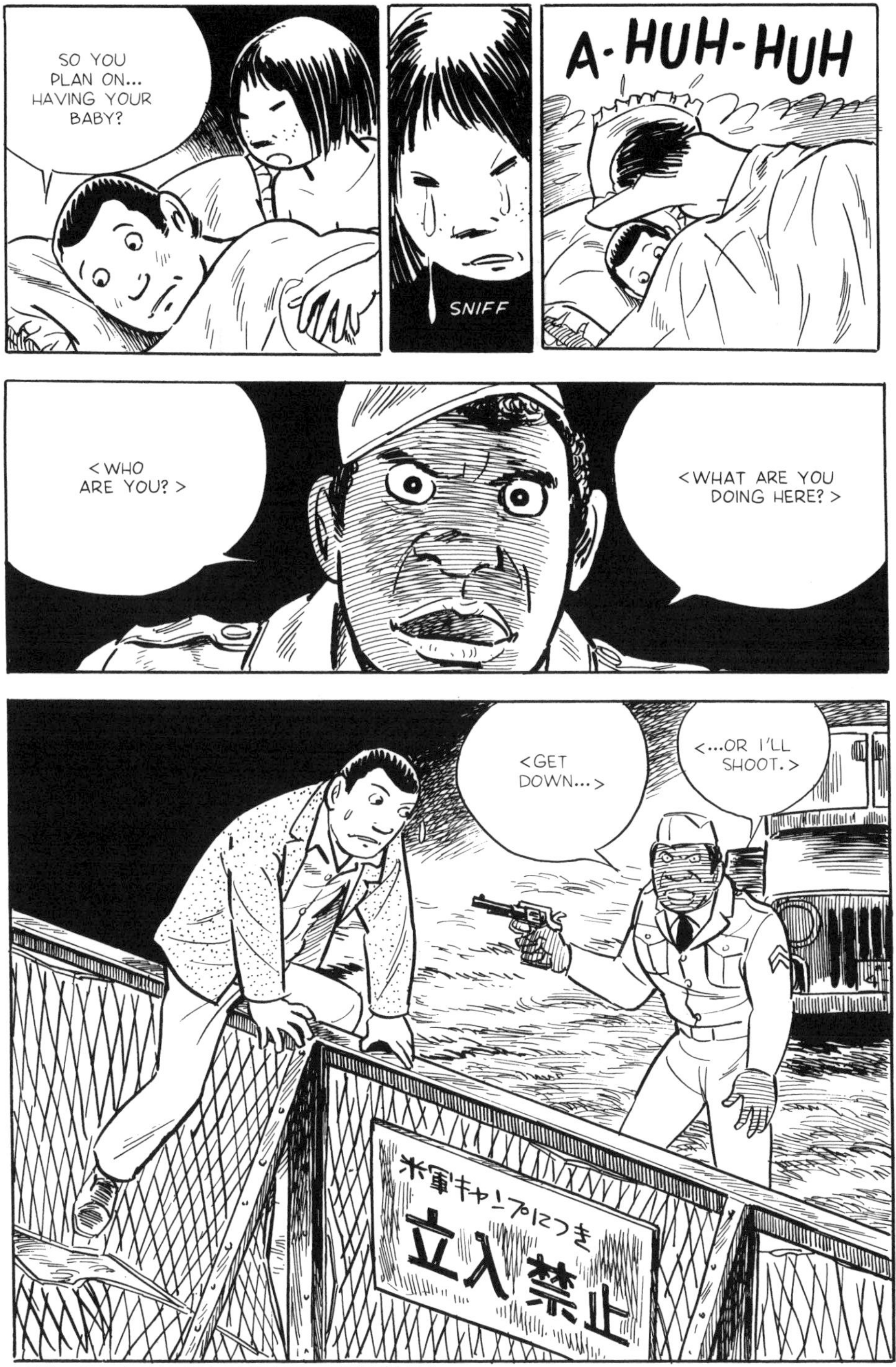
SO YOU PLAN ON... HAVING YOUR BABY?
SNIFF
A-HUH-HUH
<WHO ARE YOU?>
<WHAT ARE YOU DOING HERE?>
<GET DOWN...>
<...OR I'LL SHOOT.>
米軍キャンプにつき
立入禁止
SIGN: U.S. MILITARY BASE/ NO TRESPASSING

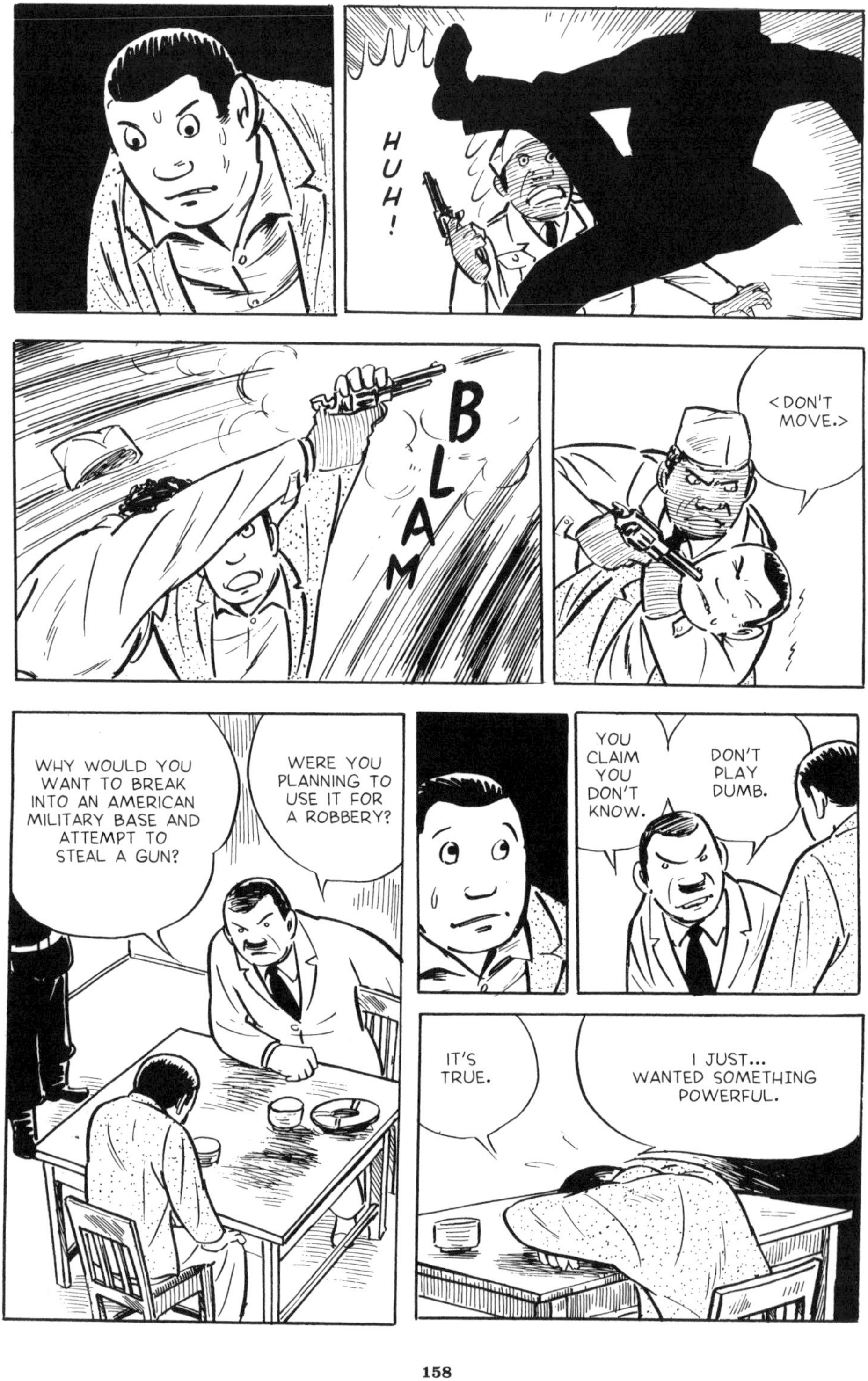
HUH!
BLAM
<DON'T MOVE.>
WHY WOULD YOU WANT TO BREAK INTO AN AMERICAN MILITARY BASE AND ATTEMPT TO STEAL A GUN?
WERE YOU PLANNING TO USE IT FOR A ROBBERY?
YOU CLAIM YOU DON'T KNOW.
DON'T PLAY DUMB.
IT'S TRUE.
I JUST... WANTED SOMETHING POWERFUL.

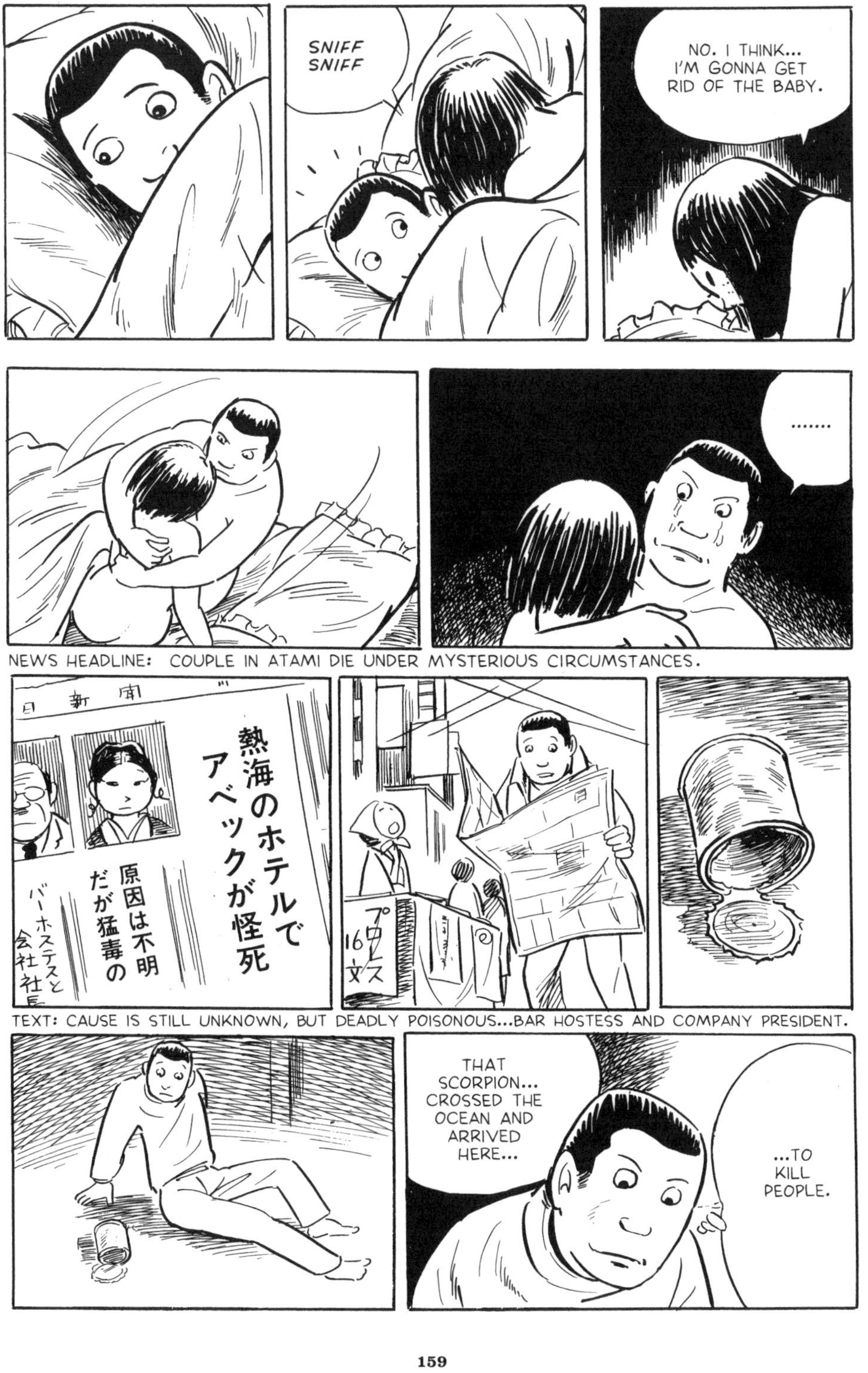
SNIFF SNIFF
NO. I THINK... I'M GONNA GET RID OF THE BABY.
....
NEWS HEADLINE: COUPLE IN ATAMI DIE UNDER MYSTERIOUS CIRCUMSTANCES.
熱海のホテルでアベックが怪死
原因は不明だが猛毒の
バーホステスと会社社長
プロレス 16文
TEXT: CAUSE IS STILL UNKNOWN, BUT DEADLY POISONOUS...BAR HOSTESS AND COMPANY PRESIDENT.
THAT SCORPION... CROSSED THE OCEAN AND ARRIVED HERE...
...TO KILL PEOPLE.

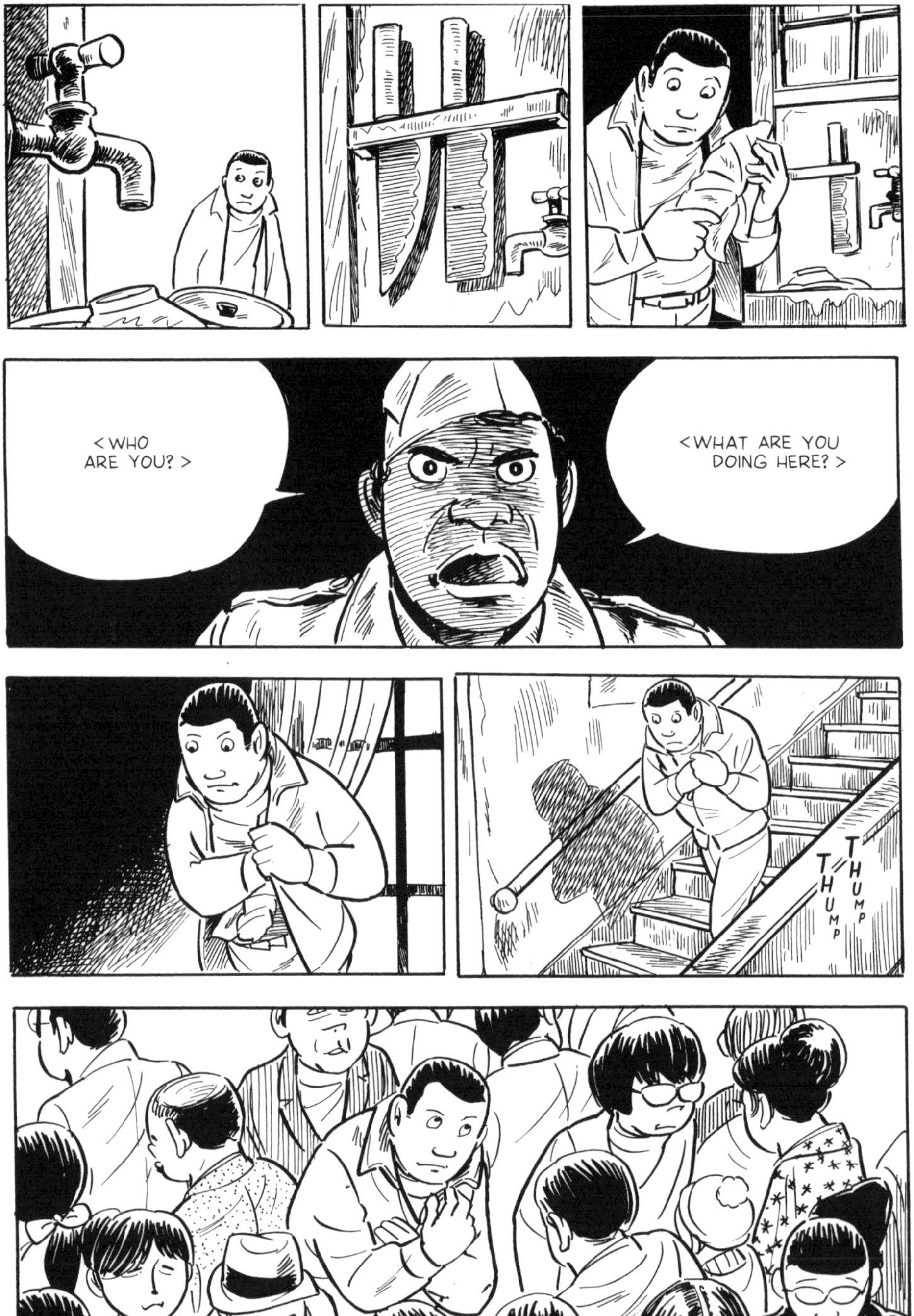
<WHO ARE YOU?>
<WHAT ARE YOU DOING HERE?>
THUMP
THUMP

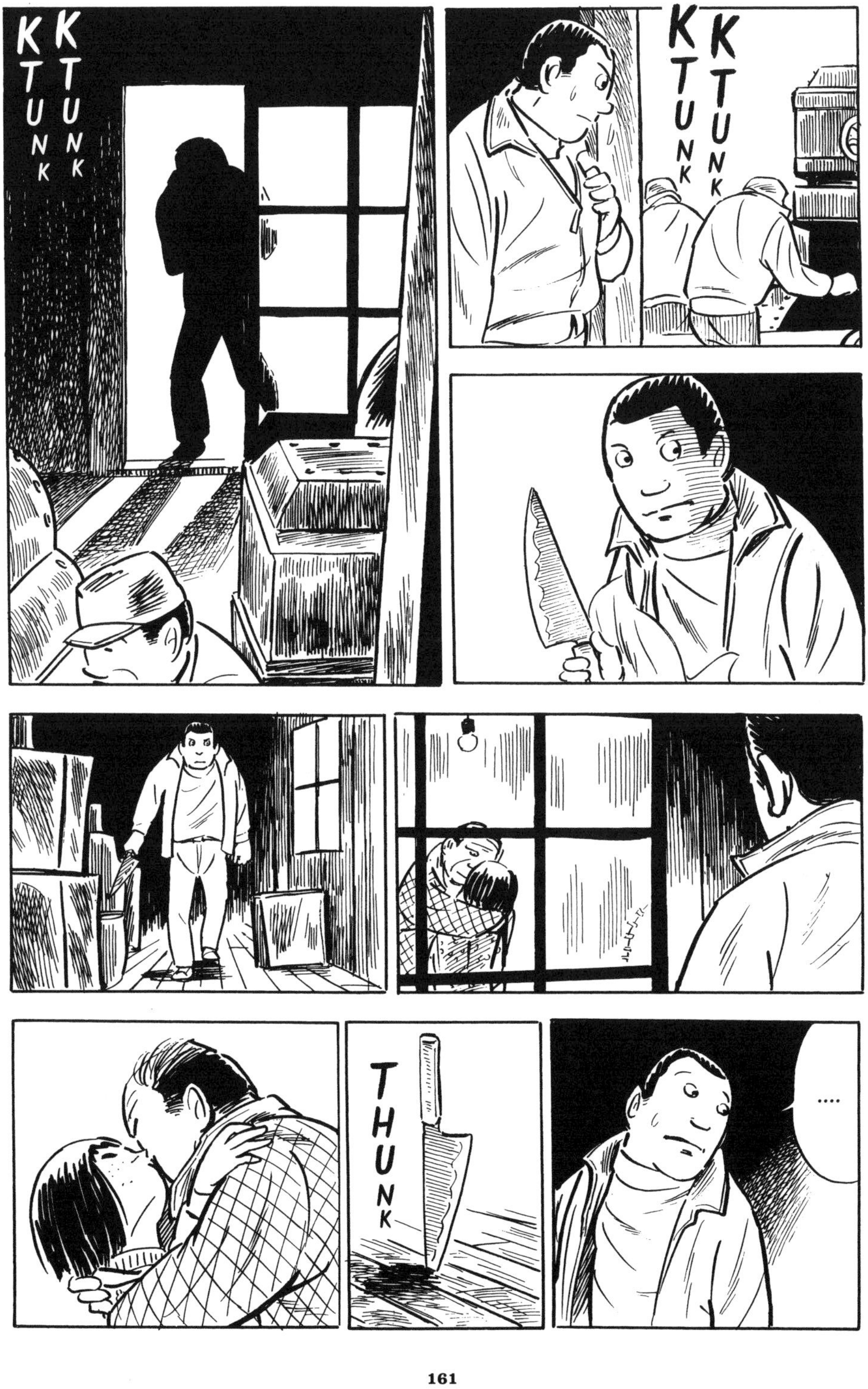
KTUNK KTUNK
KTUNK KTUNK
THUNK
....

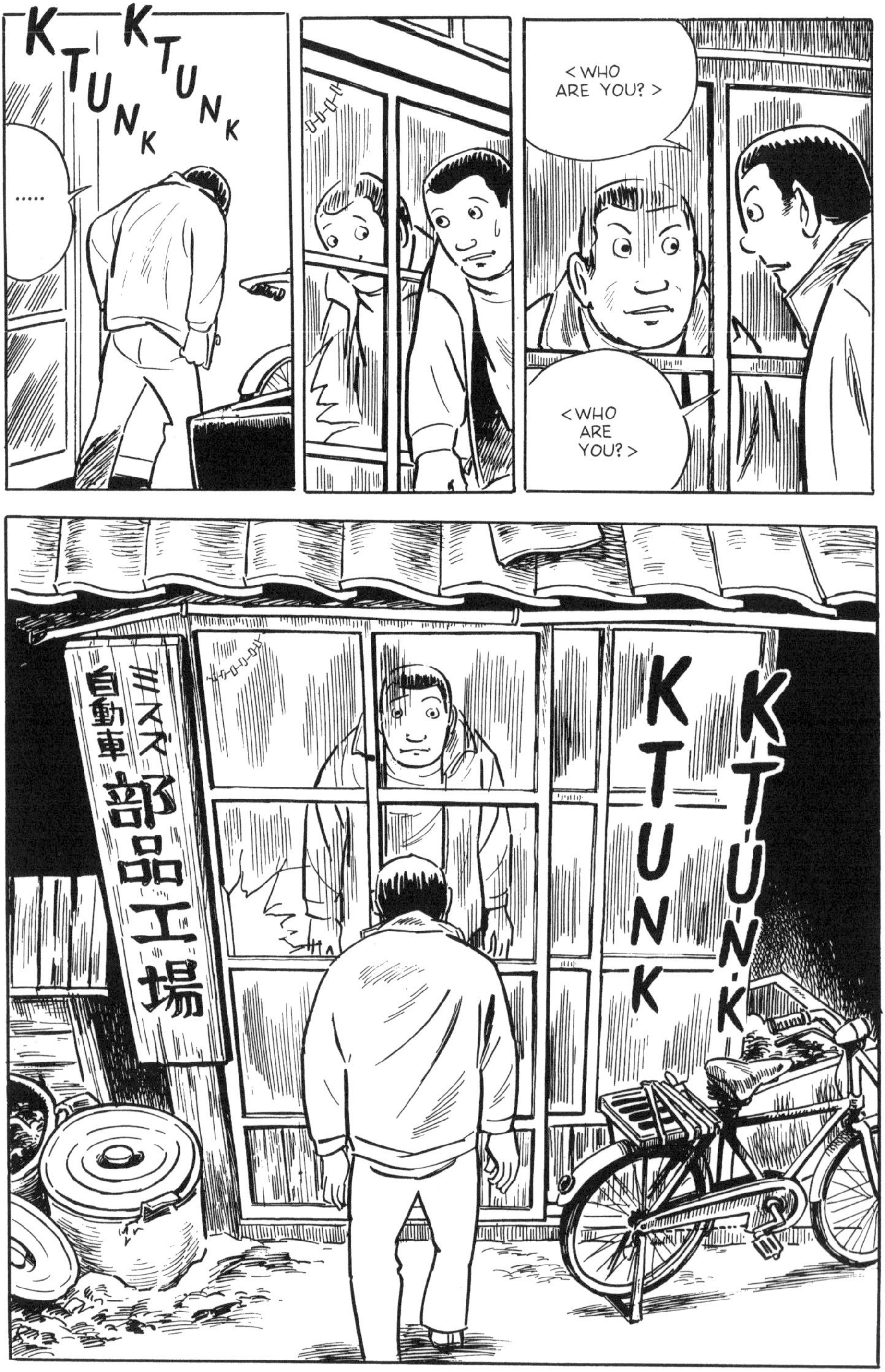
K TUNK K TUNK
.....
<WHO ARE YOU?>
<WHO ARE YOU?>
ミスズ 自動車 部品工場
K TUNK K TUNK

BEDRIDDEN

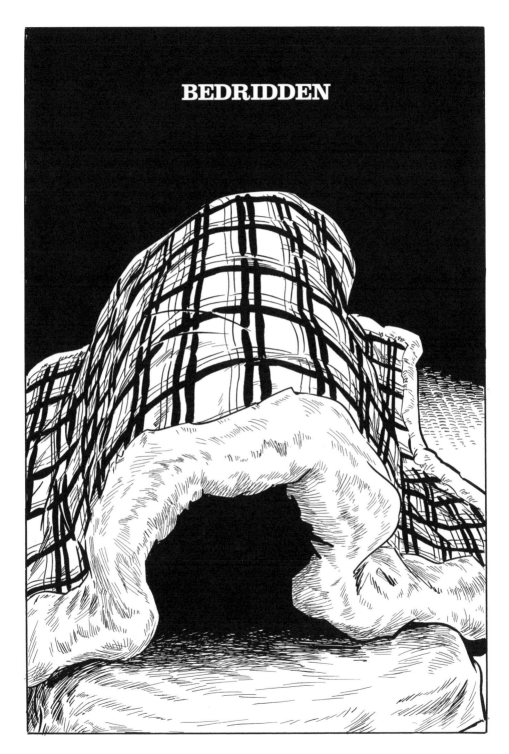

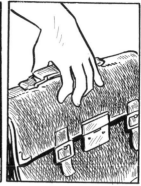

I'M OFF TO WORK.

YOU JUST REST EASY, ALL RIGHT?

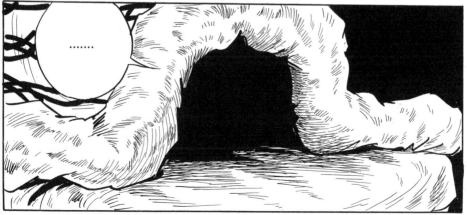

......

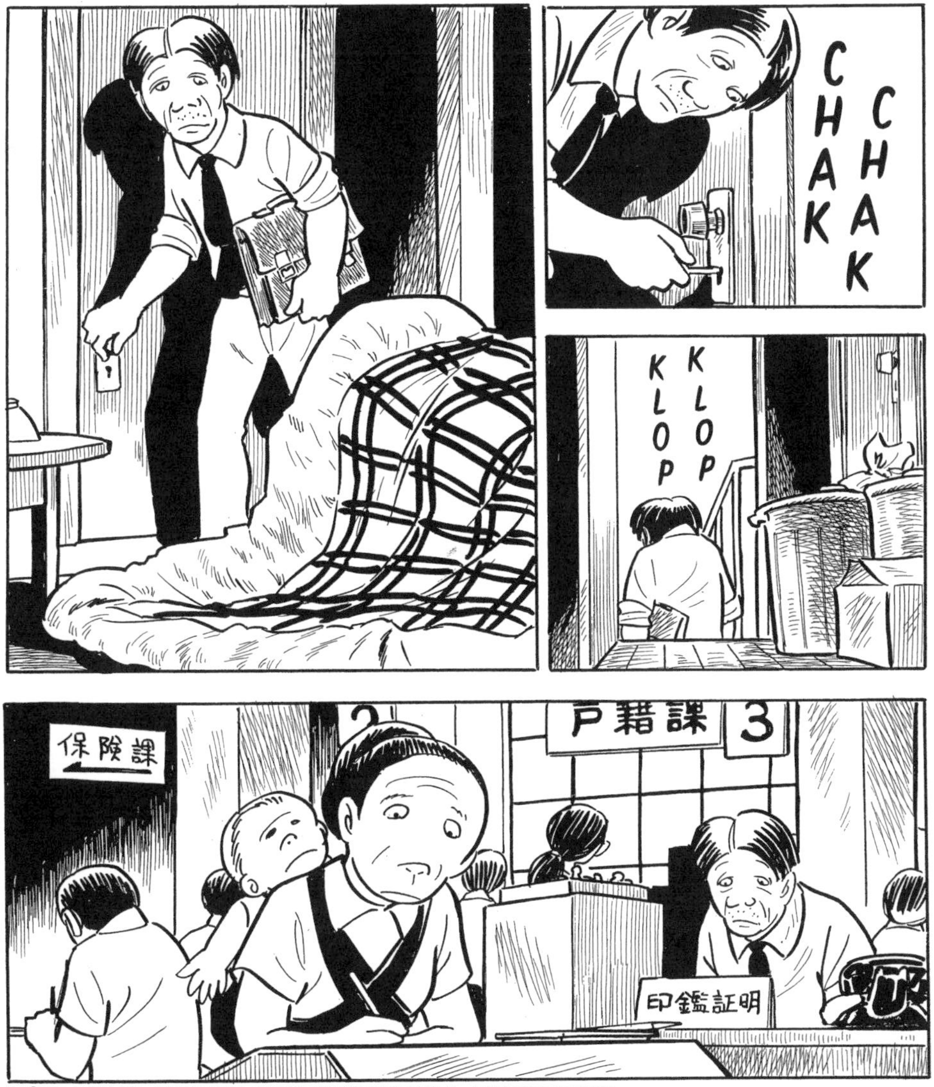
CHAK
CHAK
KLOP
KLOP
保険課
戸籍課
3
印鑑証明

SIGNS: MEDICAL INSURANCE OFFICE/ REGISTRY/ SEAL AUTHENTICATION

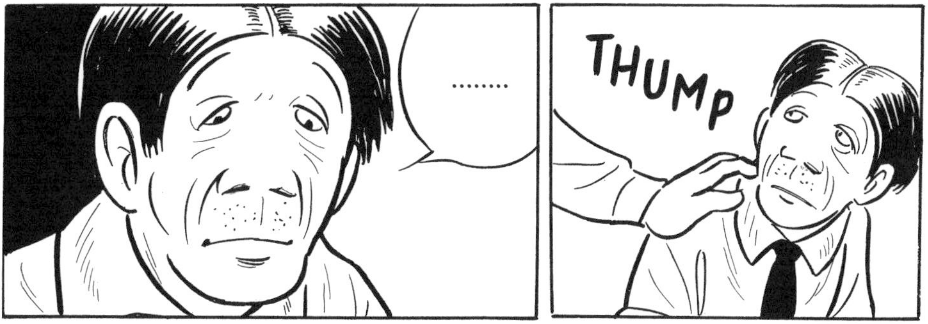
....
THUMP

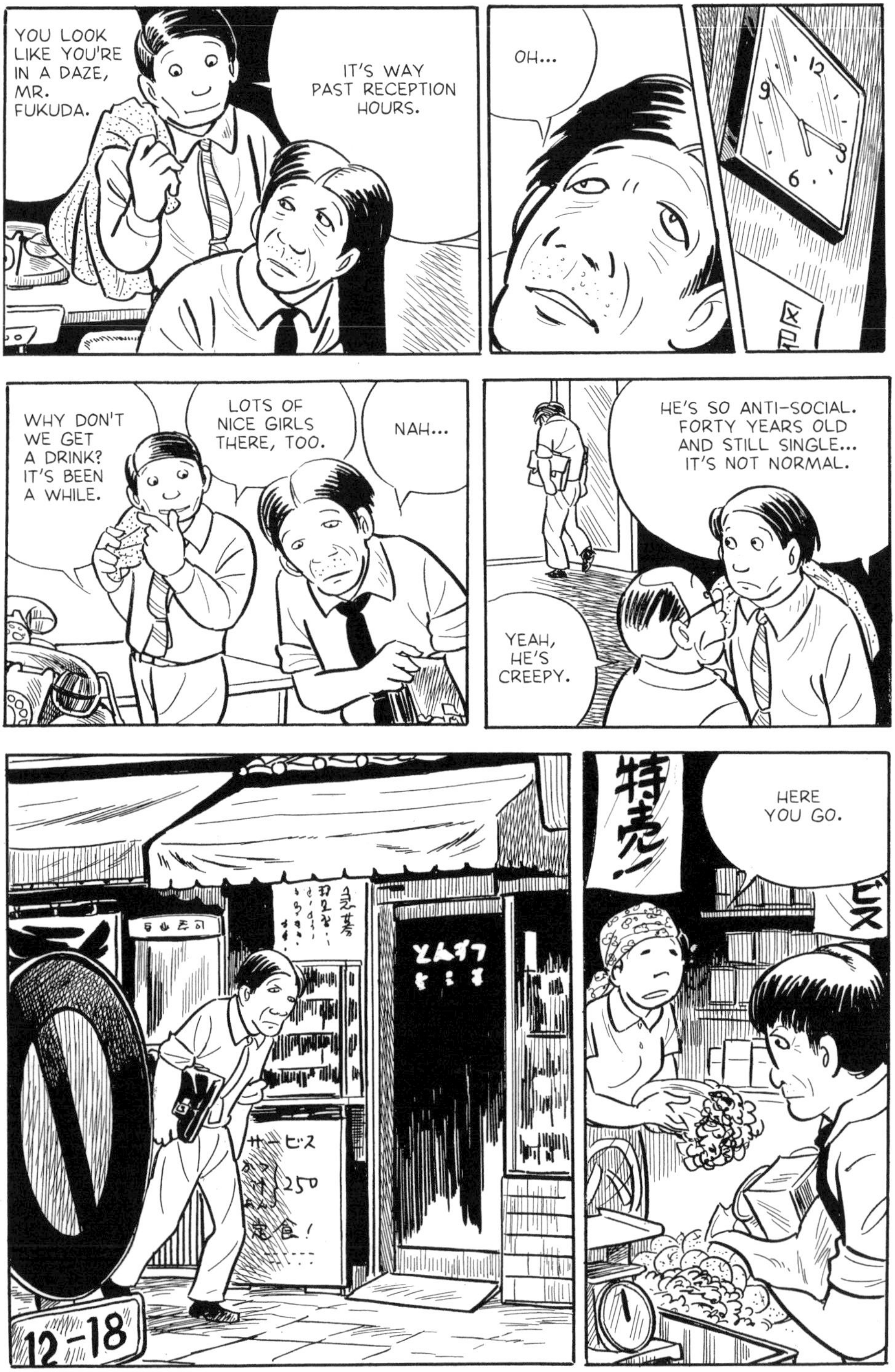
YOU LOOK LIKE YOU'RE IN A DAZE, MR. FUKUDA.
IT'S WAY PAST RECEPTION HOURS.
OH...
WHY DON'T WE GET A DRINK? IT'S BEEN A WHILE.
LOTS OF NICE GIRLS THERE, TOO.
NAH...
HE'S SO ANTI-SOCIAL. FORTY YEARS OLD AND STILL SINGLE... IT'S NOT NORMAL.
YEAH, HE'S CREEPY.
サービス
250
定食!
12-18
特売!!
HERE YOU GO.

CHAK

YOU MUST BE HUNGRY. I'LL MAKE YOUR DINNER RIGHT NOW.

MILK

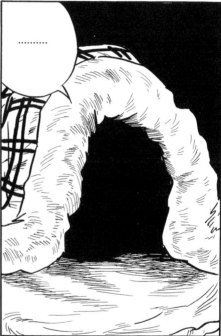

....

AHH...

YE-E-S... AHH...

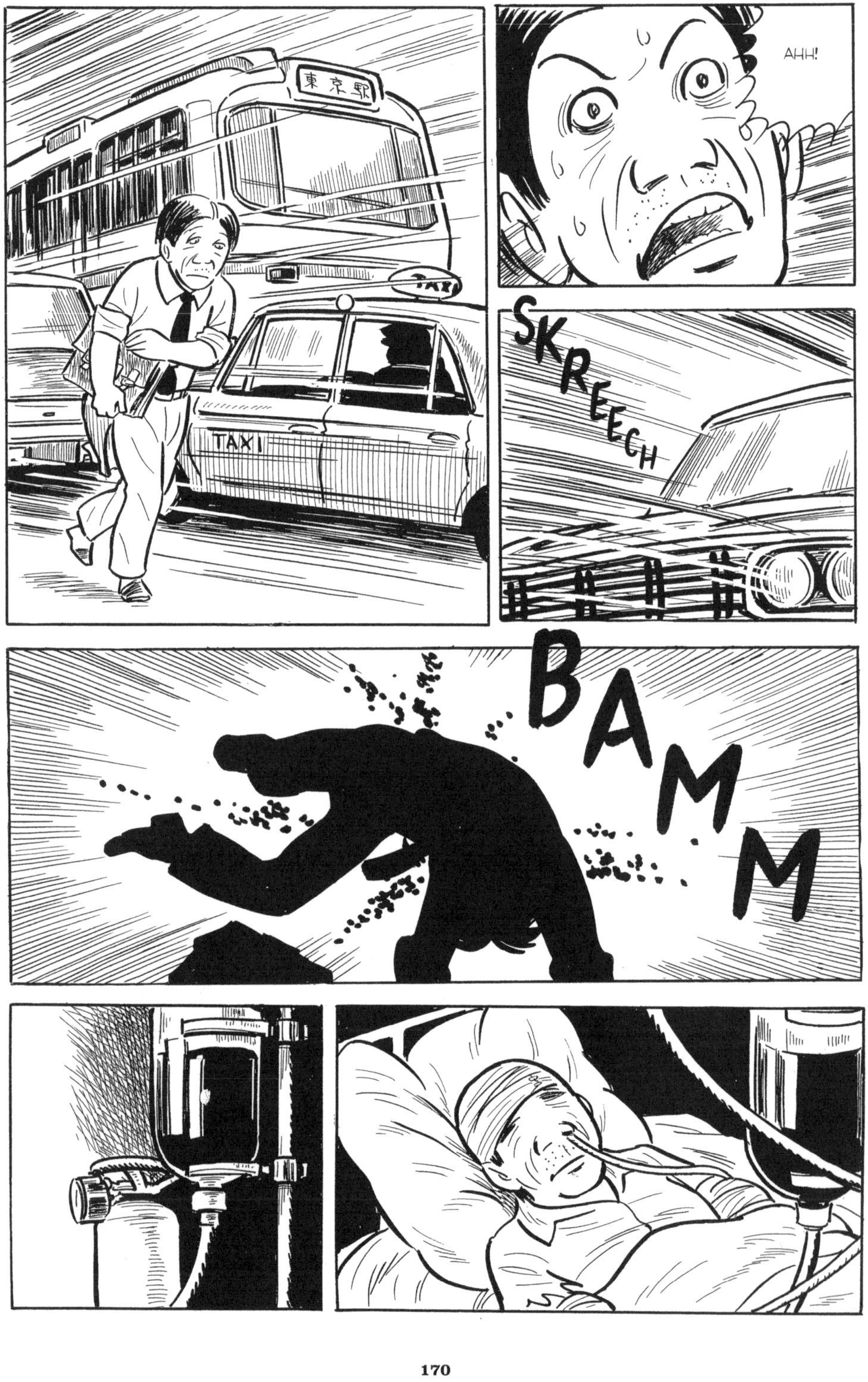
東京駅
TAXI
AHH!
SKREEECH
BAMM

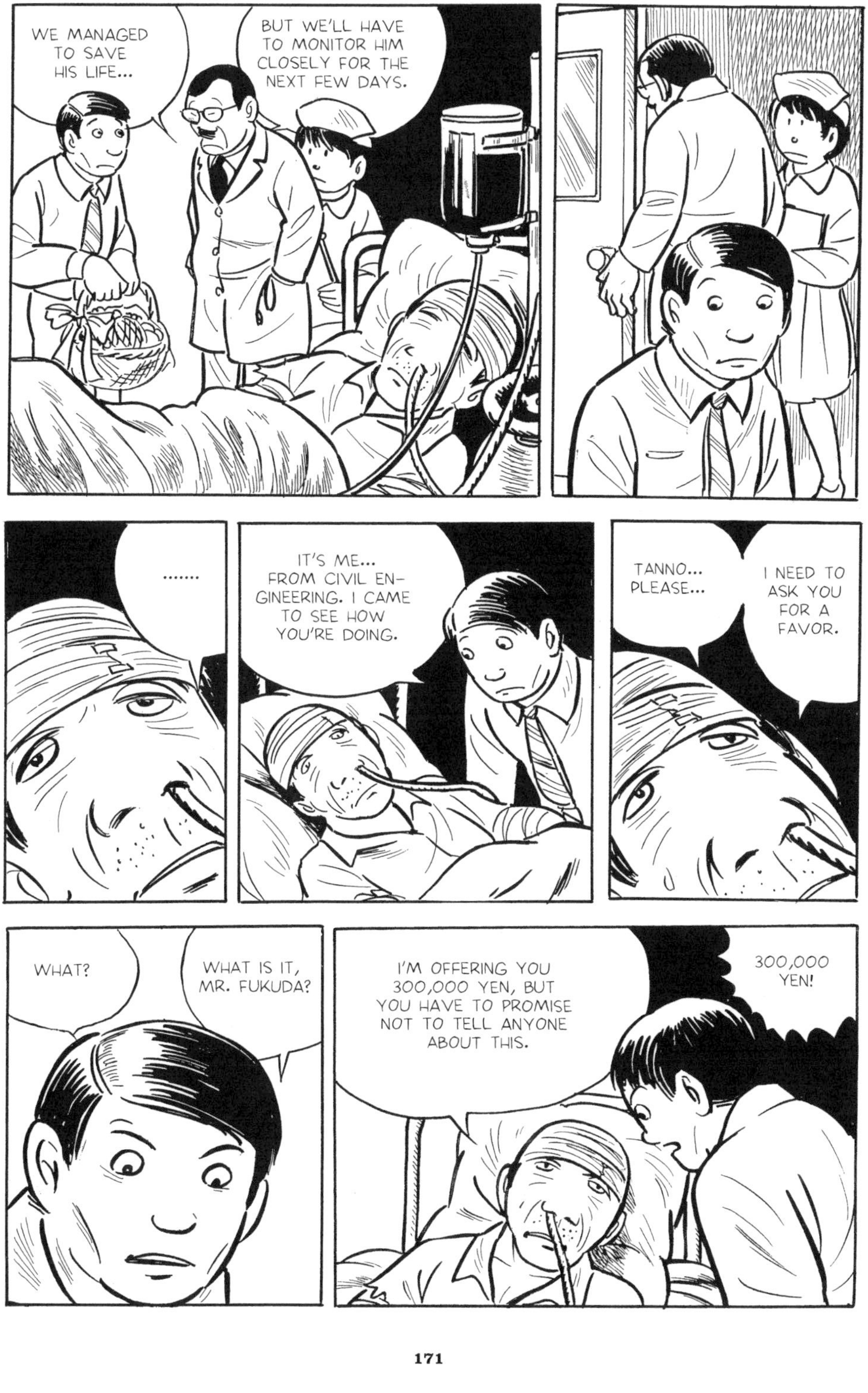
WE MANAGED TO SAVE HIS LIFE...
BUT WE'LL HAVE TO MONITOR HIM CLOSELY FOR THE NEXT FEW DAYS.
....
IT'S ME... FROM CIVIL ENGINEERING. I CAME TO SEE HOW YOU'RE DOING.
TANNO... PLEASE...
I NEED TO ASK YOU FOR A FAVOR.
WHAT?
WHAT IS IT, MR. FUKUDA?
I'M OFFERING YOU 300,000 YEN, BUT YOU HAVE TO PROMISE NOT TO TELL ANYONE ABOUT THIS.
300,000 YEN!

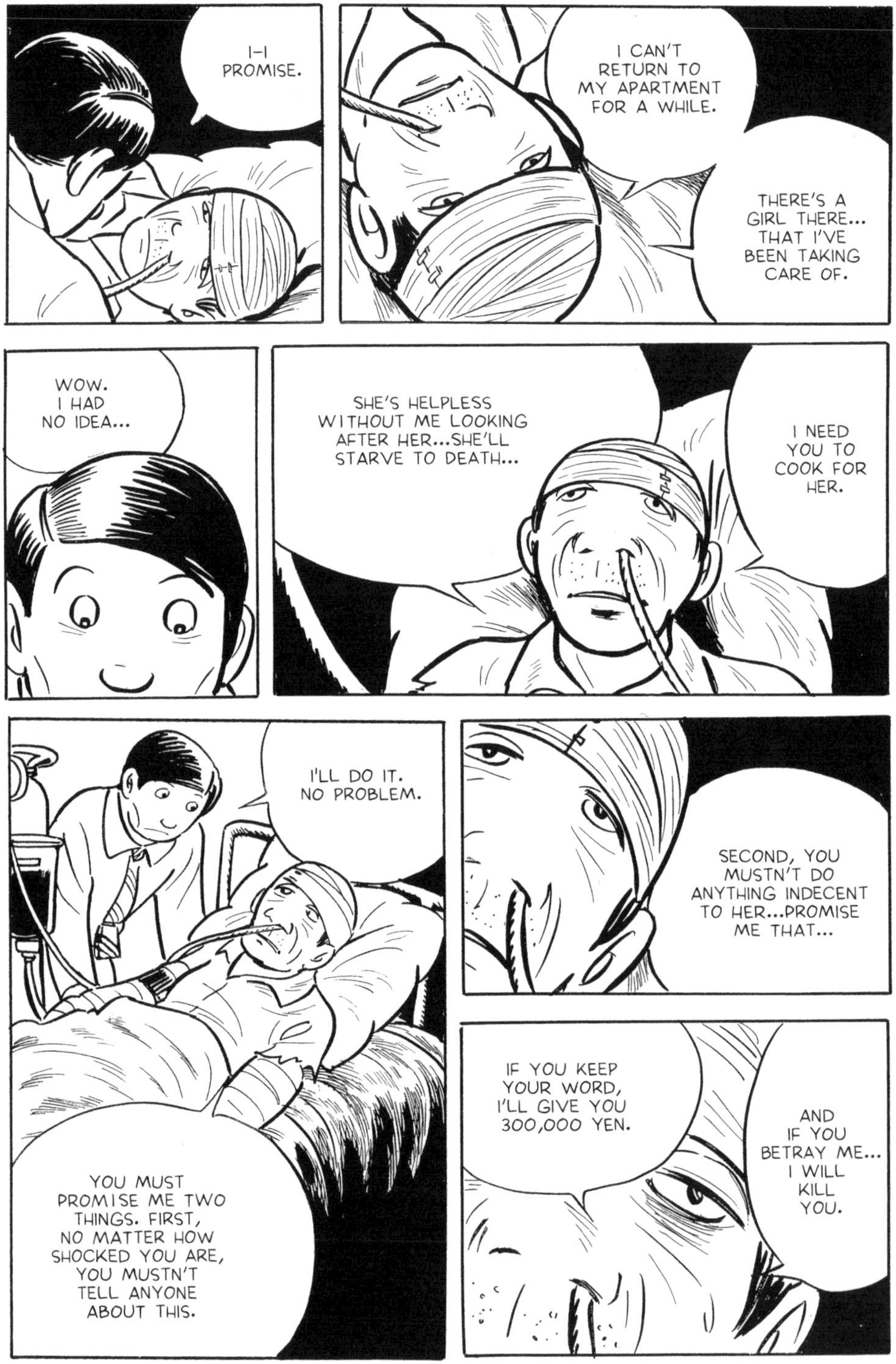
I-I PROMISE.
I CAN'T RETURN TO MY APARTMENT FOR A WHILE.
THERE'S A GIRL THERE... THAT I'VE BEEN TAKING CARE OF.
WOW. I HAD NO IDEA...
SHE'S HELPLESS WITHOUT ME LOOKING AFTER HER...SHE'LL STARVE TO DEATH...
I NEED YOU TO COOK FOR HER.
I'LL DO IT. NO PROBLEM.
YOU MUST PROMISE ME TWO THINGS. FIRST, NO MATTER HOW SHOCKED YOU ARE, YOU MUSTN'T TELL ANYONE ABOUT THIS.
SECOND, YOU MUSTN'T DO ANYTHING INDECENT TO HER...PROMISE ME THAT...
IF YOU KEEP YOUR WORD, I'LL GIVE YOU 300,000 YEN.
AND IF YOU BETRAY ME... I WILL KILL YOU.

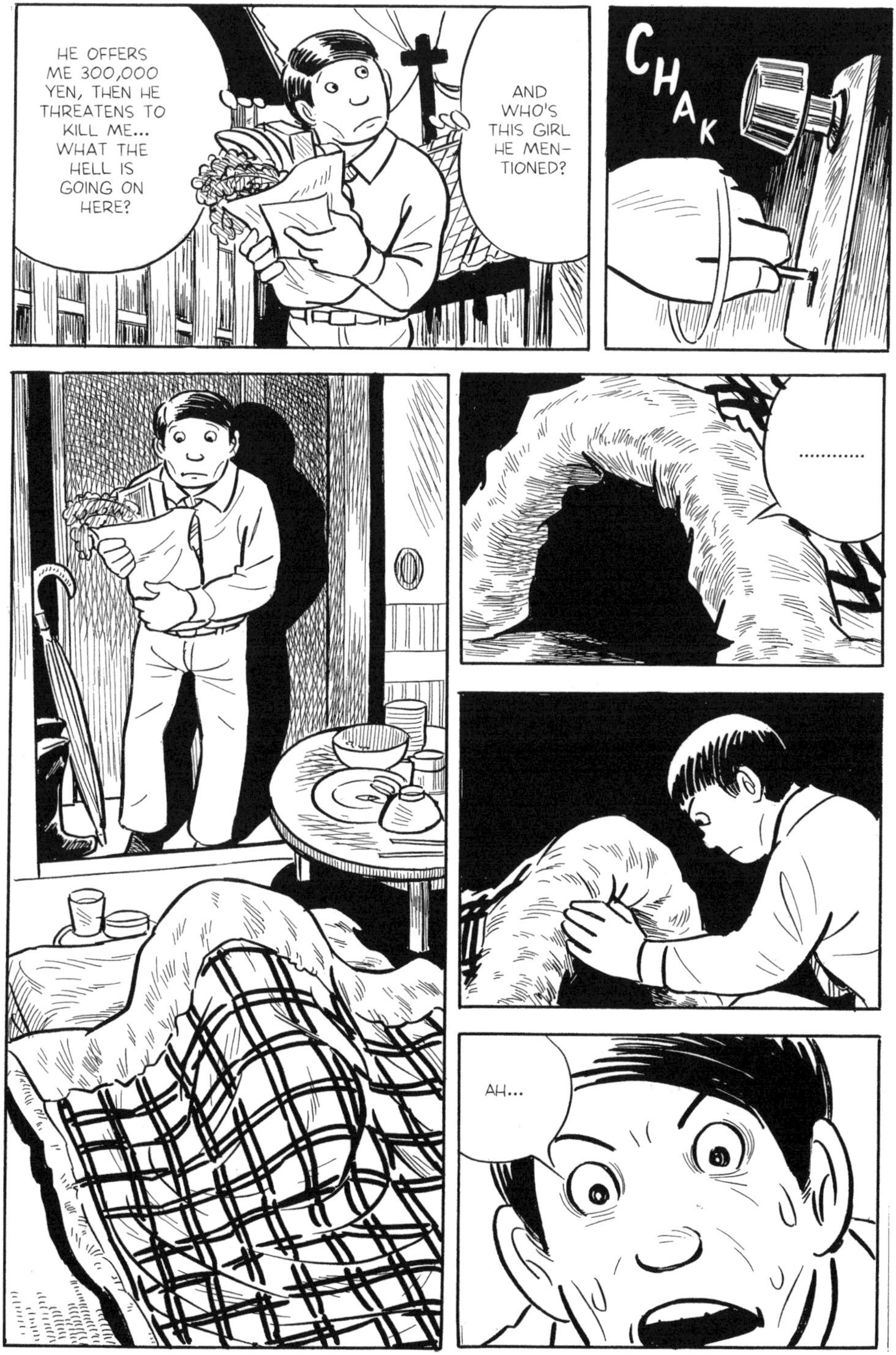
HE OFFERS ME 300,000 YEN, THEN HE THREATENS TO KILL ME... WHAT THE HELL IS GOING ON HERE?
AND WHO'S THIS GIRL HE MENTIONED?
CHAK
....
AH...

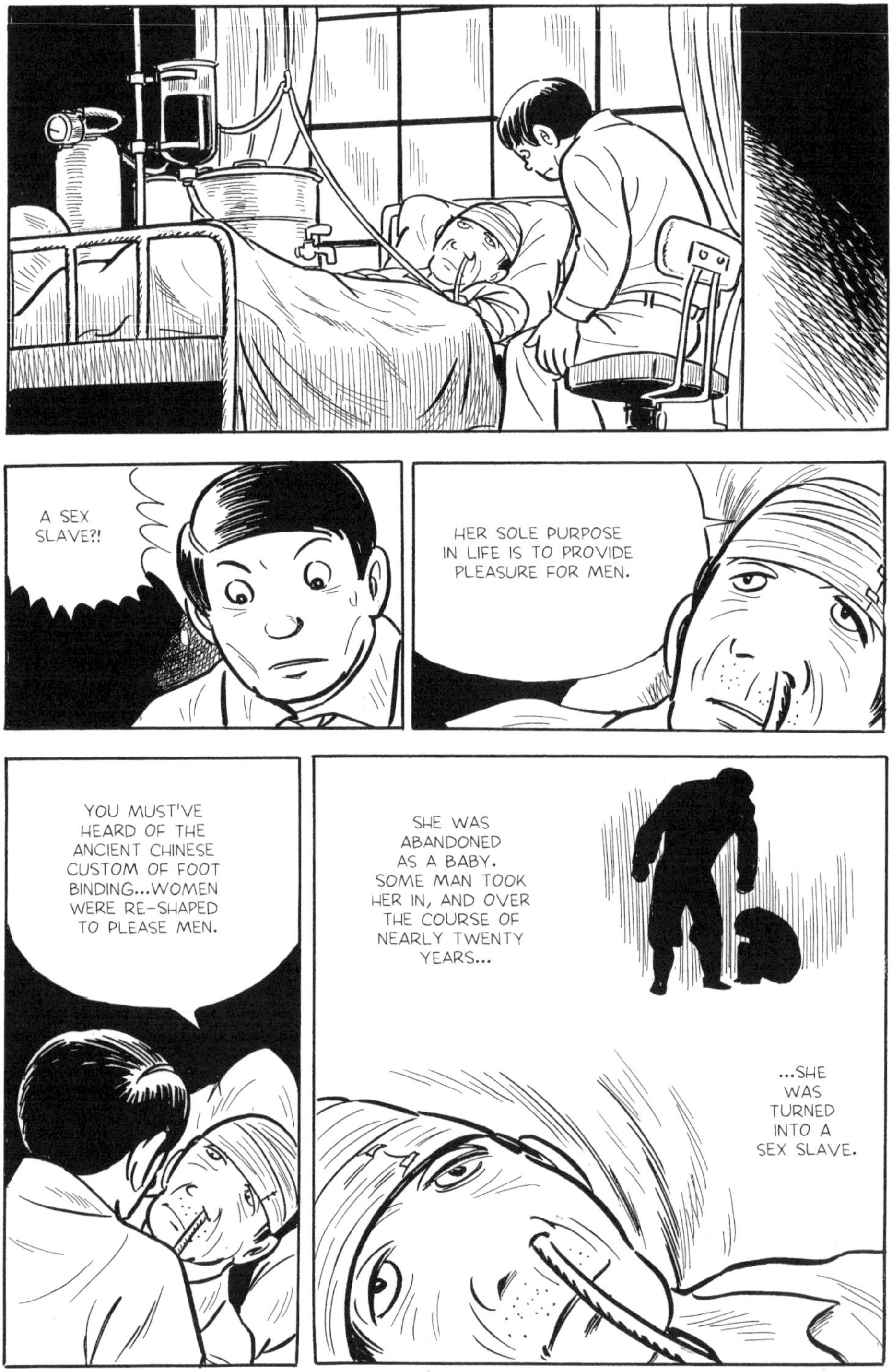
A SEX SLAVE?!
HER SOLE PURPOSE IN LIFE IS TO PROVIDE PLEASURE FOR MEN.
YOU MUST'VE HEARD OF THE ANCIENT CHINESE CUSTOM OF FOOT BINDING...WOMEN WERE RE-SHAPED TO PLEASE MEN.
SHE WAS ABANDONED AS A BABY. SOME MAN TOOK HER IN, AND OVER THE COURSE OF NEARLY TWENTY YEARS...
...SHE WAS TURNED INTO A SEX SLAVE.

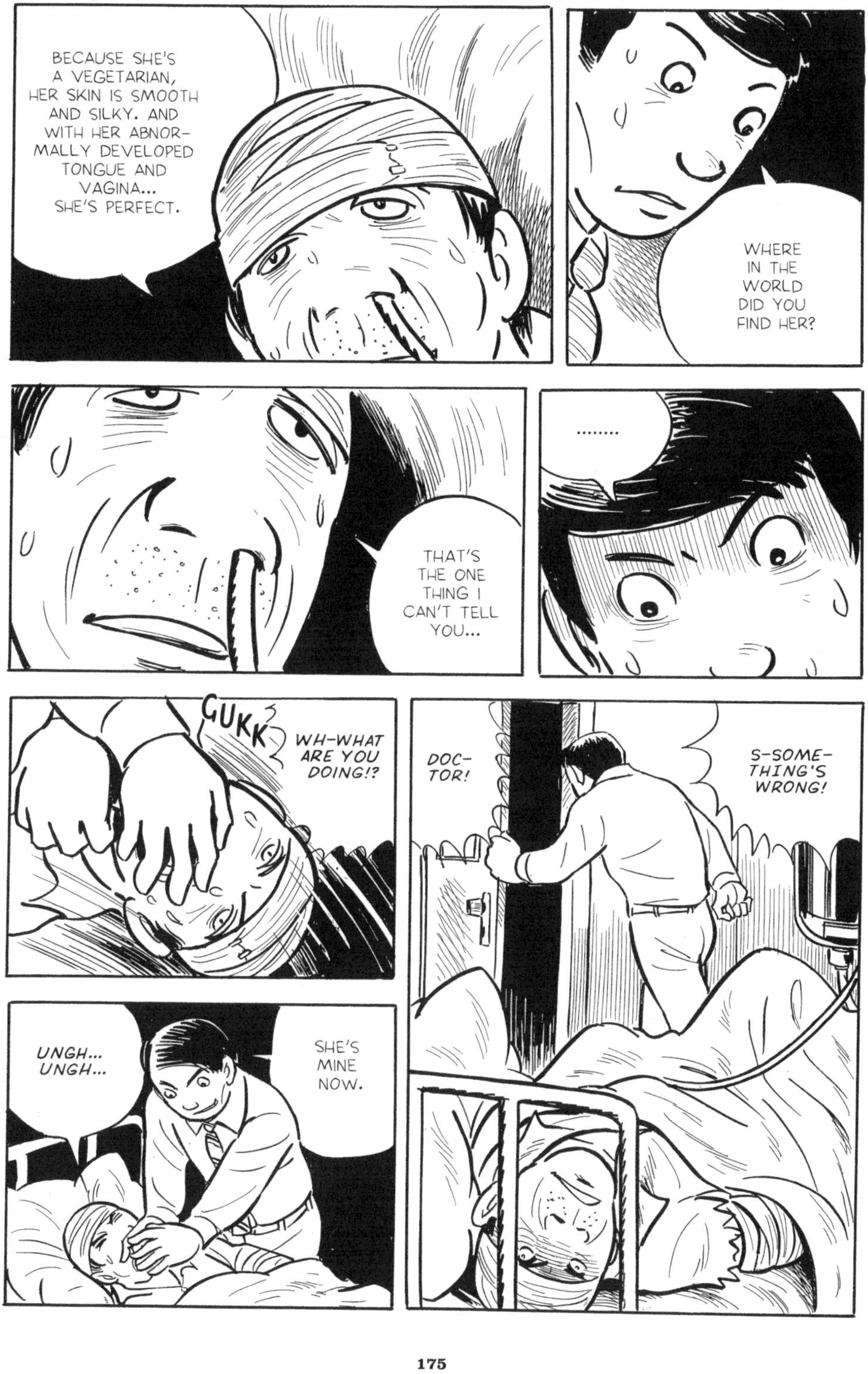

BECAUSE SHE'S A VEGETARIAN, HER SKIN IS SMOOTH AND SILKY. AND WITH HER ABNORMALLY DEVELOPED TONGUE AND VAGINA... SHE'S PERFECT.
WHERE IN THE WORLD DID YOU FIND HER?
THAT'S THE ONE THING I CAN'T TELL YOU...
....
GUKK
WH-WHAT ARE YOU DOING!?
UNGH... UNGH...
SHE'S MINE NOW.
DOC-TOR!
S-SOME-THING'S WRONG!

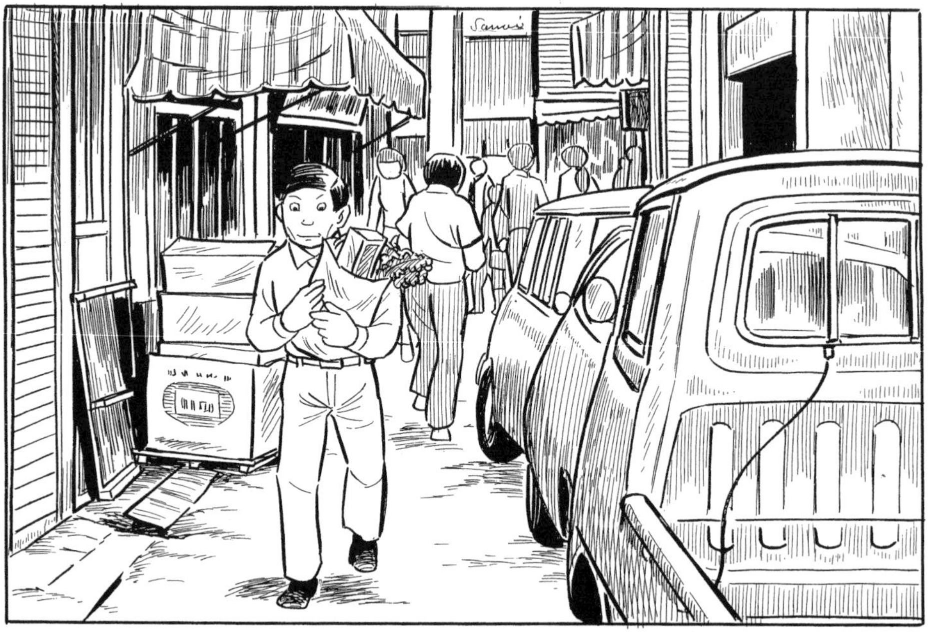

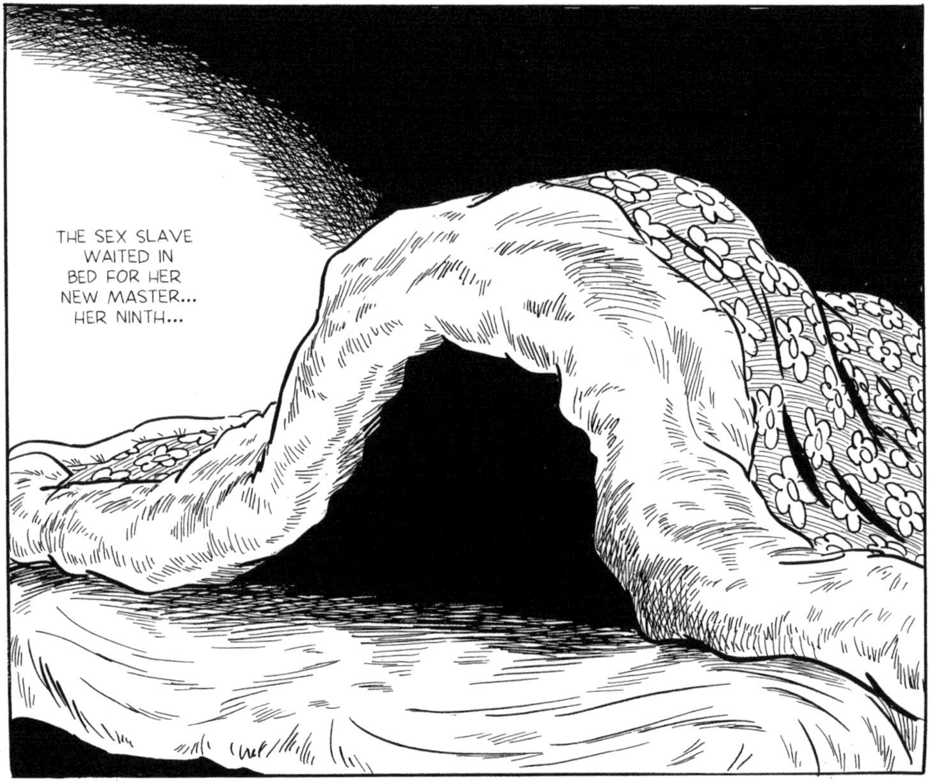
THE SEX SLAVE WAITED IN BED FOR HER NEW MASTER... HER NINTH...

MY HITLER

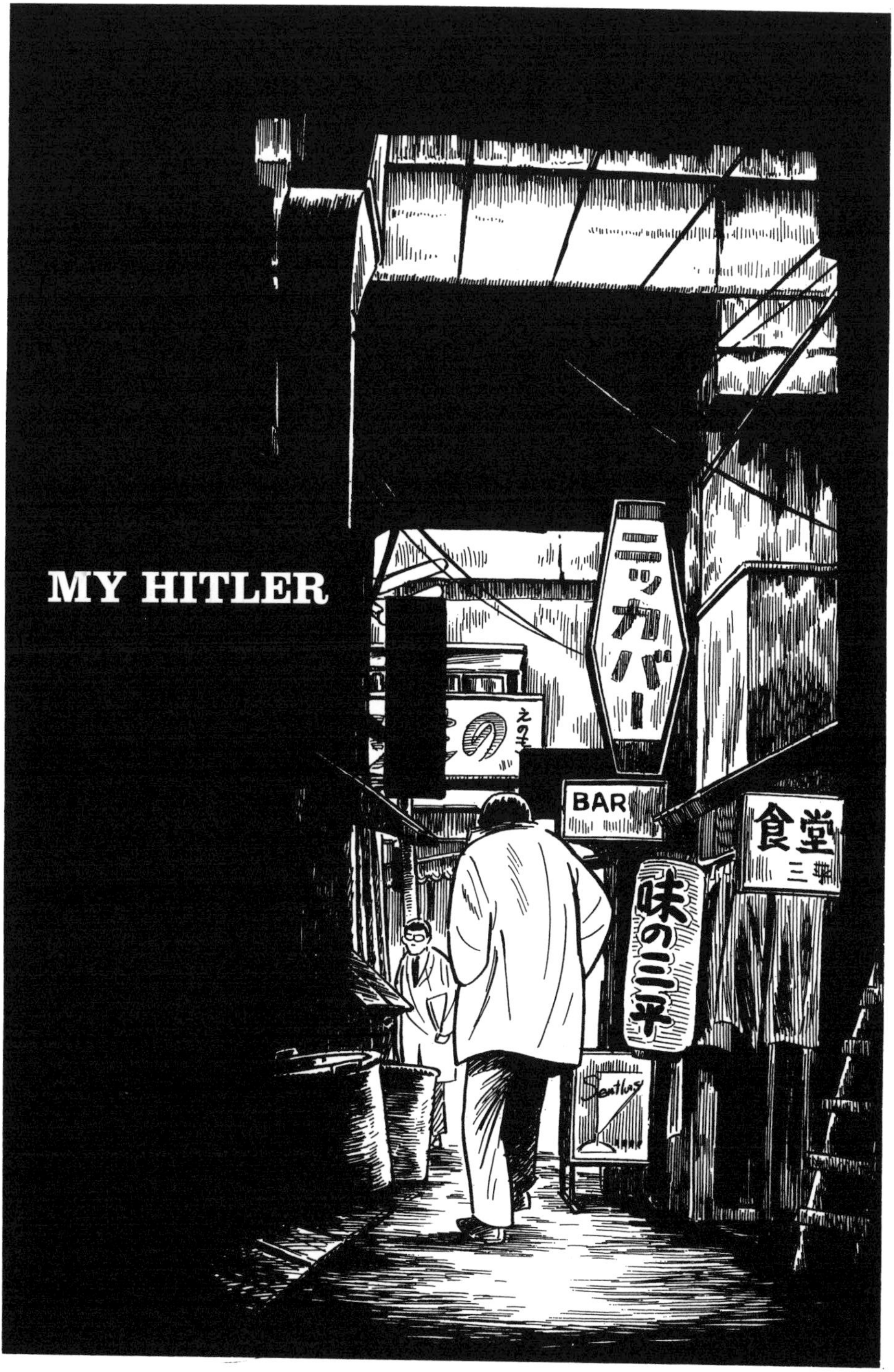
ニッカバー
BAR
食堂
味の三平

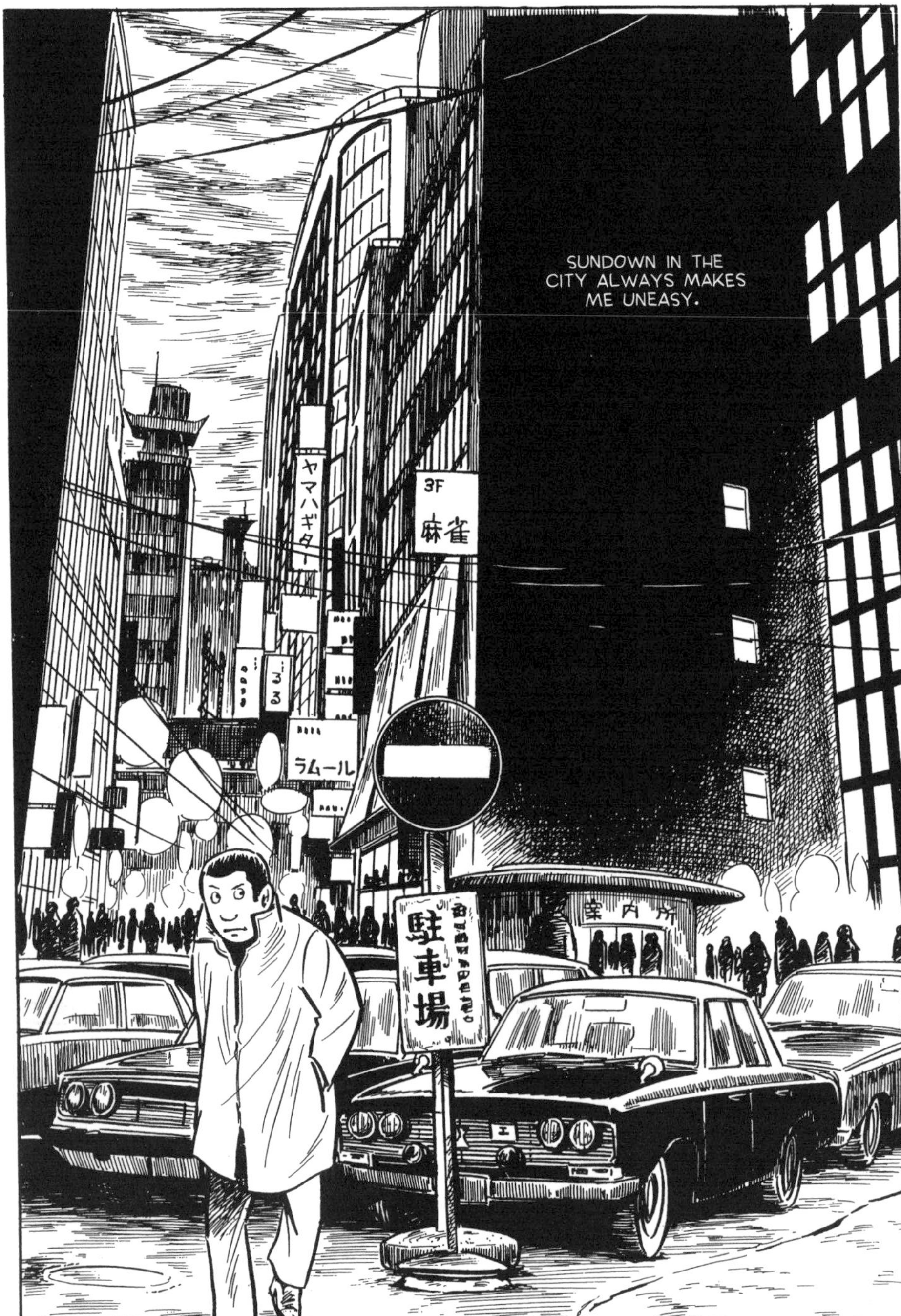
SUNDOWN IN THE CITY ALWAYS MAKES ME UNEASY.
ヤマハギター
3F 麻雀
ラムール
駐車場
案内所

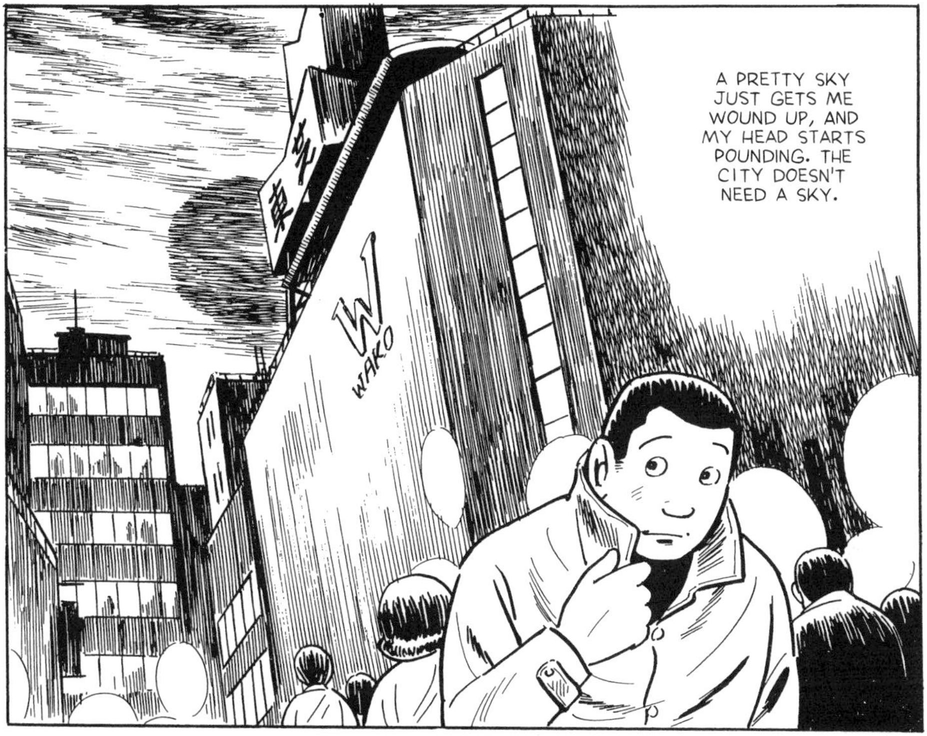
A PRETTY SKY JUST GETS ME WOUND UP, AND MY HEAD STARTS POUNDING. THE CITY DOESN'T NEED A SKY.
WAKO

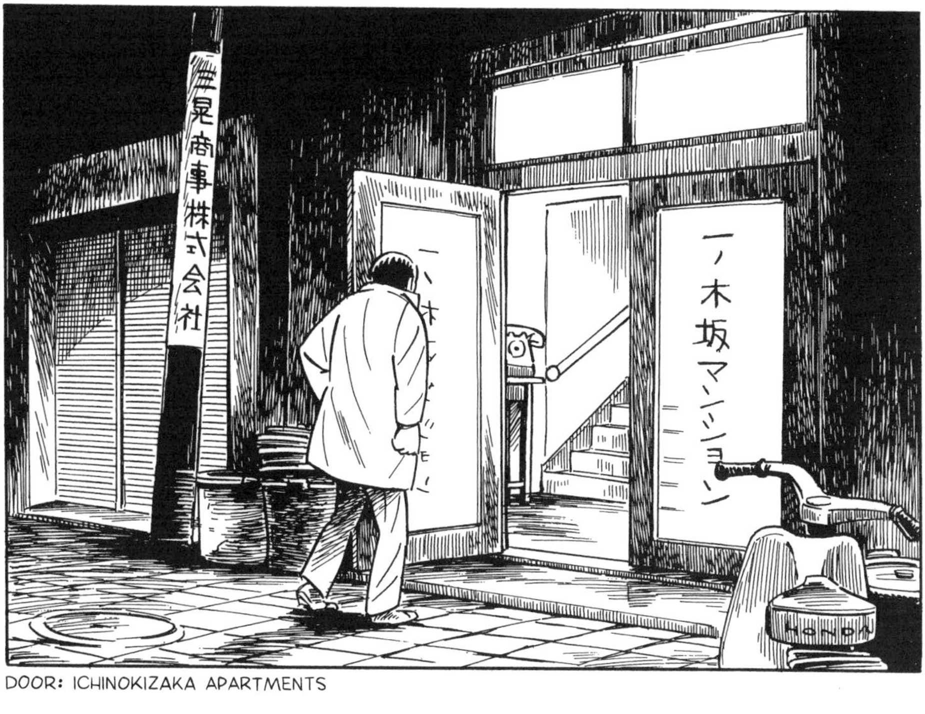
三晃商事株式会社
一ノ木坂マンション
HONDA
DOOR: ICHINOKIZAKA APARTMENTS

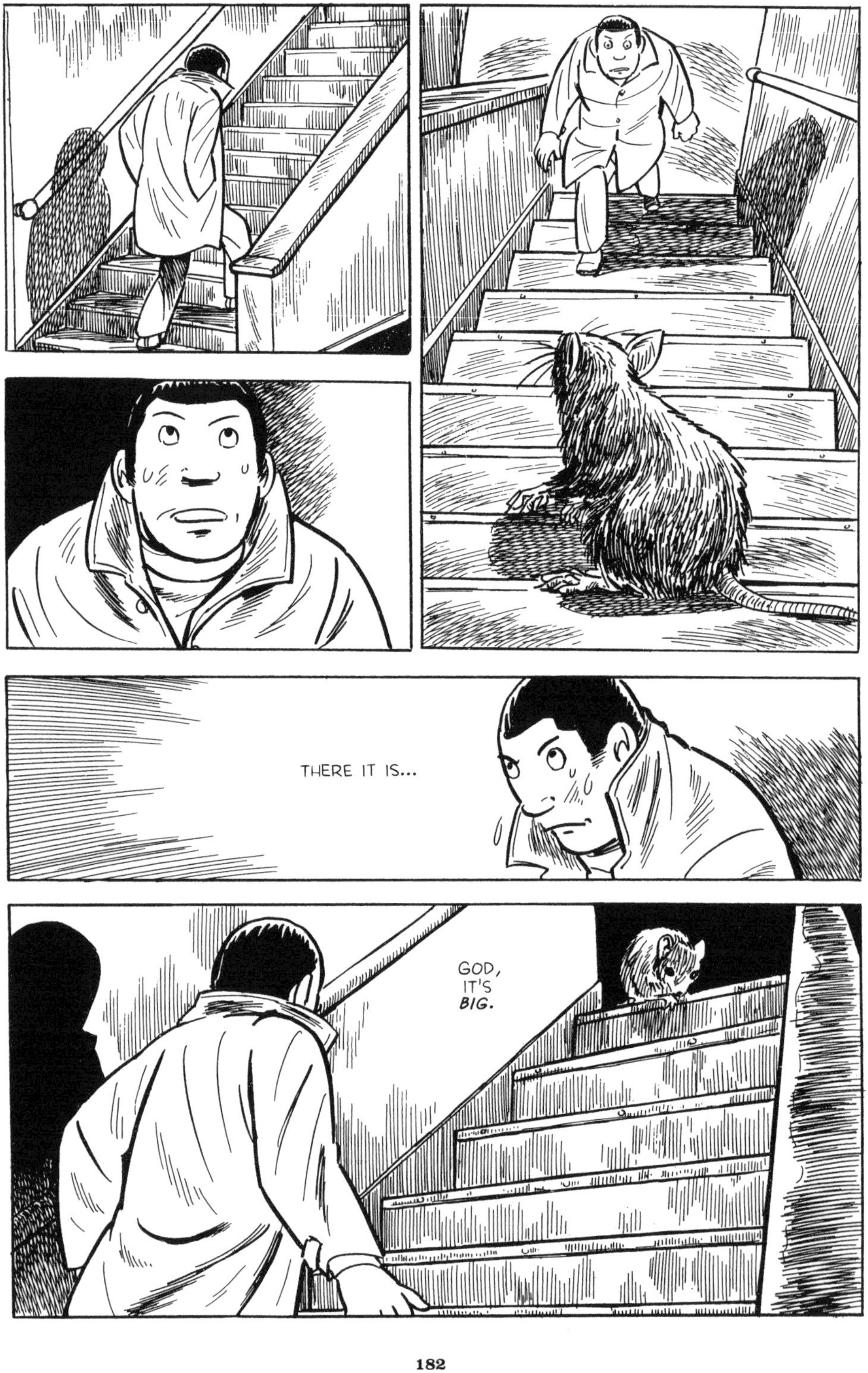
THERE IT IS...
GOD, IT'S *BIG.*

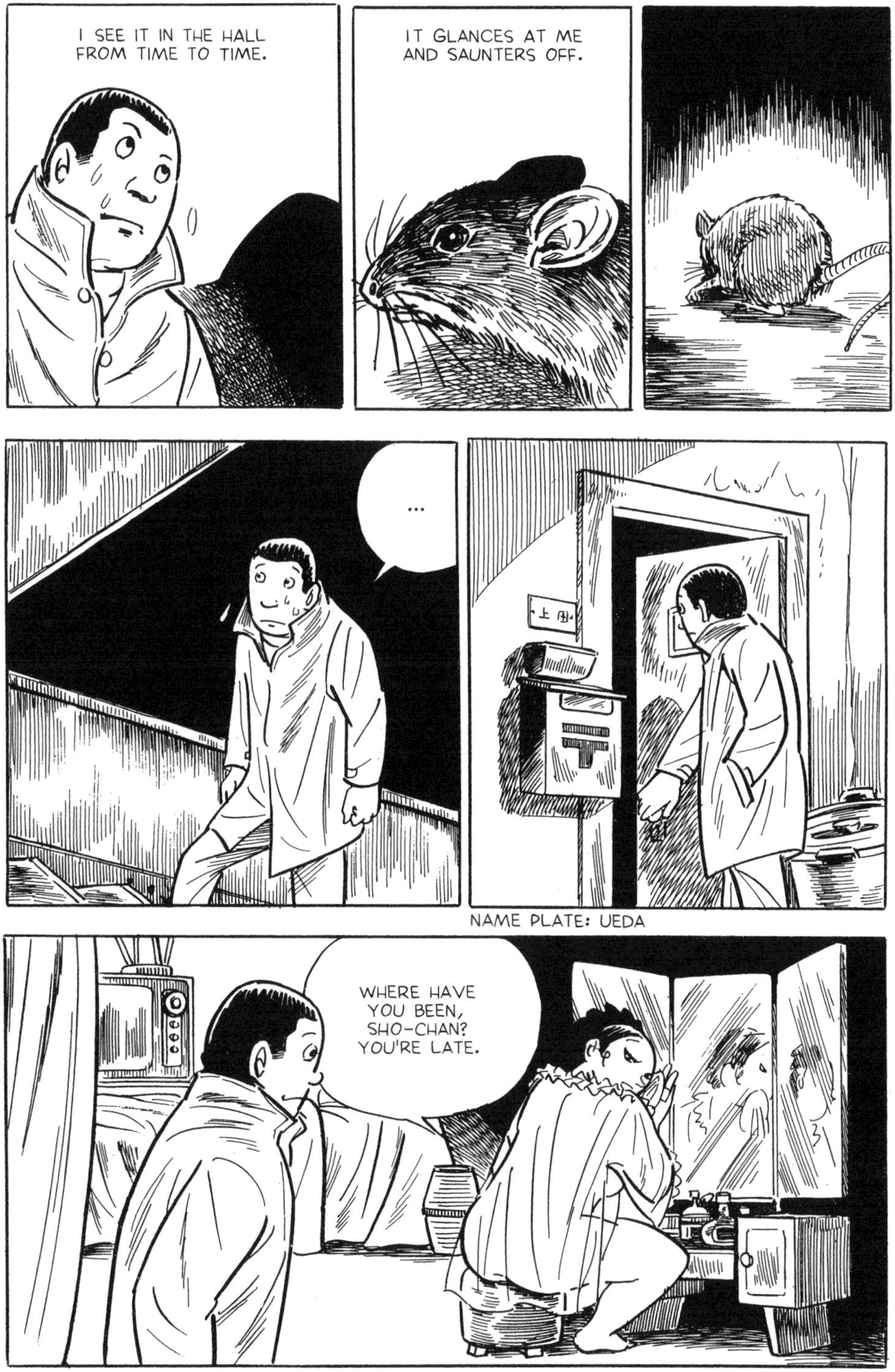
I SEE IT IN THE HALL FROM TIME TO TIME.
IT GLANCES AT ME AND SAUNTERS OFF.
...
NAME PLATE: UEDA
WHERE HAVE YOU BEEN, SHO-CHAN? YOU'RE LATE.

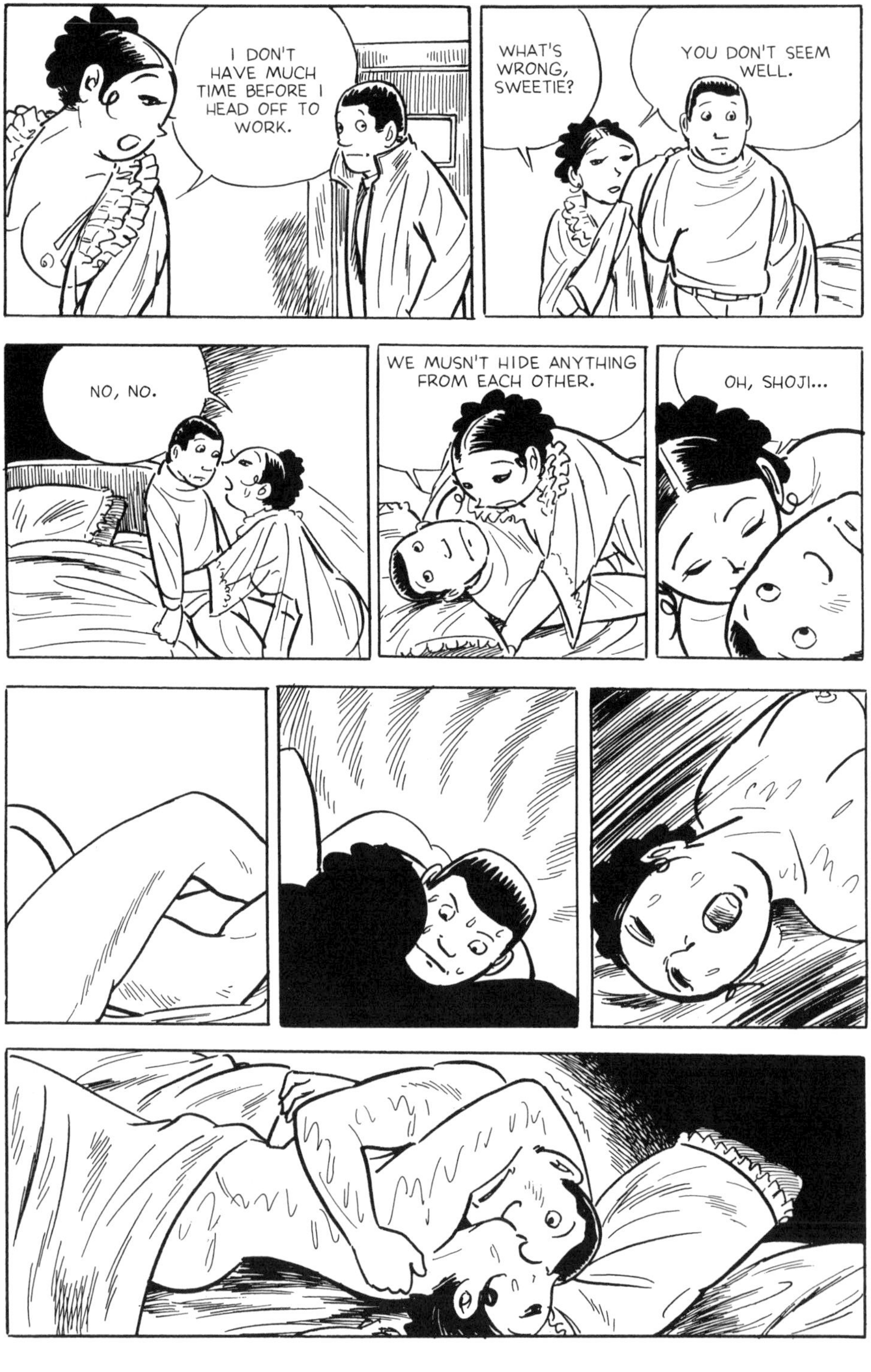
I DON'T HAVE MUCH TIME BEFORE I HEAD OFF TO WORK.
WHAT'S WRONG, SWEETIE?
YOU DON'T SEEM WELL.
NO, NO.
WE MUSN'T HIDE ANYTHING FROM EACH OTHER.
OH, SHOJI...

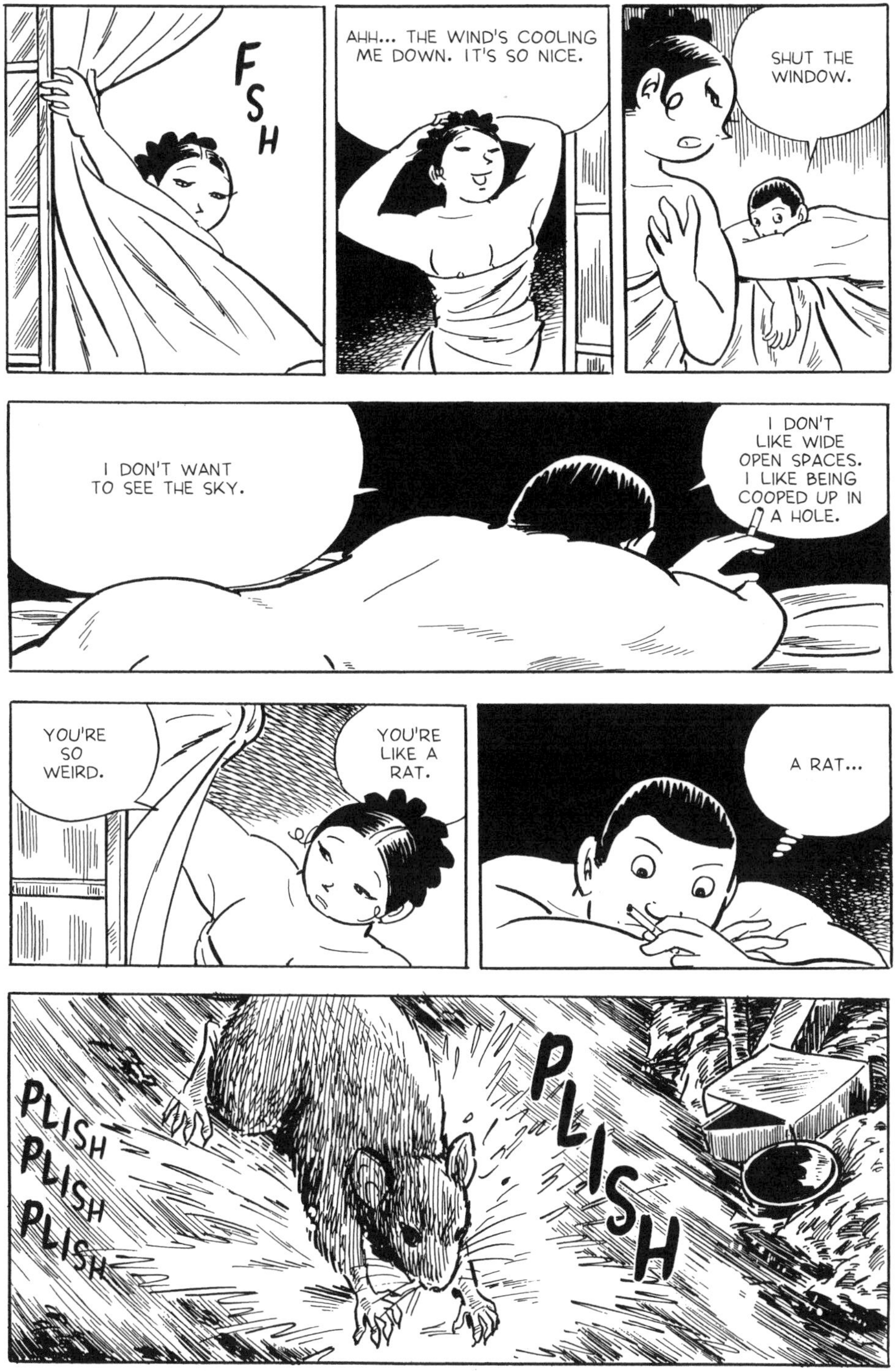
FSH
AHH... THE WIND'S COOLING ME DOWN. IT'S SO NICE.
SHUT THE WINDOW.
I DON'T WANT TO SEE THE SKY.
I DON'T LIKE WIDE OPEN SPACES. I LIKE BEING COOPED UP IN A HOLE.
YOU'RE SO WEIRD.
YOU'RE LIKE A RAT.
A RAT...
PLISH PLISH PLISH PLISH
PLISH

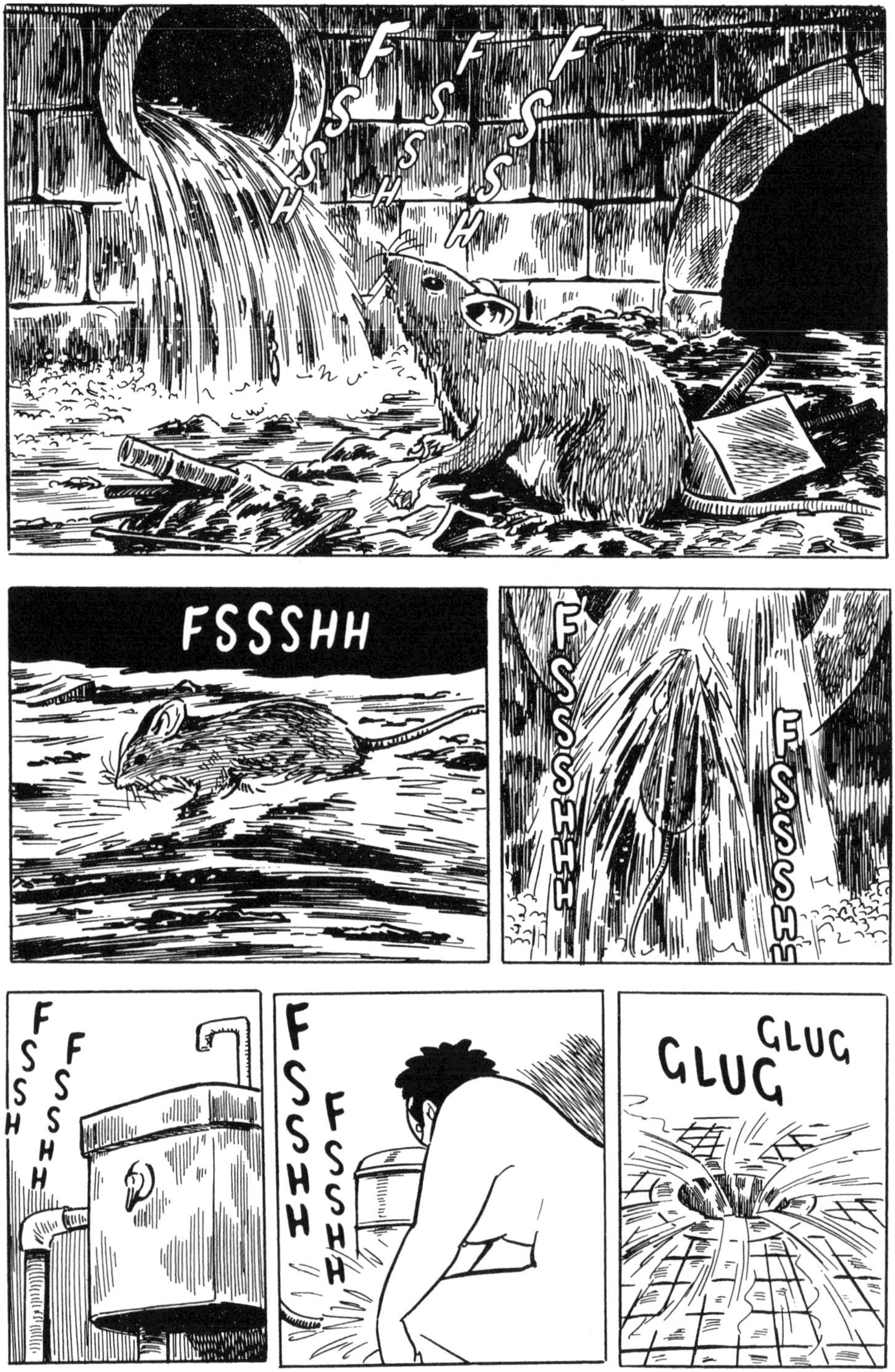
FSSH
FSSH
FSSSH
FSSSHH
FSSSHHH
FSSSHH
FSSH
FSSSHH
FSSHH
FSSSHH
GLUG
GLUG

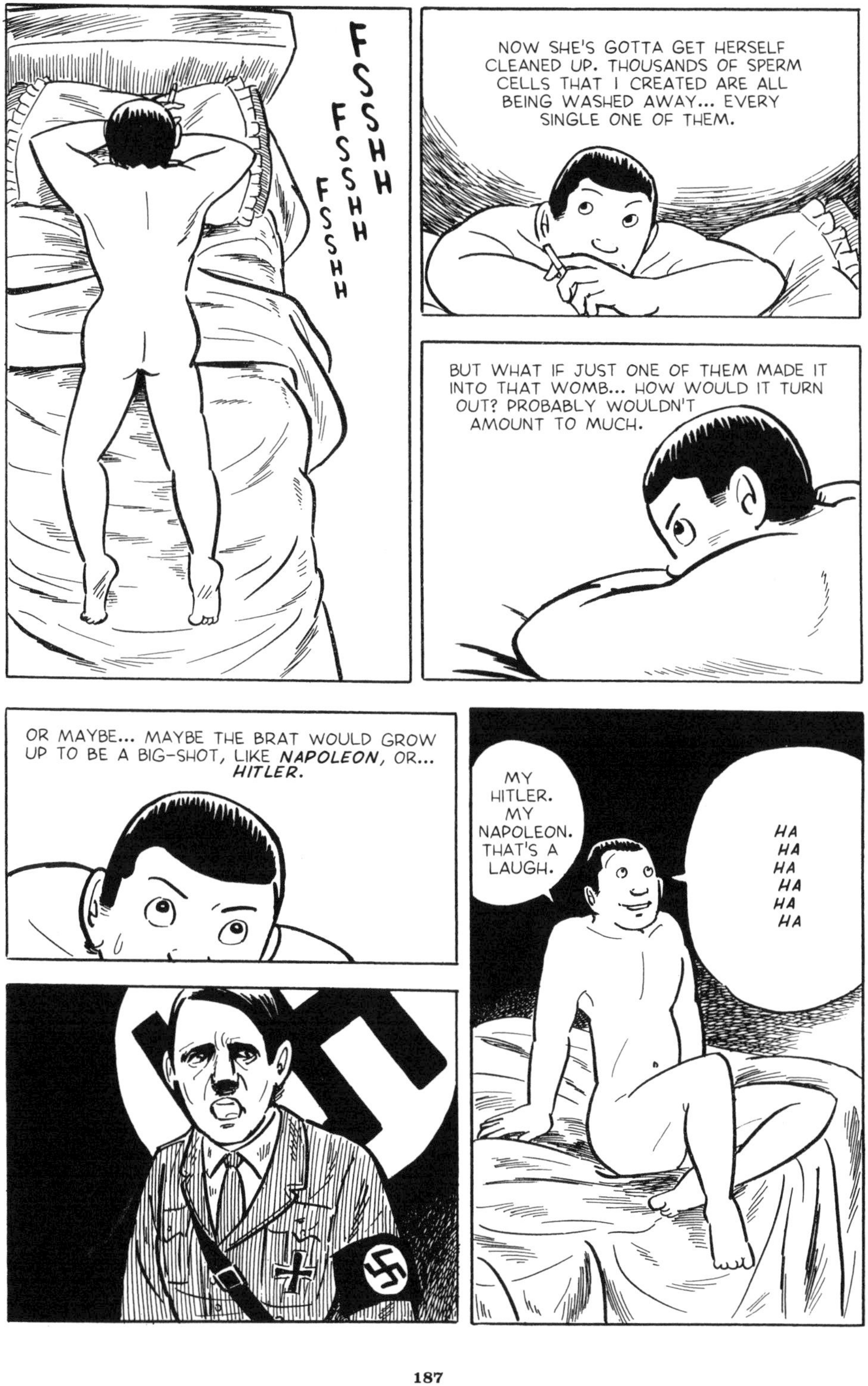
FSSHH
FSSHH
FSSHH
FSSHH
NOW SHE'S GOTTA GET HERSELF CLEANED UP. THOUSANDS OF SPERM CELLS THAT I CREATED ARE ALL BEING WASHED AWAY... EVERY SINGLE ONE OF THEM.
BUT WHAT IF JUST ONE OF THEM MADE IT INTO THAT WOMB... HOW WOULD IT TURN OUT? PROBABLY WOULDN'T AMOUNT TO MUCH.
OR MAYBE... MAYBE THE BRAT WOULD GROW UP TO BE A BIG-SHOT, LIKE ***NAPOLEON***, OR... ***HITLER***.
MY HITLER. MY NAPOLEON. THAT'S A LAUGH.
HA HA HA HA HA HA

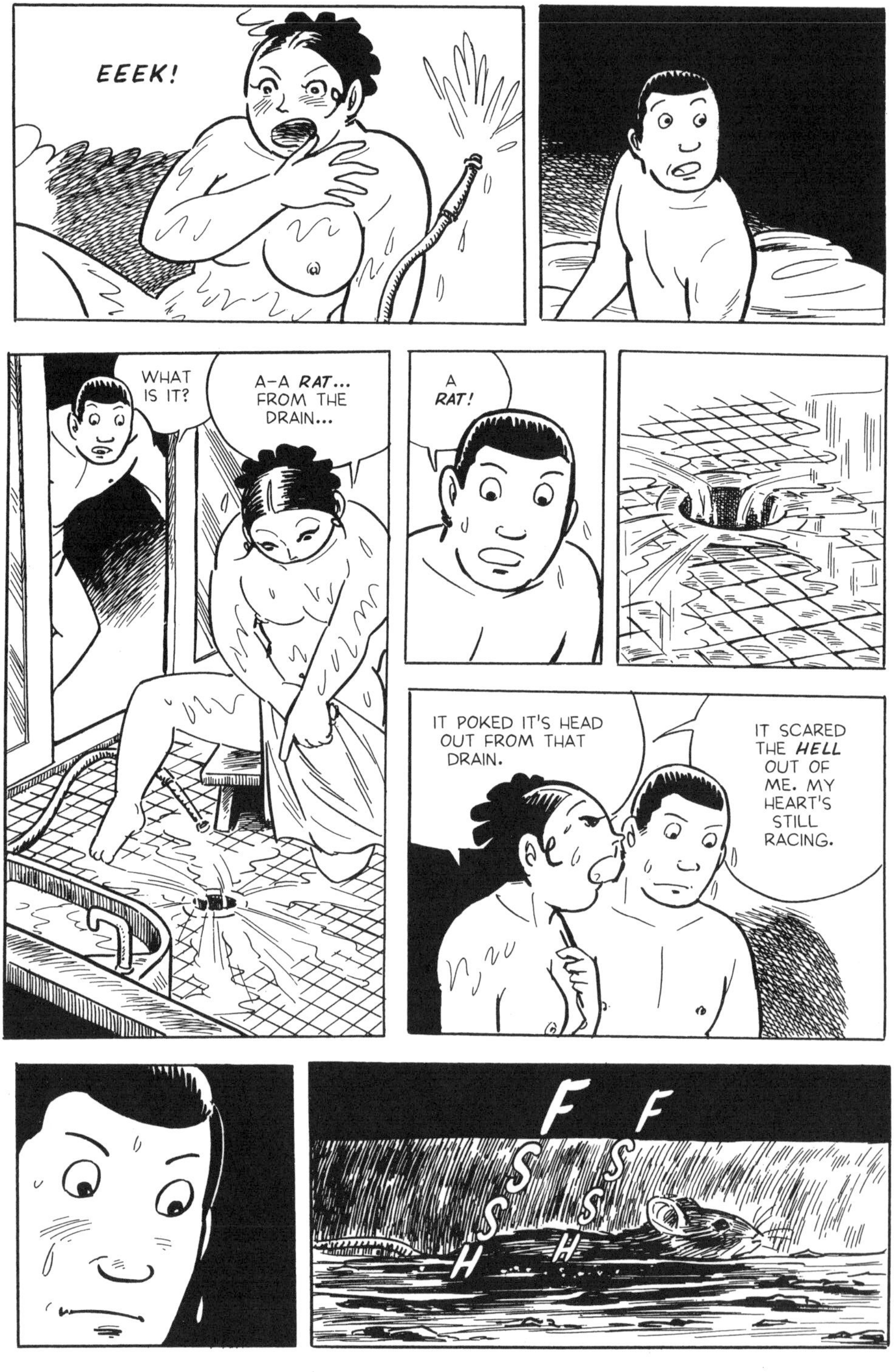
EEEK!
WHAT IS IT?
A-A RAT... FROM THE DRAIN...
A RAT!
IT POKED IT'S HEAD OUT FROM THAT DRAIN.
IT SCARED THE HELL OUT OF ME. MY HEART'S STILL RACING.
FFSSSSHH
FSSHH

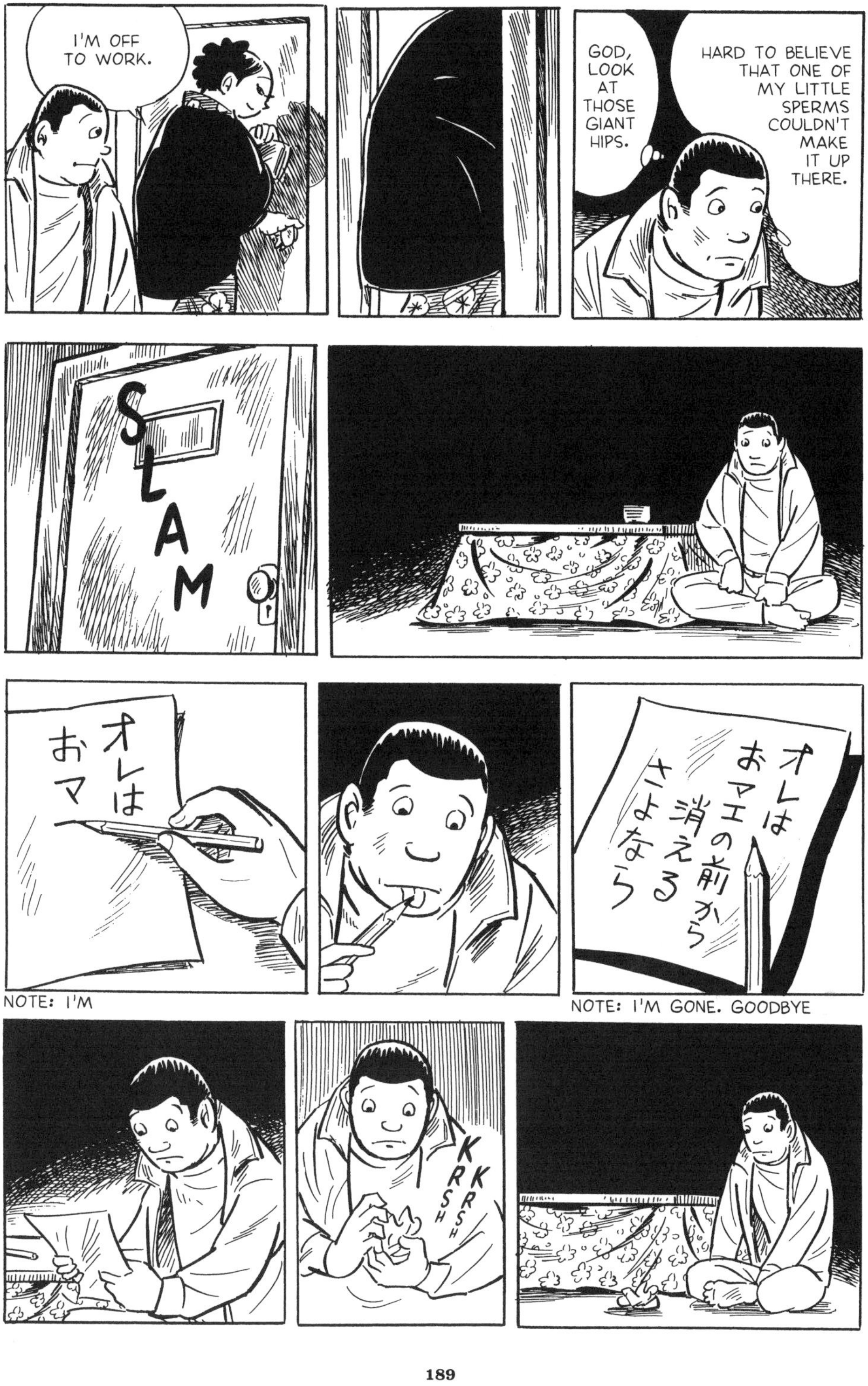
I'M OFF TO WORK.
GOD, LOOK AT THOSE GIANT HIPS.
HARD TO BELIEVE THAT ONE OF MY LITTLE SPERMS COULDN'T MAKE IT UP THERE.
SLAM
オレは
おマ
NOTE: I'M
オレは
おマエの前から
消える
さよなら
NOTE: I'M GONE. GOODBYE
KRSH
KRSH

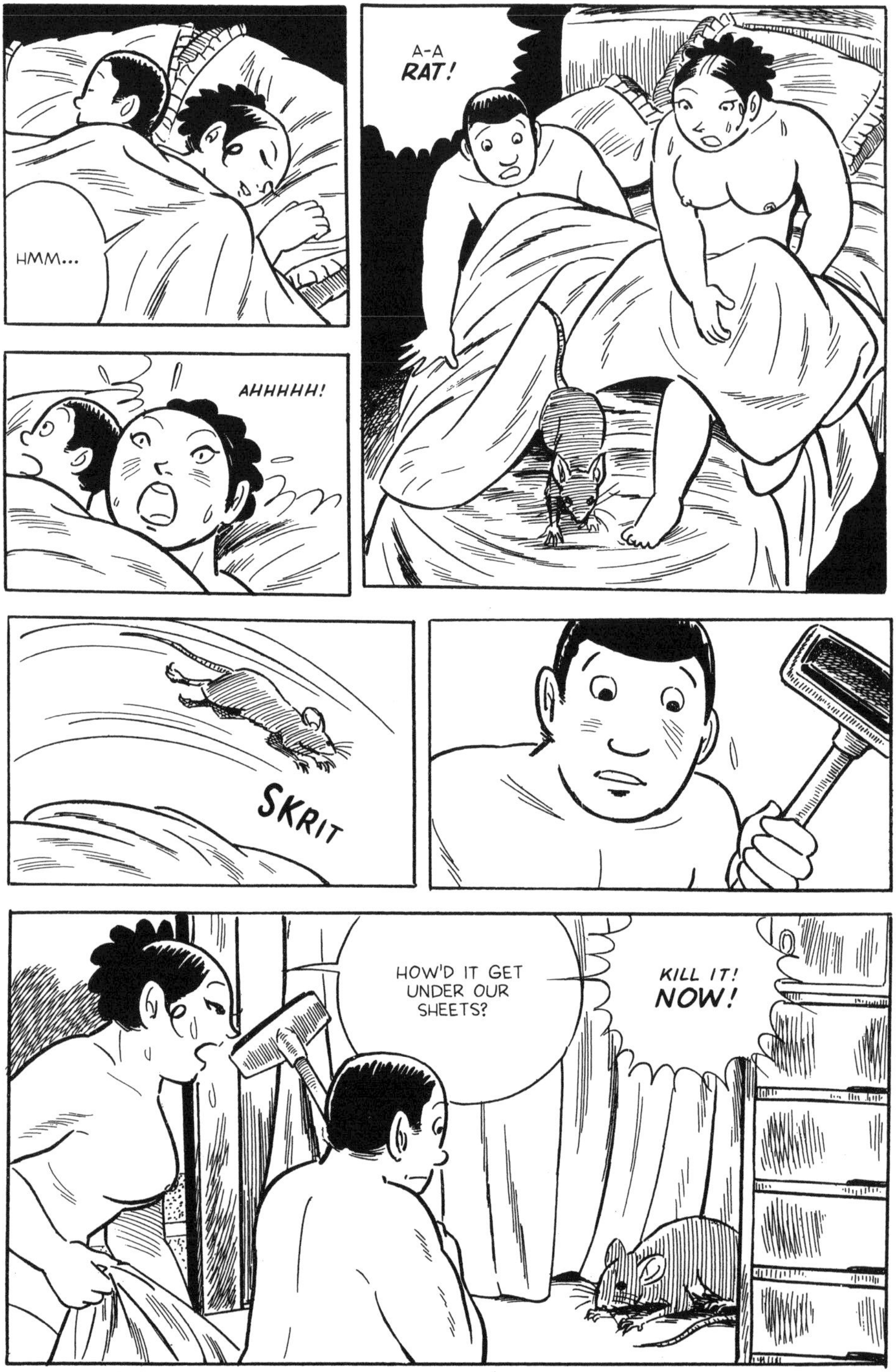
HMM...
A-A
RAT!
AHHHHH!
SKRIT
HOW'D IT GET UNDER OUR SHEETS?
KILL IT! NOW!

C'MON!

KILL IT NOW!

GET OUT OF HERE.

SCRAM.

WHY DIDN'T YOU KILL IT?

IT'S GONNA COME BACK...

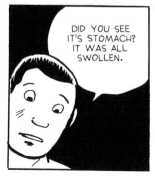

DID YOU SEE IT'S STOMACH? IT WAS ALL SWOLLEN.

...

OH, GEEZ...

I'M WIDE AWAKE NOW.

HEY, COME ON.

THIS MUNDANE RITUAL...

WHAT GOOD IS IT?

IT'S A POINTLESS ACT...

I MAY AS WELL BE EJACULATING INTO THE DRAIN THAT LEADS DOWN INTO THE DARK SEWER.

WE'LL PROBABLY END UP BEING WASHED AWAY BY THE SEWAGE, TOO.

I DON'T HAVE THE COURAGE...

...TO FIGHT AGAINST THE SEWER'S FLOW...

FFFF SSSS HHHH

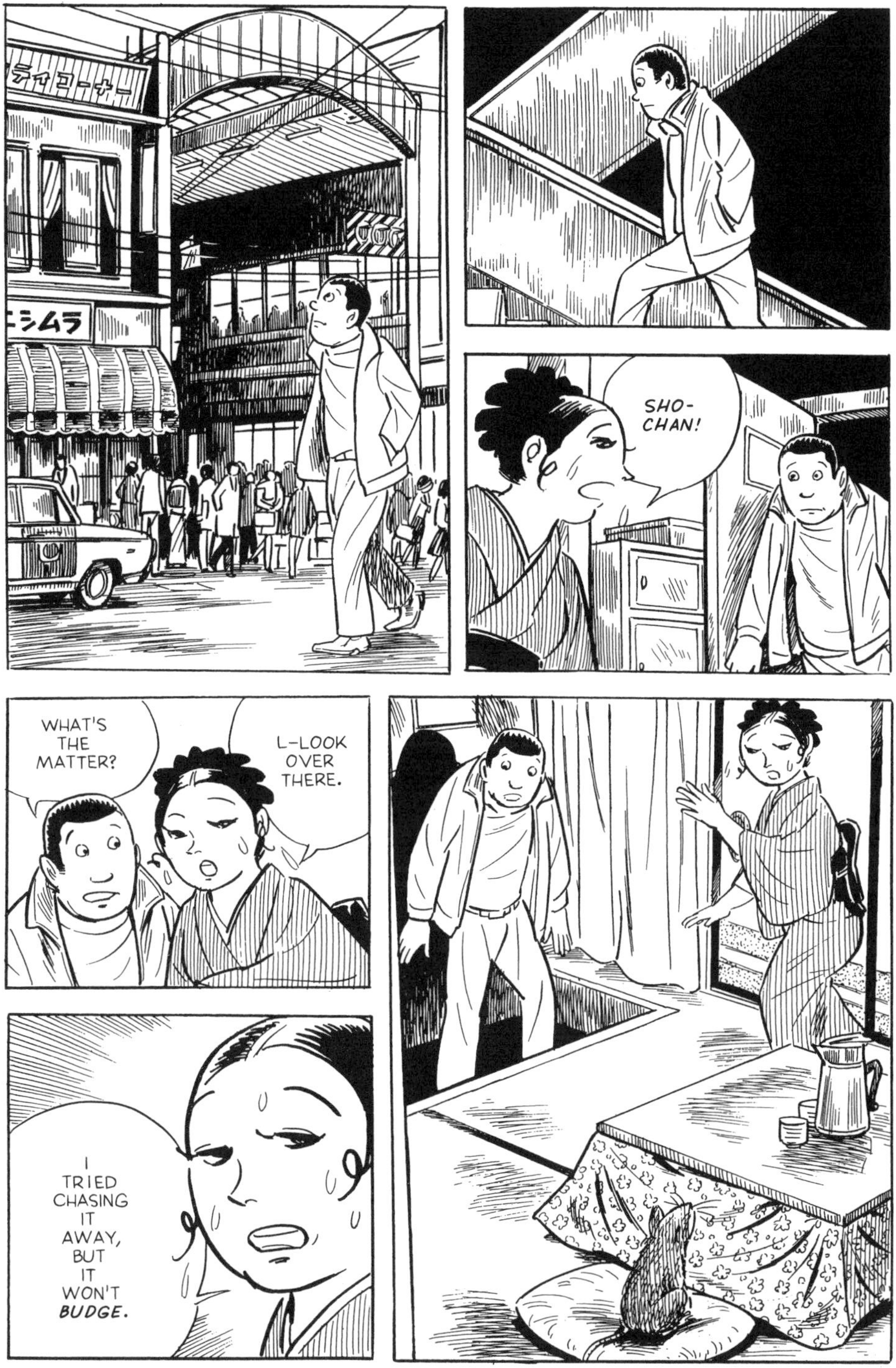
ティコーナー
シムラ
SHO-CHAN!
WHAT'S THE MATTER?
L-LOOK OVER THERE.
I TRIED CHASING IT AWAY, BUT IT WON'T *BUDGE*.

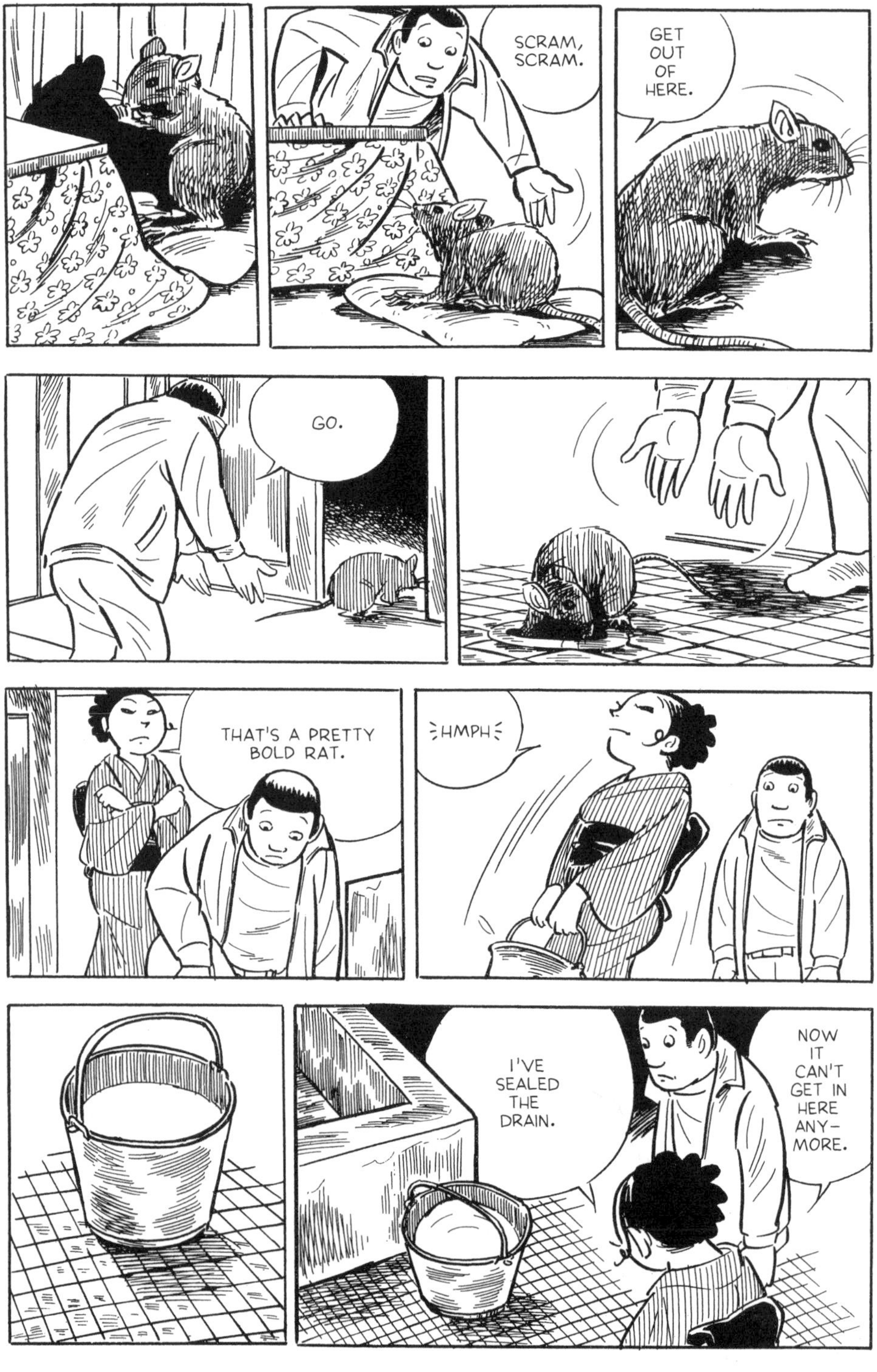
SCRAM, SCRAM.
GET OUT OF HERE.
GO.
THAT'S A PRETTY BOLD RAT.
HMPH
I'VE SEALED THE DRAIN.
NOW IT CAN'T GET IN HERE ANY- MORE.

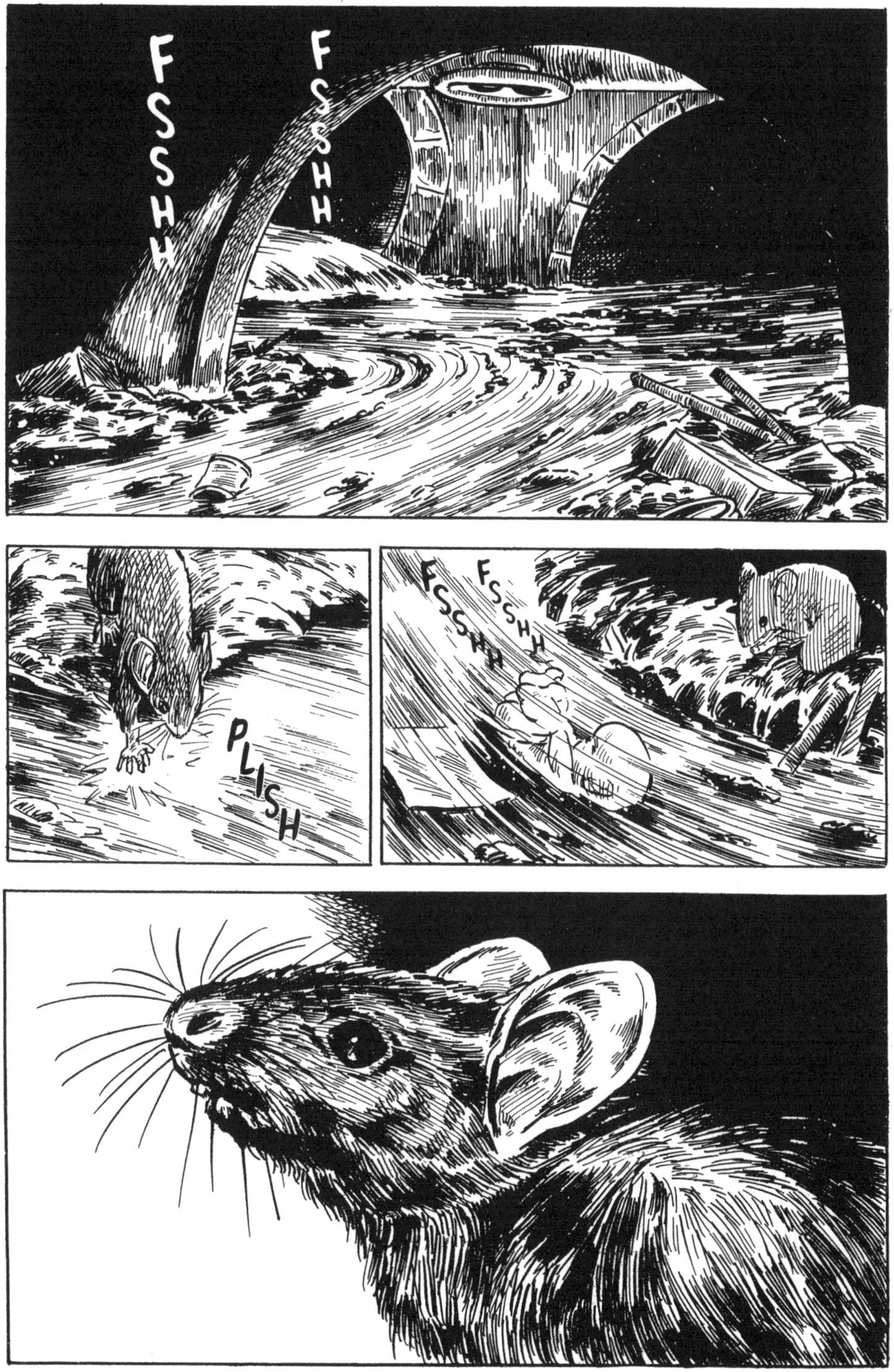
FSSHH
FSSHH
PLISH
FSSHH
FSSHH

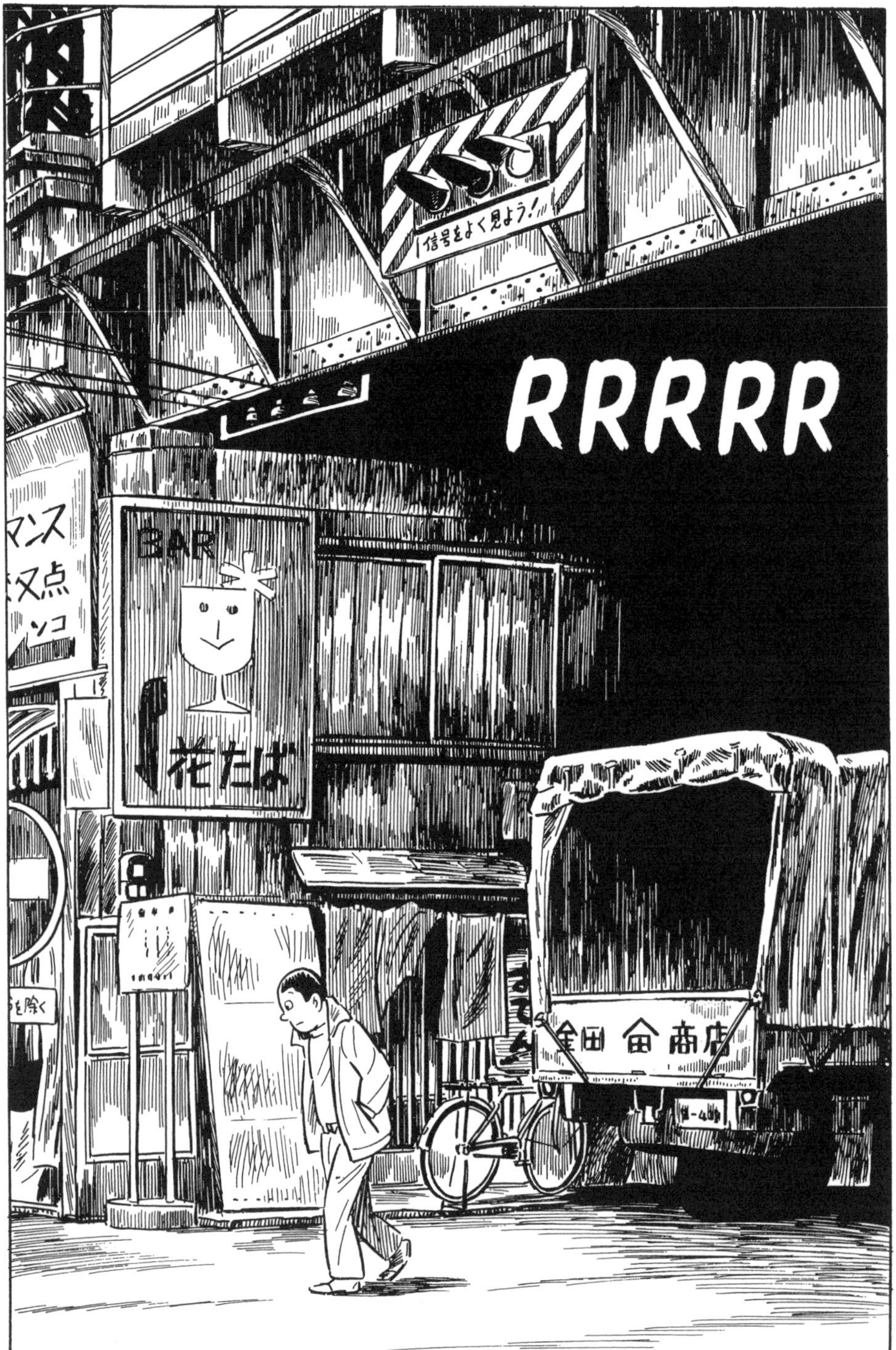
信号をよく見よう!
RRRRR
BAR
花たば

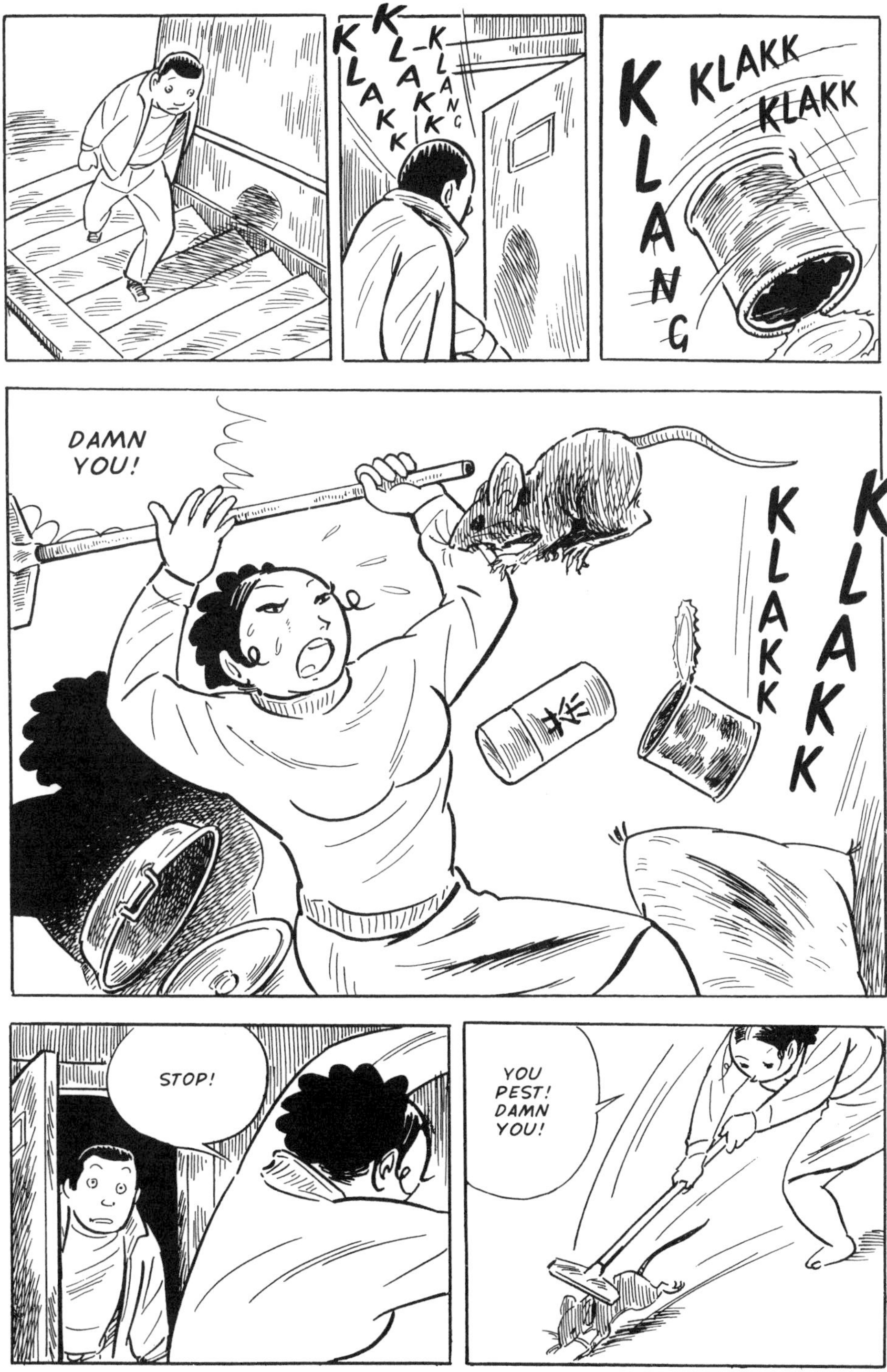
KLAKK
KLAKK
KLANG
KLANG
KLAKK
KLAKK
DAMN YOU!
KLAKK
KLAKK
STOP!
YOU PEST! DAMN YOU!

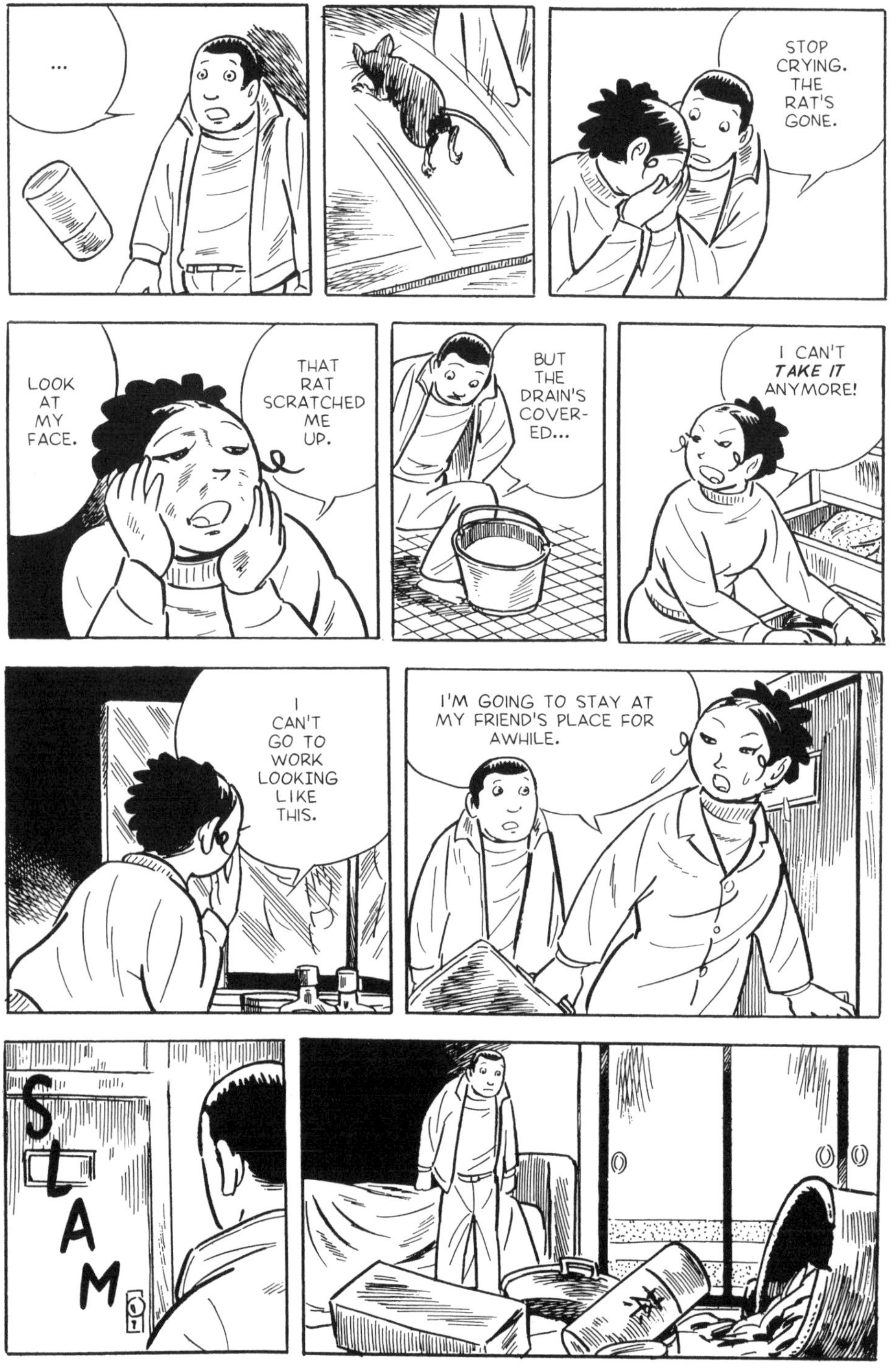
...
STOP CRYING. THE RAT'S GONE.
LOOK AT MY FACE.
THAT RAT SCRATCHED ME UP.
BUT THE DRAIN'S COVER-ED...
I CAN'T *TAKE IT* ANYMORE!
I CAN'T GO TO WORK LOOKING LIKE THIS.
I'M GOING TO STAY AT MY FRIEND'S PLACE FOR AWHILE.
SLAM

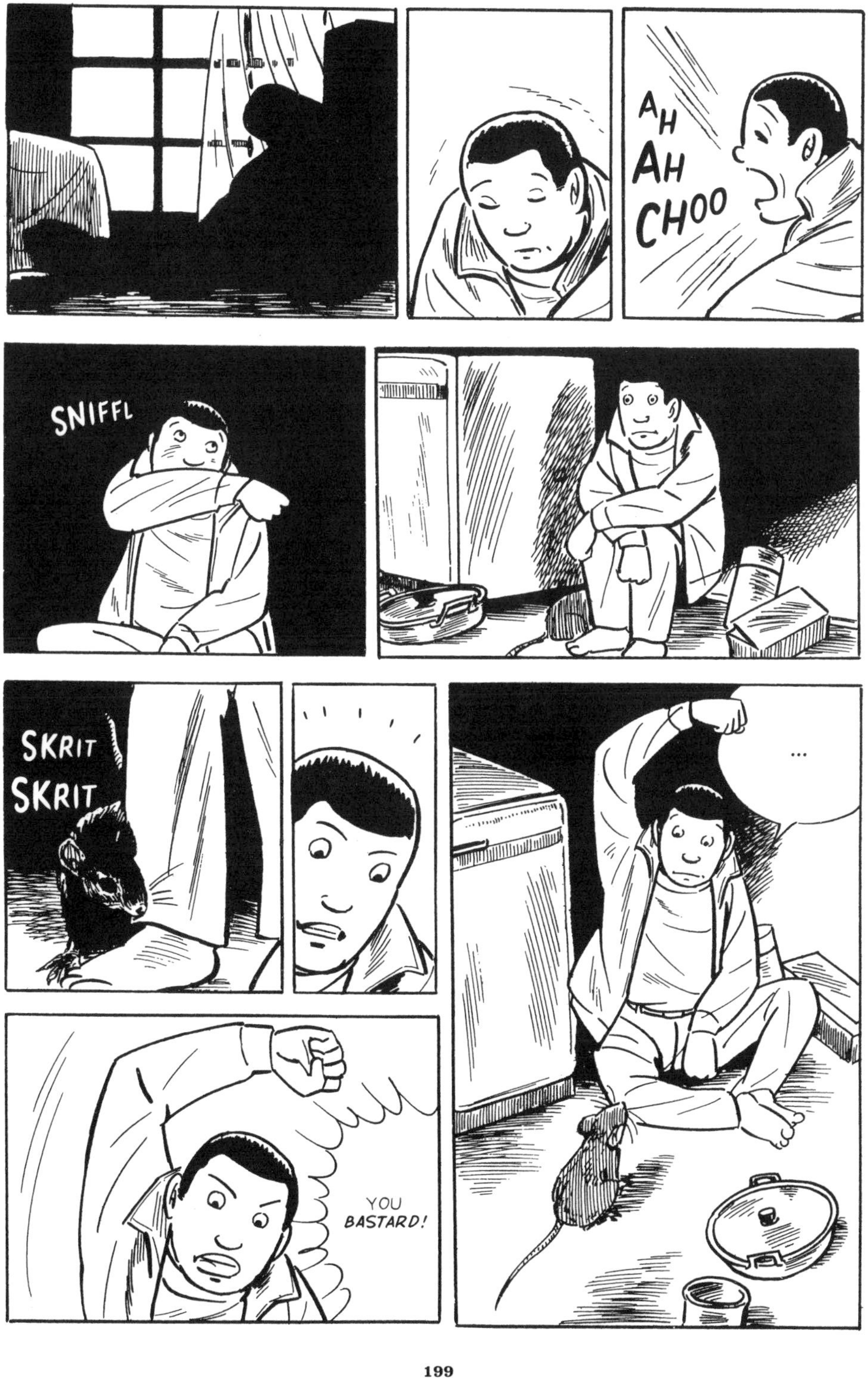
AH
AH
CHOO
SNIFFL
SKRIT
SKRIT
YOU BASTARD!
...

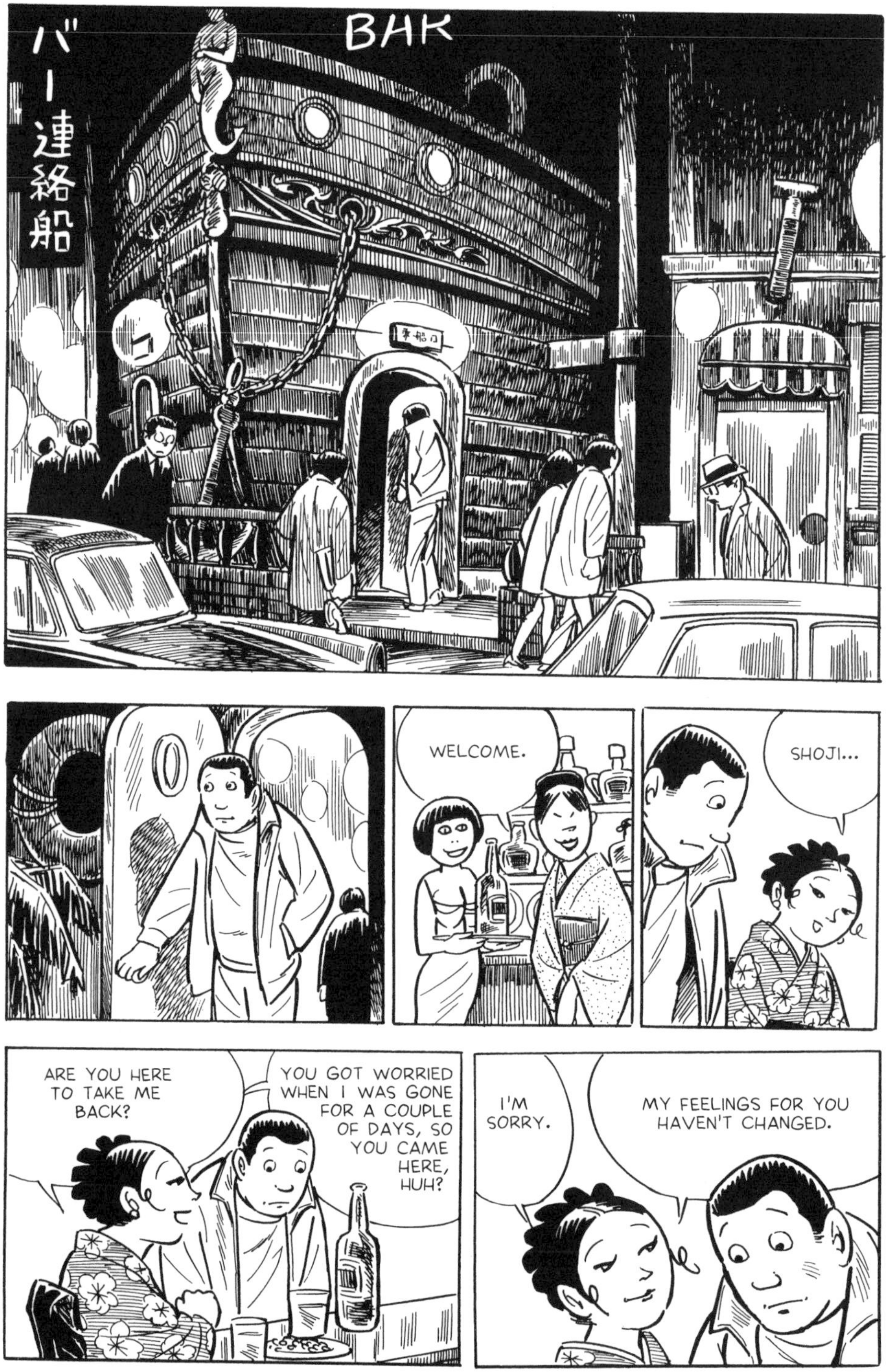
バー連絡船
BAR
WELCOME.
SHOJI...
ARE YOU HERE TO TAKE ME BACK?
YOU GOT WORRIED WHEN I WAS GONE FOR A COUPLE OF DAYS, SO YOU CAME HERE, HUH?
I'M SORRY.
MY FEELINGS FOR YOU HAVEN'T CHANGED.

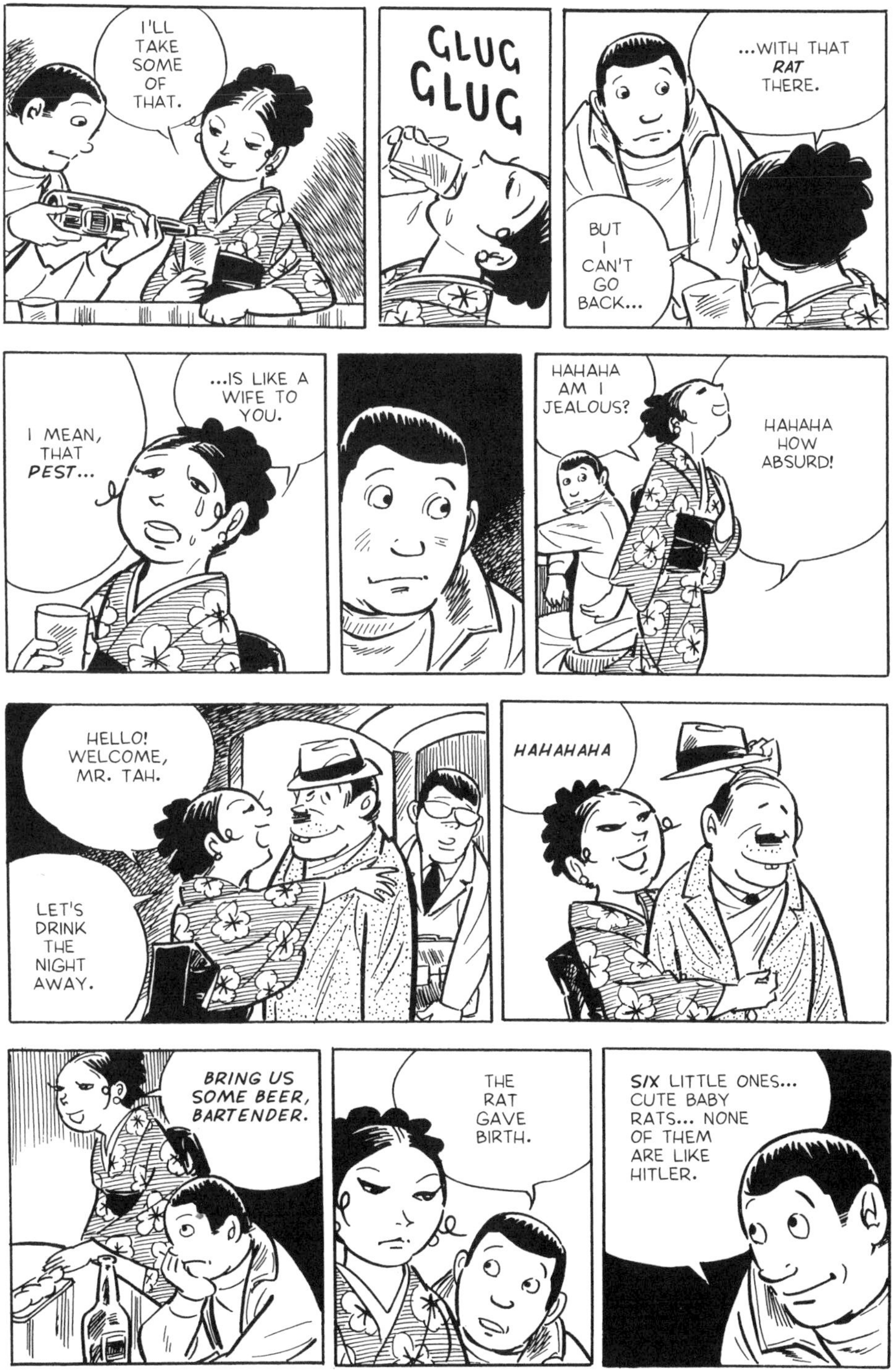
I'LL TAKE SOME OF THAT.
GLUG GLUG
...WITH THAT RAT THERE.
BUT I CAN'T GO BACK...
I MEAN, THAT PEST...
...IS LIKE A WIFE TO YOU.
HAHAHA AM I JEALOUS?
HAHAHA HOW ABSURD!
HELLO! WELCOME, MR. TAH.
LET'S DRINK THE NIGHT AWAY.
HAHAHAHA
BRING US SOME BEER, BARTENDER.
THE RAT GAVE BIRTH.
SIX LITTLE ONES... CUTE BABY RATS... NONE OF THEM ARE LIKE HITLER.

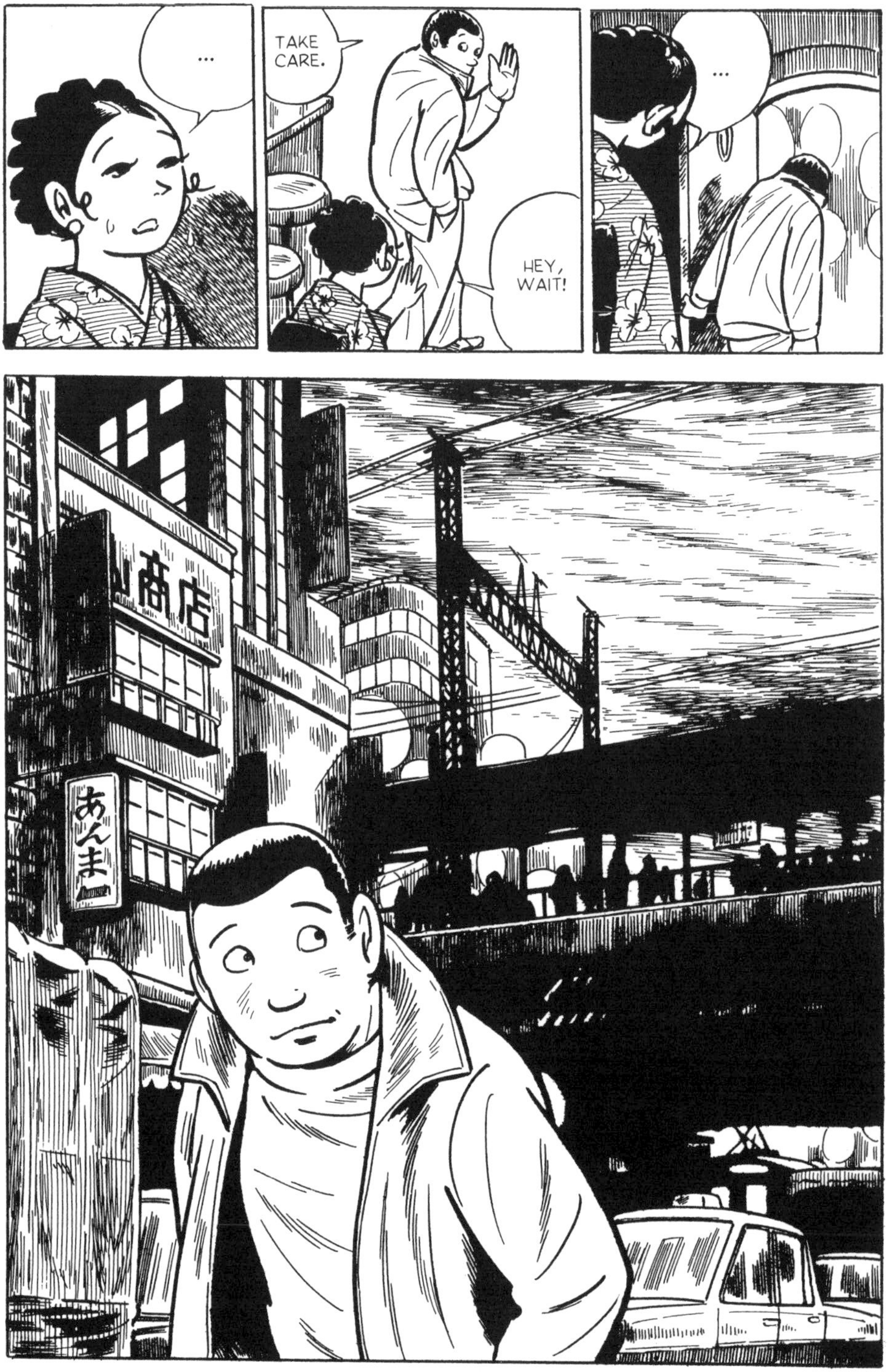
...
TAKE CARE.
HEY, WAIT!
...
商店
あんま

Q & A with YOSHIHIRO TATSUMI

This written interview was conducted in December, 2004 with the invaluable assistance of Mitsuhiro Asakawa, Beatrice Marechal, and Yuji Oniki.

ADRIAN TOMINE: *Where were these stories (from 1969) originally published? Since the majority of them are eight pages long, it seems like they might have been a regular feature in a magazine, perhaps? And what about the longer stories, such as "Who Are You?" and "My Hitler"?*

YOSHIHIRO TATSUMI: The eight–page pieces from 1969 were all published in a bi–weekly magazine called *Gekiga–Young*. A minor company published this young men's magazine, so the print runs were limited. I was only given eight pages [per issue], though, because I had no reputation as a *manga* artist for young men's magazines. I had more freedom (relatively speaking) with the page count for "My Hitler" and "Who Are You?" because they were published in *dojin–shi* magazines .[1]

AT: *Can you talk a little about your life and circumstances at the time you drew these stories?*

YT: At the time, I was a publisher of *manga* graphic novels for book lending shops.[2] I would publish three to four books per month, each with a print run of 2,500–3,200. We had six in–house artists and five to six freelancers. Of course I was publishing my own work, too, but I was so busy running the business, I didn't have much time to work on my own material. As for making a living, I had a hard enough time getting my checks cleared [for the publishing business] at the bank, so it was a hard life.

AT: *What was the comics business like in Japan at this time?*

YT: As Japan entered its period of high–growth

---

[1] Independent "vanity–press" *manga* publications.

[2] Similar to today's video rental stores, *manga* lending shops were popular in Japan in the 1950s and 60s.

economics, the demand for *manga* distributed through the lending shop system (which was so unique to Japan) started to decline. Meanwhile, *manga*–oriented magazines really began to take off as the *manga* boom approached.

AT: *There seems to be a common thread that runs through these stories, at least in terms of thematic focus. Do you remember what guided your interests towards these types of characters and stories?*

YT: Because my stories weren't acknowledged, I felt like I was an outcast. Even though I was only drawing *manga*, I felt I had to be sincere in my work. So I took an interest in the working class who lived around me. I wanted to provide slice–of–life portraits in my *manga*.

AT: *What about other influences in general? Were there any comic books, artists, films, novels, etc. that had a significant impact on you or your work?*

YT: My influences: police reports and other human interest articles in the papers. I hardly read any *manga*.

AT: *Can you describe the working process you used for these stories? What type of art supplies were you using? Did you have any assistants working for you at this time? And if so, what were their duties?*

YT: I would always have about twenty story ideas, and once I was given an assignment, I would come up with the layout (pencil sketches on memo paper) for three stories. I would show these to my editor to determine the final one. My art supplies were Kent paper and pens with calligraphy ink. I only began using an assistant in 1973.

AT: *What was the public reaction to these stories at the time they were published?*

YT: I didn't get much response. The occasional letters I got from readers tended to be long, difficult critiques of my work.

AT: *How do you feel about this work being translated and published in North America now?*

YT: First of all, I am extremely grateful to Adrian. I feel very fortunate to have these works published in the U.S. Still, these stories from 1969 are only an introduction to my work. The true scope of my work can be understood only after you have read my later stories.

AT: *Can you describe your present–day endeavors? Are you working on any comic projects right now? I've heard that you also run a bookshop...is this accurate?*

YT: Currently I run a used bookstore for *manga* collectors. It is mainly a mail order business with a quarterly catalogue. I have been slowly accumulating short stories that will be collected into a single volume.

AT: *Is there anything else you'd like English–speaking readers to know about you or your work?*

YT: Since my work has been largely unavailable in English–speaking countries, I doubt most readers have heard of me. I myself am a very normal person. Please do not interpret these stories as representative of the author's personality.

Yoshihiro Tatsumi, circa 1969.

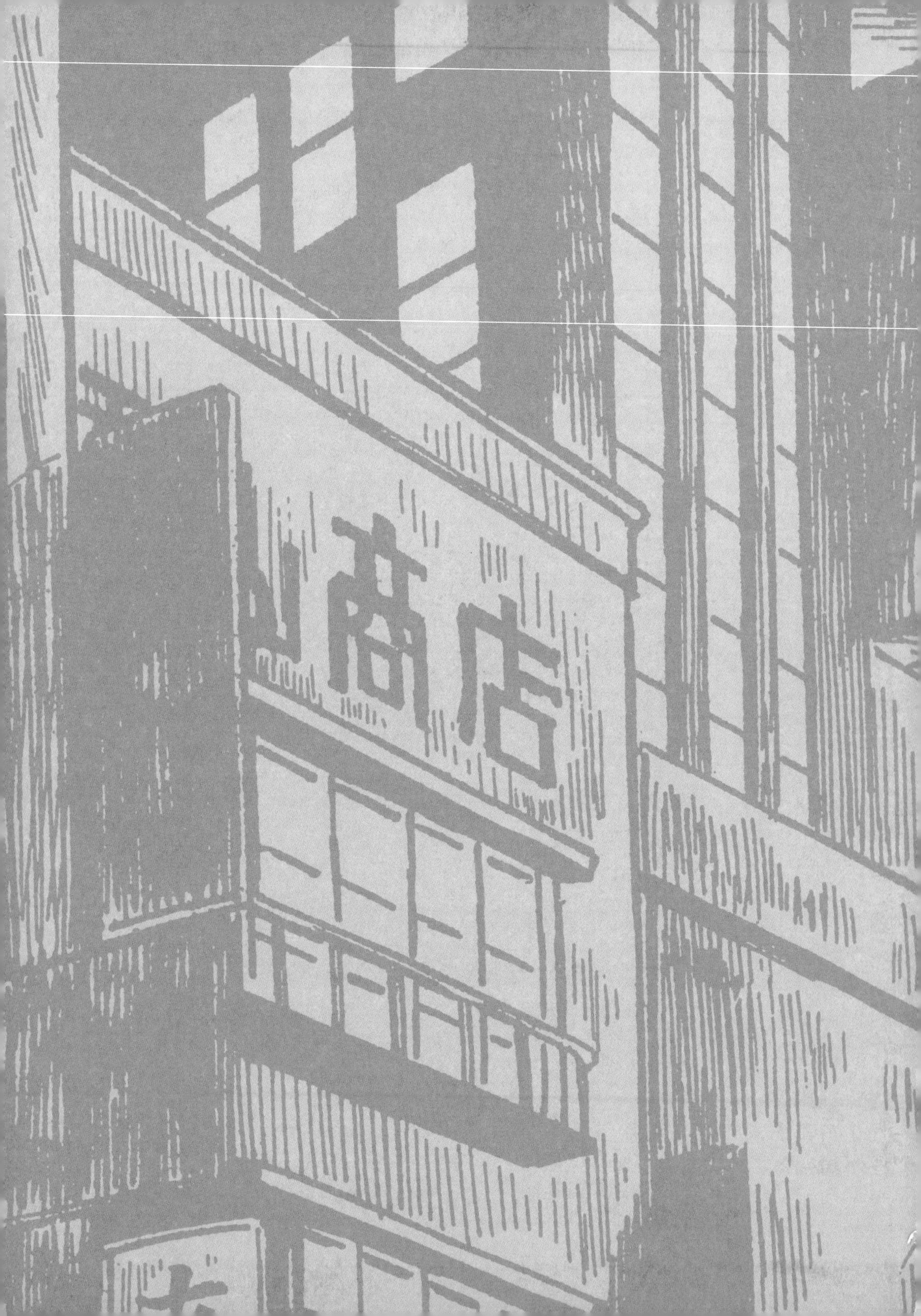
商店